By Bread Alone

By Bread Alone

The Bible through the Eyes of the Hungry

Sheila E. McGinn, Lai Ling Elizabeth Ngan, and Ahida Calderón
Pilarski, editors

Fortress Press
Minneapolis

BY BREAD ALONE

The Bible through the Eyes of the Hungry

Chapter 1 was the presidential address delivered at the Seventy-Second International Meeting of the Catholic Biblical Association of America, held at Creighton University, Omaha, Nebraska, 1–4 August 2009. Originally published in *CBQ* 72, no. 1 (2010) 1–14, it has been slightly modified and is reprinted here with permission.

An earlier version of chapter 10 was printed in *Conversations with the Biblical World: Proceedings of the Eastern Great Lakes and Midwest Region Society of Biblical Literature* 32 (2013): 175–202.

Cover design: Laurie Ingram

Cover image: *Supper at Emmaus*, Caravaggio,Pinacoteca di Brera/The Bridgeman Art Library

Library of Congress Cataloging-in-Publication Data is available

Print ISBN: 978-1-4514-6550-1

eBook ISBN: 978-1-4514-7244-8

Manufactured in the U.S.A.

This book was produced using PressBooks.com, and PDF rendering was done by PrinceXML.

Contents

Acknowledgements

The editors would like to thank the officers and members of the Catholic Biblical Association (CBA) for providing the context in which this project could come to fruition. In particular, we offer our hearty thanks to the members of the CBA Feminist Biblical Hermeneutics Task Force, who contributed greatly to this project from its conception to "birth," and to other CBA colleagues who offered criticism and encouragement as the project progressed. Especially worthy of mention are Sallie J. Latkovich and Seung Ai Yang, who offered responses to the initial draft of the volume at the 2013 CBA meeting. Also, our deep gratitude goes to one of our authors, Linda Maloney, who prepared the index. Neil Elliott, CBA member and our editor at Fortress Press, also contributed to the development of the volume and offered the vision and unfailing support that sustained us when the initial energy and excitement threatened to fade away.

Carson Bay, Meagan Howe, and Jurell Sison, MA students at John Carroll University, helped with various editorial duties, some interesting and (let's be honest) some not so much. Running down sources and checking fonts are necessary though often thankless tasks. This time, at least, we want to make sure they do not remain thankless, so kudos and commendations.

Sincere thanks are due to the general editors of the *Catholic Biblical Quarterly* and *Conversations with the Biblical World*, respectively, for permission to reprint Kathleen O'Connor's presidential address and the revised version of the essay by Sheila E. McGinn and Megan T. Wilson-Reitz that appears here as chapter 11.

As editors, we would like to take the opportunity also to thank our respective academic institutions for their overarching support: John Carroll University, Baylor University, and Saint Anselm College.

Finally, thank you to all the students, community, members, friends, and "family" who helped us along the way as we made our halting steps along the path of listening more intently, with ears to hear the voices of the hungry and eyes to see their faces in the pages of the Scriptures.

Foreword

Christine Vladimiroff, OSB

I recall from my childhood a part of my Russian heritage, a ceremonial blessing exchanged by host and guest: "Bread, that this house may never know hunger, salt, that life may always have savor." The reader of this book will be the recipient of another rich blessing with both the substance and flavor of the hermeneutic of hunger.

You are both host and guest in a communal exegesis on hunger. A host because this book is a call to be a coparticipant in uncovering the revelatory content of Scripture, and a guest, as it is also an invitation to sit still and to reflect on the suffering and privation of the time.

These pages present mothers in anguish, unable to feed their children; animals, emaciated, starving; the parched earth ravaged by the greed and contempt of those who walked its surface in that other time. It was another time—wasn't it?

You will come into a space of searching for meaning and relevance. What is the experience of God in desolation? It is not difficult to make the transition to the sociopolitical time we inhabit. You may begin to view hunger from the eyes of the hungry that you see on the streets where you live, in the soup kitchens and pantries where you serve, poverty in the coin you give the beggar with dirty, outstretched hand. The authors engage you to make the practical application, to begin your walk through the reality of your life, your place and time. You may come to realize the importance of perceiving (with a critical eye) the antagonism between a person's life and his or her conscience. Indifference becomes an unacceptable luxury when one reads the Scripture through the hearts of those for whom a bit of bread is an experience of God.

The reader is led through the biblical accounts of prophets warning a people of their errant ways, consoling a people with a glimpse of a compassionate God. The lamentations echo the human search for meaning in suffering and the enduring hope that anchors one to the reality of a future different from the suffering of the present. The kaleidoscope of images from past to present is the background with which we participate in communal exegesis. Transformation will not take place unless we sit with the text in the sociopolitical reality that is the context of our lives. The mystical experience of God invites us to enter into the text and our reality simultaneously. We are not to be silent bystanders. Blinders must be removed, for shadows must not obscure our sight as we read the text in our cultural situation. The blessing I give you, reader: "Bread that you may never know hunger, salt that your life may always have savor, courage that you may never turn away from the hunger of any other, and gratitude to the God who cares for us all, who nourishes all creation with love and beauty."

Introduction: The Bible through the Eyes of the Hungry

Lai Ling Elizabeth Ngan, Ahida Calderón Pilarski, and Sheila E. McGinn

One of Jesus' more famous sayings appears in the scene of his temptation in the desert (Matt. 4:1-11; Luke 4:1-13). After fasting for "forty days and forty nights" (v. 2), Satan tempts Jesus to "turn these stones into bread" (v. 3). Jesus retorts that the human person lives "not by bread alone . . . but by every word that comes from the mouth of God" (v. 4).

This pious sentiment, when combined with a phrase from Jesus' defense of the woman who anointed him ("the poor you will always have with you"; Mark 14:7 and parallels), has led to disastrous consequences in Christian attitudes toward poverty and injustice. After all, many Christians have been able to argue, Jesus himself said that poverty is an inevitable factor in human society. Why should we trouble ourselves about it? So what if someone is hungry? The Christian's duty is not to feed them but to bring the word of God to the poor. As long as they hear the gospel, Christians have done their job.

Why "By Bread Alone"?

While somewhat overstated, perhaps to the point of caricature, this synopsis makes clear the essential problem of the proof-textual use of these two sayings. Jesus refused bread for himself; he did not deny it to someone else. Indeed, one need only compare the stories of his miraculous feedings of the multitudes to see that he was remembered for quite the opposite (see, e.g., Mark 6:33-44; John 6). To choose to fast is one thing; to stand idly while others go hungry is quite another.

As for the second passage, Jesus did not enjoin the disciples to do nothing, since there will always be poor among us. Rather, his defense of the prophetic woman's action served to ridicule the onlookers' hollow objection to her use of the oil for his messianic anointing (Mark 14:8; Matt. 26:12). The Johannine version makes explicit what may be implicit in the synoptic version of this scene: the protest was motivated by avarice (John 12:6), not by concern for the poor. Jesus' words were not a rebuke of the concern being voiced, but its intensification: the poor are *always* in need, and thus constitute a ceaseless claim on the faithful. His words invoked the words of Torah: "*Since there will never cease to be some in need on the earth*, I therefore command you, 'Open your hand to the poor and needy neighbor in your land'" (Deut. 15:11; emphasis added). Elsewhere in the New Testament we find a repetition of Third Isaiah's claim (Isa. 58:6-10) that those who are faithful to God "share [their] bread with the hungry and bring the homeless poor into [their] house" (Isa. 58:7; cf. Matt. 25:31-46; James 2:15;17).

While we would not want to argue that "bread alone" is sufficient to a biblical understanding of salvation, we have chosen this title as an explicit corrective to the distortion of the biblical message by self-proclaimed Christians who espouse a radical laissez-faire economic policy (à la Ayn Rand), who value a hyperindividualism over the common good, and who foster antipathy toward the poor. This extreme social Darwinism has been coated with a thin veneer of piety, with proponents arguing that the poor need "not bread alone," but the gospel (alone). Yet how can one speak of "gospel" when it has been eviscerated of the good news Jesus preached and enacted? The open table, healing works, and other aspects of Jesus' liberating praxis cannot be dismissed as tangential or irrelevant to his proclamation of the in-breaking reign of God. In harmony with the message of "the Law and the Prophets," Jesus affirmed the inseparability of honor for God and love of neighbor—a love to be expressed in concrete actions to remedy the plight of the poor and foster the common good.

The Genesis of the Project

By Bread Alone is a collaborative work that grows out of the Feminist Biblical Hermeneutics (FBH) Task Force of the Catholic Biblical Association of America (CBA). Scholars have contributed articles in this volume that focus on the important and urgent issue of hunger so as to explore, understand, and articulate a feminist perspective that is biblically based and socially relevant. This collection of essays is modeled after an earlier project of the Task Force that culminated in the publication of *Earth, Wind, and Fire: Biblical and Theological Perspectives on Creation*, edited by Carol Dempsey and Mary Margaret Pazdan, published by Liturgical Press in 2004.

The present project began in 2008 at the Seventy-First International Meeting of the CBA at Fordham University, New

York City, when Kathleen O'Connor led a communal exegesis of Isaiah 58, on fasting and true religion. This exercise involved three movements: (1) the twenty-two participants, all feminist biblical scholars, first dialogued with one another about their present contexts in personal, national, and global terms; (2) this was followed by a critical analysis of the biblical text; and (3) a reexamination of our contemporary contexts in light of the communal exegesis. The communal aspect is significant because the diverse background of the participants adds richness and texture to the interpretation, and most importantly, it involves the *praxis*[1] of the critical dimension of a feminist perspective. The experience proved to be insightful and profitable and the members of the Task Force decided to engage in a similar exercise in the following years.

The selection of the topic for this project, *Hunger*, however, was inspired by Kathleen O'Connor's 2009 Presidential Address to the members of the CBA, entitled "Let All the Peoples Praise You: Biblical Studies and a Hermeneutics of Hunger." In her presentation, O'Connor introduced and dealt briefly with the concept of a hermeneutics of hunger, and because of its relevance to the project, we dedicate the next section of this introduction to it. In 2010, a portion of the Task Force's meeting at Loyola Marymount University in Los Angeles, California, was dedicated to the planning of what came to be called the Hunger Project.

The Issue of Hunger and the Hermeneutics of Hunger

In her 2009 presidential address to the CBA, Kathleen O'Connor called its members to consider the importance of expanding the interpretive horizons of biblical studies to include a hermeneutics of hunger.[2] This concept was developed by Dorothee Sölle in her book,

---

1. We will provide a description of this concept in the next section.

The Silent Cry: Mysticism and Resistance (2001).[3] In this introduction we elaborate briefly on some key ideas at the background of Sölle's hermeneutics of hunger as it, together with O'Connor's address, inspired the contributors of this project to pursue the critical and communal analysis of selected biblical passages on the topic of hunger.

The process of communal exegesis done by the FBH Task Force began with a series of dialogues about contemporary contexts in personal, national, and global terms. This step in the interpretive process reflects not only a critical aspect of a feminist perspective, but it also constitutes a key stage in a hermeneutics of hunger. According to Julia Prinz, this hermeneutical key is part of what Sölle refers to as a *double-contextualization*. This stage foregrounds the idea that the biblical text can be experienced as revelatory and transformative only when its reading is contextualized in the reader's sociopolitical situation. "The biblical text cannot speak into a vacuum but needs to have an historical subject to be able to create an experience."[4] In addition to the historical subject undergoing the experience, the biblical text itself also must be contextualized through critical analysis focusing on its own sociohistorical dimensions. Prinz observes that "Sölle does not question the method of historical criticism . . . itself, but critiques its omission of any transition into the socio-political reality of the corresponding time of the exegesis. The lack of this transition is for Sölle the core of problematic exegesis, which perpetuates social injustice and silently legitimizes human atrocities."[5]

2. Kathleen M. O'Connor, "Let All the Peoples Praise You: Biblical Studies and a Hermeneutics of Hunger," *CBQ* 72, no. 1 (2010): 1–14; reprinted herein as chapter 1.

3. Dorothee Sölle, *The Silent Cry: Mysticism and Resistance*, trans. Barbara Rumscheidt and Martin Rumscheidt (Minneapolis: Fortress, 2001).

4. Julia D. E. Prinz, *Endangering Hunger for God: Johann Baptist Metz and Dorothee Sölle at the Interface of Biblical Hermeneutics and Christian Spirituality*, Religion-Geschichte-Gessellschaft, Fundamentaltheologische Studien 44 (Berlin: LIT, 2007), 23.

5. Prinz, *Endangering Hunger for God*, 22.

The choice of words here is far from capricious: Sölle's insight about the importance of such double-contextualization emerges out of her confrontation with Auschwitz.[6]

The present volume takes up the challenge of addressing this double-contextualization of text and reader.[7] It includes some contributions that are the product of the communal exegesis described above (see Maloney and Beavis) as well as several other essays aimed at exploring the sociohistorical context(s) of selected biblical texts, with an eye to the socioeconomic-political context of the hungry—both those mentioned or intimated in the texts and those in our own times. The basic purpose of all the essays is to help the contemporary, first-world reader develop a different field of vision for the biblical texts—one that *sees* and *hears* those who hunger, both those mentioned or intimated in the texts and those in our own world today. We view this as a necessary first step to engaging the revelatory text as it speaks to, for, and with those who hunger and thirst for food, water, shelter, clothing, freedom, respect, meaning, integrity, and all the fundamental needs of a fully human life. We hope to help readers shift the interpretive center of gravity to begin reading in solidarity with the hungry.

A hermeneutic of hunger provides "an interpretative stance that engages the religious content of Christian traditions and feeds the world's physical and spiritual hungers."[8] Embedded in this perspective are two interpretive mediations that allowed O'Connor to establish a connection between a hermeneutic of hunger as applied to mysticism (in the work of Sölle) and the work done in the field of biblical

6. Prinz describes thoroughly the three important momentums (personal-political awakenings) in the life of Dorothee Sölle that shaped her understanding and proposal for a hermeneutics of hunger. See Prinz, *Endangering Hunger for God*, 1–50.

7. Although the contributors of this volume understand the significance of a double-contextualization "as a single process" in a hermeneutics of hunger, the work presented here comprises merely a first step in this direction. A subsequent volume will continue this challenge.

8. O'Connor, "Let All the Peoples Praise You," 1.

studies. In the first mediation one can relate the aims of mysticism with the theological dimension of biblical texts; the latter comprises the relationship between academic exegesis and the theological content of traditions informed by biblical texts. The second mediation is methodological. The hermeneutics of hunger incorporates methodological insights that may assist in repairing common hermeneutical breaches in the process of biblical interpretation.

This introduction elaborates briefly on these two mediations to show the relevance of a hermeneutics of hunger to contemporary biblical interpretation and to highlight the ways in which the essays in this volume respond to O'Connor's call to biblical scholars to expand their interpretive horizons. We hope the interpretive lens of a hermeneutics of hunger will enable contemporary biblical scholars and readers to engage some of the pragmatic and theological dimensions of hunger as they appear in the biblical text.

An engaged interpretive stance has similar dynamics to what mystics call the *unio mystica* (mystical union). The mystical tradition interprets fulfillment of every commandment as a moment of mystical union. When the will of a person "can become identical with the will of God," actions are "an expression of this unity."[9] Sölle was able to unveil and restore this key aspect of mysticism by bringing into her analysis a hermeneutics of hunger.

I. Reading through a Hermeneutics of Hunger: Mysticism and the Theological Dimension of Biblical Texts

Sölle provides three central ideas to understand the correlation established in the first interpretive mediation (that is, the correlation of the aims of mysticism and the theological dimension of biblical

9. Sölle, *Silent Cry*, 54.

texts): (1) the location of mysticism in religion, (2) the definition of mysticism, and (3) a criterion to determine genuine mysticism.

1. Sölle begins by asserting that "all living religion represents a unity of three elements that . . . we may call the institutional, the intellectual, and the mystical."[10] Just as mysticism finds its essential location at the center of a *living* religion, the theological dimension of biblical texts finds its proper central place when the process of biblical interpretation is interconnected with a religious tradition. Furthermore, according to Sölle, this clarification of the appropriate location of mysticism—that is, within a living religion—sets the foundations for its definition, which is our next point.

2. Mysticism involves *cognitio Dei experimentalis* (the knowledge of God through and from experience). Sölle explains that this definition elicits two possible ways of understanding God, the ordered way and the extraordinary way. While the former points to a kind of knowledge that is dogmatically legitimated and hierarchically directed, the latter rests on experiment and experience, which cannot be fully institutionalized. Sölle argues that people can rediscover the permanent reality of religious experience by refocusing on the extraordinary way;[11] a hermeneutics of hunger supports this core element.After presenting four contrasting and valid interpretations of Genesis 11 (grounded on scientific historical-critical approaches), O'Connor alludes to these extraordinary ways of understanding God when speaking about the theology of this biblical passage: "This God speaks to unsettle, to breed confusion, and to overthrow the dominance of one tongue, one way to speak,

10. Ibid., 1.
11. Ibid., 45.

one way to understand our neighbors. This is the 'unsettled and "unsettling" God' who removes the shields of protection erected when everyone must think, speak, and act alike."[12] O'Connor clarifies that, although historical-critical studies are essential to academic exegesis, scholars and readers alike need to understand that all texts are culturally situated, linguistically multiple, and of polyglot nature. When biblical texts are critically read from different readers' *social locations*,[13] contrasting and extraordinary theological reflections may result. Prinz affirms Sölle's critique of these dynamics: "If the historical-critical method 'frees' people of the political responsibility through reading the biblical text . . . then [it] denies the biblical text its function as the 'Word of God' that inherently creates and recreates humanity and humanness."[14] How, then, to recognize what belongs to the theological dimension? The third idea addresses this point.

3. In the process of rediscovering the permanent reality of religious experience that emerges through experiential modes of understanding God, Sölle offers one key criterion for identifying a genuine mysticism. The same criterion also may be used to rediscover the theological dimension of biblical texts. The genuineness of mysticism is rooted in its ethical dimension. This ethics rests in the affirmation that we are all creatures of God, and that God desires fullness of life for all.[15] Sölle continues, "Whatever destroys this basic experience . . . suspends this commonness of God, hence, also destroys the very writings of ontology and ethics that genuine mysticism searches for and

---

12. O'Connor, "Let All the Peoples Praise You," 13, citing Walter Brueggemann, *An Unsettling God: The Heart of the Hebrew Bible* (Minneapolis: Fortress, 2009).
13. More information about this concept and its connection to *praxis* can be found in the section on methodology.
14. Prinz, *Endangering Hunger for God*, 21–22.
15. Sölle, *Silent Cry*, 54.

lives out."[16] This criterion is central to any engaged conversation about the theological dimensions and meanings of biblical texts. O'Connor observes that feminist interpretation, a leading inquiry in this kind of conversation about the meaning of texts, has learned, and teaches that "interpretation is both illuminated and obscured by the interpreter's cultural contexts."[17] Every generation must reengage this critical conversation with the biblical texts so that the fullness of life for all becomes a reality in their own time.

These three preliminary ideas set the background and vision to understand the methodological contribution that a hermeneutics of hunger brings to the conversation, and we devote the next section to that contribution.

II. Hermeneutics of Hunger: Methodological Insights

Sölle describes a hermeneutics of hunger as an interpretive stance differentiated from a hermeneutics of suspicion.[18] While the hermeneutics of suspicion provides the foundation for ideological critique,[19] the hermeneutics of hunger seeks to recover a mode of understanding that allows for a sense of hope. "Suspicion is an element that critical consciousness cannot relinquish . . . [but] must not another hermeneutic be articulated in a world where hope itself is exiled? . . . Is suspicion our only lens? Is critical consciousness the only consciousness we have?"[20]

16. Ibid.
17. O'Connor, "Let All the Peoples Praise You," 2.
18. Sölle seems to imply that a hermeneutic of suspicion is the only lens used in feminist interpretation, which does not do justice to the work done in feminist studies in the last three decades. While a hermeneutic of suspicion was central to feminist interpretation in its early stages, it is important to distinguish feminist inquiry as an epistemological process from the different stages of its application in the history of feminist interpretation.
19. Sölle, *Silent Cry*, 46.
20. Ibid., 27.

A hermeneutics of hunger incorporates a key epistemological insight from liberation theology, the "hermeneutics of the poor [which] is one of hunger for bread and liberation."[21] From this theological-hermeneutical locus, hunger provides a common ground as one observes the realities of hunger in the Northern and Southern Hemispheres. In places where readers experience *physical hunger*, the Bible has served as "the answer to what oppression, illness, lack of education, and apathy inflict on human beings" and has driven people to seek a place where "their dignity and their right to have a life are being respected."[22] In contrast, in places where *spiritual hunger* predominates, people may find themselves trapped in a constant search for meaning, falling into the "bottomless emptiness" generated by consumerism. Depression and isolation "transport women and men into a kind of anorexia where any kind of nourishment is nauseating."[23] In such circumstances, a hunger for meaning is reflected in the "yearning to live a different kind of life."[24] A hermeneutics of hunger then provides a theological locus where liberation and life are possible, and where people can recover the lived reality of a religious experience of God. "The hermeneutic of hunger is in search of nourishment."[25]

At the core of this search is a methodological clue—a double-contextualization rooted in the critical analysis of the sociohistorical contexts of both reader and text(s). Sölle explains that the "hermeneutic of hunger elicits inquiry not only into the testimonies of mystical wisdom and ecstasy but also into their context."[26] This twofold contextualization grounds the inquiry process and assures

21. Ibid., 48.
22. Ibid.
23. Ibid.
24. Ibid.
25. Ibid., 51.
26. Ibid., 50.

its cohesiveness. "Contextuality is counterweight to a rambling pluralism of methods; it connects us back to the real actuality of the witnesses and protects our relation to the mysticism we have come to see against a false worldlessness."[27] Contextuality serves as a comparative criterion when evaluating the plurality of methods in academic exegesis. In addition, "contextuality brings together the relation between others' mystical experience and one's own search, as well as the others' and one's own praxis."[28] This last characteristic clarifies the relevance of O'Connor's invitation to develop a hermeneutical conversation that mediates the reality of "what the text meant and what it might mean now in specific places, among particular peoples."[29] Such a *praxis* constitutes a radical call to scholars and readers because understanding the readers' social locations involves more than mere description of their social contexts; it requires the readers' "involvement in their own situation, to such an extent that they begin to perceive and confront the victims of the socio-political dimensions on their locations."[30]

The imagery of hunger—a fundamental, unavoidable, and pressing human need—conveys the urgency of a call that embraces all of humanity and the whole creation. As Sölle explains when discussing the subtitle of her book, *The Silent Cry: Mysticism and Resistance*, "The 'and' between mysticism and resistance must be understood more radically . . . for one cannot think what one does not do. You cannot perceive or observe God's love by looking at others. . . . I can see God's love only when I become part of it myself."[31]

27. Ibid., 51–52.
28. Ibid., 52.
29. O'Connor, "Let All the Peoples Praise You," 2.
30. Prinz, *Endangering Hunger for God*, 45.
31. Sölle, *Silent Cry*, 6.

Introducing the Essays

The following collection of essays comprises somewhat of an experiment, an initial attempt at developing a hermeneutics-of-hunger approach to the biblical texts. Leading off with Kathleen O'Connor's 2009 CBA presidential address, the collection follows the canonical order with discussions of selected texts from Genesis, Isaiah, Jeremiah, Lamentations, Sirach, the Gospels of Mark, Luke, and *Thomas*, 1 Corinthians, and 2 Thessalonians.

The five essays from the Old Testament provide strong evidence for the importance of *re*-focusing on the topic of hunger from the eyes of the hungry. This responds to Kathleen O'Connor's call to biblical scholars to recognize and engage the world in front of the text. In her essay, O'Connor focuses on Genesis 11, the tower of Babel story, to show the contrast between the use of historical-critical method detached from the world in front of the text *versus* the multiplicity of meanings that emerges when including the contributions of scholars from various cultural perspectives who responsibly take their contexts into account. Laura Manzo's essay looks into the theological meaning of feeding the poor in Isa. 58:1-9a; she argues that this passage provides a vision of justice and a call to create a community of inclusion, humility, and generosity. Carol Dempsey explores the reference to "the great drought" in Jer. 14:1-9 and its connection to the theme of hunger and water scarcity; Dempsey relates the text's ancient historical context to contemporary times, addressing environmental and ecological implications inherent to the critical issue of hunger then and now. Lauress Wilkins studies the rhetorical function of war-related hunger in the book of Lamentations, focusing especially on its impact on women and children; her final remarks show that many of these oppressive practices continue very much unchanged today. Finally, Bradley

Gregory explores the social and theological influences in Ben Sira's view of hunger and poverty, arguing that the vision in Sirach aligns with the earlier Hebrew traditions that emphasize God's love for the poor and the necessity of social justice.

The five contributions for the New Testament offer a degree of variation in the volume, with two of the authors emphasizing the perspective of the world in front of the text. Mary Ann Beavis's essay describes a communal exegesis on Mark 6:33-44 that she led with the members of the CBA Feminist Biblical Hermeneutics Task Force. In setting the grounds for the communal reflection, Beavis interrelated two feeding stories—this one in the Gospel of Mark and a present-day story of Station 20 West in Saskatoon, Saskatchewan. Linda Maloney's contribution also incorporates a reflection that she shared in the context of a communal exegesis with the FBH Task Force. Maloney offers a pastoral reading of the parable of the Friend at Midnight (Luke 11:1-10), raising many questions about the interpretive implications of this parable for today's context(s).

The last three essays offer innovative findings that we hope will continue to spark stimulating conversations on the dynamics of hunger in ancient and contemporary times. Susan Elliott's essay analyzes the parable of the Woman's Empty Jar (of meal) in the *Gospel of Thomas* Logion 97, and concludes with a multilayered interpretation of the parable. Malou Ibita applies "point-of-view" analysis to the story of the Lord's Supper in 1 Cor. 11:17-34, providing readers with a window into the perspective of those who hunger. In the final contribution to this volume, Sheila McGinn and Megan Wilson-Reitz use linguistic analysis, sociohistorical criticism, and intertextuality to analyze 2 Thess. 3:6-15. They challenge the dominant interpretation of *ataktoi* as referring to "the lazy poor," instead arguing that it more likely refers to upwardly mobile social climbers who are being reproached for obedience to the cultural practices of the Empire instead of following the subversive norms of the reign of God.

We offer this collection of essays as an invitation to join in this communal exegesis of the revelatory text, focusing on the lived realities of hunger, ancient and contemporary. Hunger was and is a real, concrete issue affecting humanity and all of creation. Only through people's praxis (from reading to action, and vice versa) might we truly be able to address and nourish the physical and spiritual hungers of this world that God has committed to our care. As Christine Vladimiroff so simply and yet eloquently stated in the preface, the task at hand is to read the Scriptures by conforming our hearts to those for whom a bit of bread is an experience of God.

1

Let All the Peoples Praise You: Biblical Studies and a Hermeneutics of Hunger

Kathleen M. O'Connor

Let all the peoples praise you, O God, let all the peoples praise you. (Ps. 65:7)

If all the peoples are to praise God, surely the praise must be in their own speech, their own culture, their own specific place in the world. And if the field of biblical studies is to contribute to this global chorus of praise, it requires a hermeneutic of hunger.[1] I borrow the phrase "hermeneutics of hunger" from Dorothee Sölle, the late German theologian, who said that theology was in need of more

---

1. Dorothee Sölle, *The Silent Cry: Mysticism and Resistance*, trans. Barbara Rumscheidt and Martin Rumscheidt (Minneapolis: Fortress, 2001), 45–49.

than a hermeneutic of suspicion, more than an interpretive mode that critiqued the text to reveal its oppressive powers. To that I add, more than a historical-critical analysis that leaves the text in the past as if its meaning for today were self-evident or, more likely, outside the scope of scholarly work. What Sölle proposed by a "hermeneutic of hunger" is an interpretive stance that engages the religious content of Christian traditions and feeds the world's physical and spiritual hungers. In a similar vein, I agree deeply with the admonitions that the Bishops' Synod addressed to Catholic Biblical Scholars.[2] "While current academic exegesis, including Catholic exegesis, operates on a very high level with regard to historical-critical methodology . . . , one cannot say the same regarding study of the theological dimension of the Biblical texts."[3] The result is that the Bible becomes for its readers a book only of the past, by now incapable of speaking to our present. Under these conditions, biblical exegesis risks becoming no more than historiography and the history of literature.[4] This ecclesial statement and, in different ways, Sölle's hermeneutics of hunger come close to naming what has always engaged me most about our field, that is, the hermeneutical conversation between what the text meant and what it might mean now in specific places, among particular peoples.[5] In the strictest sense, the purpose of our work as a learned society, related in a variety of ways to Roman Catholicism, is the conversation between ancient text and present world, the

2. Synod of Roman Catholic Bishops, 12th Ordinary General Assembly, "The Word of God in the Life and Mission of the Church," *Instrumentum Laboris* (Vatican City, 2008), http://www.vatican.va/roman_curia/synod/documents/rc_synod_doc_20080511_instrlabor-xii-assembly_en.html.
3. *Instrumentum Laboris* 25.
4. "The second consequence, perhaps even more grave, is the disappearance of the hermeneutics of faith indicated in *Dei Verbum*. In the place of a believing hermeneutics, a positivistic and secular hermeneutics insinuates itself, denying the possibility of either the presence, or the accessibility, of the divine in the history of humanity" ("Word of God," prop. 26).
5. See Kathleen M. O'Connor, "Crossing Borders: Biblical Studies in a Trans-Cultural World," in *Teaching the Bible: The Discourses and Politics of Biblical Pedagogy*, ed. Fernando F. Segovia and Mary Ann Tolbert (Maryknoll, NY: Orbis, 1998), 322–37.

discovery and creation of meanings. Whatever philological, historical, archaeological, sociological, and comparative ancient Near Eastern materials are brought to bear on interpretation, the text's power for a wider audience than scholars consists, at least in part, in being put back together as a literary and theological document. Some among us already do this in a wide variety of forums. My thesis is this: biblical studies can better fulfill its promise to church and world if more among us were to expand our methods beyond historical-critical approaches toward a hermeneutic of hunger. To do so may require a transformation of perspectives something akin to what has been happening in feminist biblical studies for decades. Feminist interpretation engages in global conversations about the meanings of texts and has learned what many among us now take for granted—that interpretation is both illuminated and obscured by the interpreter's cultural contexts.[6] To make my argument, I turn to the so-called tower of Babel text in Gen. 11:1-9 (hereafter Genesis 11). After a brief rhetorical analysis of the passage, I present a recent scholarly scuffle about the text, occurring largely in the *Journal of Biblical Literature*, followed by readings from other parts of the world that engage in a self-conscious hermeneutics of hunger. I conclude with reflections on the passage from my perspective as a Roman Catholic woman in the United States.

---

6. See recently D. M. Premnath, ed., *Border Crossings: Cross-Cultural Hermeneutics* (Maryknoll, NY: Orbis, 2007); and R. S. Sugirtharajah, ed., *Still at the Margins: Biblical Scholarship Fifteen Years after the Voices from the Margin* (Edinburgh: T & T Clark, 2007).

Genesis 11:1-9

A. Translation

Part 1: Human Actions

v. 1. Now [ויהי] all the earth [כל הארץ] [had] one tongue [שפה אחת] and the same words.

v. 2. Now [ויהי] when they migrated from the east, they found a plain in the land of Shinar. And they settled there [שם].

v. 3. And they said [ואמרו] each to his neighbor [רעהו]: "Come [הבה], let us make bricks, and let us completely burn them." And they had [להם] bricks for stone, and they had [להם] bitumen for pitch.

v. 4. And they said [ויאמרו]: "Come [הבה], let us build for ourselves [נבנה-לנו] a city and a tower [עיר ומגדל] with its head in the heavens. And let us make a name for ourselves [ונעשה-לנו שם] lest we be scattered [נפוץ] upon the face [על-פני] of all the earth" [כל הארץ].

Part 2: Divine Actions and Conclusions

v. 5. And YHWH came down [וירד] to see the city and the tower [את-העיר ואת-המגדל] that the children [sons] of humankind had built.

v. 6. And YHWH said [ויאמר]: "Look, they are one people with one tongue [ושפה אחת] to them all. And this is the beginning of what they will do,[7] and now nothing will be cut off from them of all they plan to do.

v. 7. Come [הבה], let us go down [נרדה] and let us there [שם] baffle[8] [ונבלה] their tongue [שפתם] so that each will not understand the tongue [שפת] of his neighbor" [רעהו].

---

7. Barry Bandstra, *Genesis 1–11: A Handbook on the Hebrew Text*, Baylor Handbook on the Hebrew Bible (Waco: Baylor University Press, 2008), 565.

8. Everett Fox's term (*The Five Books of Moses: Genesis, Exodus, Leviticus, Numbers, Deuteronomy: A New Translation with Introductions, Commentary, and Notes*, Schocken Bible 1 [New York: Schocken, 1995], 49) for the Hebrew verb with the primary meaning "to confuse," which also mirrors the sound play of the text.

v. 8. YHWH scattered [ויפץ] them from there [שם] upon the face of [על-פני] all the earth [כל-הארץ]. And they stopped building [לבנת] the city [העיר].

v. 9. Therefore, the city is named [שמה] Babel [בבל][9] because there [שם] YHWH baffled [בלל] the tongue [שפת] of all the earth [כל-הארץ]. And from there [ומשם] YHWH scattered them [הפיצם] upon the face of [על-פני] all the earth [כל-הארץ].

In my view, Gen. 11:1-9 is best understood as a language world, a thing of beauty, a work of art that refuses reduction to a single meaning. Language forges the unity of the people in the text; words unify the text itself, even as God's words move everything in the opposite direction toward the baffling of speech.[10] Although there are many ways to divide the text, I identify two units: Human Actions (vv. 1-4) and Divine Actions and Conclusions (vv. 5-9).

B. The Verbal Structure

One way to approach the literary structure of the passage is through its many verbal repetitions. Words repeat within each unit, and across the two units.

Words Repeat within Each Unit

Words Repeating within Part 1

"Now," ויהי (vv. 1 and 2) "And they said," ויאמרו (vv. 3 and 4) "For themselves," להם (v. 3 twice) "Come," הבה (vv. 3 and 4)

---

9. Bandstra (*Genesis 1–11*, 575) translates "he called its name" on the grounds that YHWH is the presumed agent, as in the next clause.
10. The text has at work both centripetal and centrifugal literary forces, according to Bernhard W. Anderson, "The Tower of Babel: Unity and Diversity in God's Creation," in *From Creation to New Creation: Old Testament Perspectives*, OBT (Minneapolis: Fortress, 1994), 165–68.

Words Repeating within Part 2

"Came Down," וירד and נרדה (vv. 5 and 7) "Baffled," ונבלה and בלל (vv. 7 and 9) "YHWH," יהוה (vv. 5, 6, 8, 9 [twice])

Words and Phrases Repeating across the Two Units to Fashion a Unified Whole

"All the earth," כל-הארץ (vv. 1, 4, and vv. 8, 9) "Upon the face of," על-פני (v. 4 and vv. 8, 9) "One tongue," שפה אחת (vv. 1, 6), "their tongue," שפתם (v. 7), and "tongue of," שפת (vv. 7, 9) "Scattered," נפוץ (v. 4) and ויפץ, הפיצם (vv. 8, 9) "Said," "And they said," ויאמרו (vv. 3 and 4) and ויאמר יהוה (v. 6) "Build," נבנה (v. 4) and לבנת (v. 8) "City," עיר (v. 4) and העיר (v. 8) "Name," שם (v. 4) and שמה (v. 9) "There," שם (v. 2) and משם, שם (vv. 7, 8, 9 [twice]) Whatever might be the origins of Genesis 11, and whatever original sources might now thread through it, the passage is a unified composition[11] of two balanced parts with a conclusion in v. 9. The text is a silken weave of words, a fabric of threaded language about language—artful, economical, evocative, turning back upon and echoing itself in a narrative précis about speech. Because language is so closely interwoven across the passage, it is hard to imagine that Genesis 11 could be a compression of two previously existing sources, as Hermann Gunkel proposed.[12] Despite his appreciation of source criticism, Joel S. Baden also challenges Gunkel's assessment of the text as an amalgam of two sources.[13] "Genesis 11:1-9," he writes, "shows none of the hallmarks of a

---

11. See Joel S. Baden, "The Tower of Babel: A Case Study in the Competing Methods of Historical and Modern Literary Criticism," *JBL* 128 (2009): 209–24, here 217, for a source-critical look at the text's composition.

12. Hermann Gunkel, *Genesis*, trans. Mark Biddle, 3rd ed., 1910, Mercer Library of Biblical Studies (Macon, GA: Mercer University Press, 1997) 94–102; and see Baden, "Tower of Babel," 209–24.

13. Baden, "Tower of Babel," 217–18.

composite text: contradictions, doublets, or other narrative inconsistencies."[14]

C. The Narrative Flow of the Passage

Part 1 (11:1-4)

Even as words unify the text, the narrative flow confuses it. Part 1 begins in harmony, unanimity of tongue, one set of words for "all the earth." The migrating population moves as one to settle "there" (םש) in the land of Shinar. The settlers think together and then speak together as one undifferentiated mass, with the intensifying action verb "Come," combined with the cohortative "let us make." "Come, let us make."[15] The unified thinkers and speakers now become unified makers of bricks and bitumen. Again, they speak with an action verb and cohortative, "Come, let us build for ourselves a city and tower," and with these words, the unified thinkers, speakers, and makers (v. 3) become unified builders (v. 4). Finally, with a third cohortative, they tell why they should do these things: "Let us make a name for ourselves lest we be scattered." They are a singular community, an undifferentiated collective, an entity, uniform in thought, word, and deed. The act of building city and tower is itself a form of language, that is, an expression of desire and fear "lest we be scattered" (v. 4). To realize their desires and forestall their fears, all must think, speak, and act alike. Uniformity is a shield against unspecified dangers. Among them, there is no report of conflict, disharmony, or disruption; there is no other thought, no other voice. Such is life in Babel.

---

14. Ibid., 217. Baden challenges literary criticism for failing "to prove" the unity of the text.

15. According to Bruce K. Waltke and M. O'Connor (*An Introduction to Biblical Hebrew Syntax* [Winona Lake, IN: Eisenbrauns, 1990] 34.5.1a, 21 [575]), "The effect of the plural cohortative is frequently heightened by a verb of motion in the imperative, which functions as an auxiliary or interjection" (574).

Part 2 (11:5-9)

Divine speech in part 2 unravels all the human efforts in part 1. Rather than bringing further cohesion, divine language baffles, disturbs, and destroys. YHWH "comes down" to see what humans have built, and YHWH "said" (ויאמר) what the narrator has already said: "They are one people with one tongue" (שפה אחת). To this, YHWH adds the observation that this is only the beginning of what they can think, scheme, or plan to do, however one translates זמם. Next, YHWH continues to speak and also acts, and each of these engagements with humans has a consequence. YHWH's speech mirrors the grammatical pattern of human speech, employing the cohortative twice and repeating the hortatory action word: "Come, let us go down [נרדה] and let us there baffle [ונבלה] their tongue" (v. 7). The consequence of the divine tongue-baffling is that humans cannot understand their neighbors. But for YHWH, baffled tongues are not enough. In v. 8, YHWH acts to scatter (ויפץ) the people from there (שם) upon the face of all the earth (כל-הארץ). The consequence of divine scattering is the end of city building (v. 8). The story could end here, but three interrelated conclusions summarize it and explain it (v. 9):

1. The city is named Babel.
2. There the tongue of all the earth is baffled.
3. And from there, humans are scattered upon the face of all the earth.

The city and tower disappear, and building ceases, not because of divine destruction but because of divine scattering. When YHWH scatters the humans, everyone—*every single human being*—becomes a migrant, a refugee, and a displaced person who cannot understand the language.[16] Genesis 11 celebrates language through verbal repetitions and narrative flow. Its compressed lines; parallel constructions; wordplays; and repeated sounds, words, and phrases make it as much poetry as prose. Possible meanings appear as tones and hints in a rippling swirl of sounds and words.[17] A perfect postmodern template of the world, the text baffles us by defying reduction to a single meaning, even as it begs for a hermeneutic of hunger.

D. Confusions of Meanings

The text contains confusions that enact and perform the baffling of tongues. Nearly every line of Genesis 11 admits of multiple meanings, meanings left open by the text that lead readers along a path of ambiguity. Is the tower, for example, a work of hubris[18] or merely a city-tower, such as the tower of Shechem (Judg. 9:46)?[19] Does the people's making a name for themselves signify self-promotion in place of God,[20] or is it the means of acquiring honor by which people protect themselves?[21] Is the baffling of languages punishment for sin or a celebration of diversity of language and cultures? Vigorous debate about these and related questions enlivens current scholarly work on the passage. Where the text refuses definitive meaning, however, these interpretations each arrive at a

---

16. See Jean Pierre Ruiz, "Abram and Sarai Cross the Border: Reading Genesis 12:10-20 with People on the Move," in Premnath, *Border Crossings*, 15–34.

17. See sound plays noted by Robert Alter, *Genesis: Translation and Commentary* (New York: W. W. Norton, 1996), 47: "*Hi eimar* becomes *hiomer*," and *sham, shamayin,* and *shem,* and *balal* and Babel.

18. André LaCocque, "Whatever Happened in the Valley of Shinar? A Response to Theodore Hiebert," *JBL* 128 (2009): 29–41, here 36; and John T. Strong, "Shattering the Image of God: A Response to Theodore Hiebert's Interpretation of the Story of the Tower of Babel," *JBL* 127 (2008): 625–34, here 633.

19. Ellen van Wolde, *Words Become Worlds: Semitic Studies of Genesis 1–11*, BIS 6 (Leiden: Brill, 1994), 80–109; Theodore Hiebert, "The Tower of Babel and the Origin of the World's Cultures," *JBL* 126 (2007): 29–58, here 33–41. See Nahum M. Sarna, *Understanding Genesis*, Heritage of Biblical Israel 1 (New York: Jewish Theological Seminary, 1966), 73.

20. LaCocque,"Whatever Happened," 36.

21. So Hiebert, "Tower of Babel," 40.

claim for the "one true meaning" of the text. My survey of four recent interpretations finds a great diversity of exposition among them but a common philosophy underlying them that arises from scientific historical-critical approaches.

1. Ellen van Wolde's semiotic reading concludes that Gen. 11:1-9 is not the traditional crime-and-punishment tale that much interpretation claims for it.[22] It is not about human sin, or even much about humans at all. Rather, the scattering of humans expresses divine intention to "fill and cultivate" the earth, a commission in Gen. 1:28-29 that humans have avoided by settling in one place.[23] The text is an ecological expression that reveals the primeval history (Genesis 1–11) to be about God's relation to the created world, in which humans play a minor role, indeed.

2. Building on van Wolde's literary work, Theodore Hiebert agrees that the multiplication of languages in Genesis 11 is not punishment for the sin of human pride.[24] Like others, he notes that the tower, with its head in the heavens, is merely a tall building, mentioned only once as part of the city. The text, instead, celebrates Babylon as the cradle of civilization and the origin of diverse cultures in which God revels.

3. John T. Strong disagrees with Hiebert's diminishment of the tower.[25] Tower building in Genesis 11 is, for Strong, an act of idolatry as suggested by ancient Near Eastern victory stelae (Ashur-nasir-pal of Assyria stela [883–859 BCE]).[26] These stelae established a king's authority over conquered territory and often

22. Van Wolde, *Words Become Worlds*, 80–109.
23. Ibid., 102.
24. Hiebert, "Tower of Babel," 29–59.
25. Strong, "Shattering the Image of God," 625–34.
26. Ibid., 630.

bore the king's image. The tower of Genesis 11 is such a construction, upon which humans put their own image in the place of the divine image. According to Strong, this means that God's creation of humankind in the divine image (Gen. 1:26) has been a crashing failure. After this, only Israel, not humankind, is made in God's image.[27]

4. On source-critical grounds and with the interpretive conviction that "reception history is determinative," André LaCocque also holds to a crime-and-punishment reading.[28] The tower building is an act of prideful idolatry that plays a climactic role in the Yahwist's agenda to depict the growth of sin, later reversed in Abraham. Diversity of language and culture is the consequence of sin.

Each of these recent interpretations is insightful, lucid, and elegant, and each compels assent on some points. Yet all of them attempt to tame the text, to find one meaning, nail it down, and "prove" it objectively with the sharp eyes of the scientific exegete. Van Wolde, for example, writes, "*The point* is not the perspective of the people, but the perspective of the earth."[29] Hiebert says, "The text is exclusively about the origins of cultural difference and not about pride and punishment at all."[30] And Strong declares that the story "conveys the message that God has given up on all humankind." Only one people (i.e., Israel) is "to be made anew in that image."[31] Ironically, van Wolde objects to scholars who "present their work as 'objective datum' that is immediately evident to everyone" (she refers to Jan P. Fokkelman).[32] She adds in her critique, "Ordering

---

27. Ibid., 633–34.
28. LaCocque, "Whatever Happened," 29.
29. Van Wolde, *Words Become Worlds*, 102.
30. Hiebert, "Tower of Babel," 31.
31. Strong, "Shattering the Image of God," 628.

of the stylistic data seems in fact to be largely dependent on the exegete."[33] These studies of Genesis 11, a text that baffles attempts at one meaning, demonstrate that illusions of scientific objectivity (conscious and unconscious!) still prevail in our field, perhaps in a kind of tower building that obscures rich layers of meaning in the text and the role of interpreters in finding it.[34] Feminist biblical studies and postcolonial criticism point in other directions.

Conversion to the World

When feminist biblical study reappeared in the middle of the twentieth century, it was driven by a hermeneutic of hunger.[35] It sought and continues to seek words of life for women and others excluded both in life and in text. Euro-American feminists used methods we learned in the academy and arrived at our own universalist interpretations. But it did not take long to discover that white middle-class women were reading as if we had discovered the truth for all women. We were assuming that women readers and believers were one uniform entity everywhere, and that the text had one meaning heretofore hidden in the male domain. Soon other women in the United States—*mujerista*,[36] womanist,[37] and Asian American[38]—and women from the two-thirds world[39] began to

---

32. Van Wolde, *Words Become Worlds*, 89; J. P. Fokkelman, *Narrative Art in Genesis: Specimens of Stylistic and Structural Analysis*, SSN 17 (Assen: Van Gorcum, 1975).

33. Van Wolde, *Words Become Worlds*, 89.

34. Van Wolde (ibid., 205) acknowledges the reader's participation in meaning making across her study, yet she still holds to the view that the exegete, as opposed to the theologian, "does not focus on the current problems of mankind but on the text." Yet her ecological reading clearly has its catalyst in the current problems of humankind.

35. Kathleen M. O'Connor, "The Feminist Movement Meets the Old Testament: One Woman's Perspective," in *Engaging the Bible in a Gendered World: An Introduction to Feminist Biblical Interpretation in Honor of Katharine Doob Sakenfeld*, ed. Linda Day and Carolyn Pressler (Louisville: Westminster John Knox, 2007), 3–24; see the expansion in perspectives across the work of Elisabeth Schüssler Fiorenza from her groundbreaking *In Memory of Her: A Feminist Theological Reconstruction of Christian Origins* (New York: Crossroad, 1983) to later works, including *Sharing Her Word: Feminist Biblical Interpretation in Context* (Boston: Beacon, 1998).

reveal the entrenched biases of our race, class, and national identities, hidden behind our privilege, and to underscore how our conceptions of power relations and gender roles afflict our work. Often bitter and acrimonious, these exchanges about texts continue to reveal to Euro-American women who we are, to expand notions of communities with whom we read, and to demonstrate how texts yield interpretations dependent, in part, on contexts of interpreters. This is what the wider field of biblical studies in general has yet to appreciate, though the conversation has been going on for decades, and the culturally specific nature of interpretation is an agreed premise among many of us.[40]

A. Critical Tools Are Necessary to Protect the Text's Strangeness

In emphasizing the role of reading contexts in a hermeneutic of hunger, I am not advocating abandonment of historical-critical methods as the sine qua non of our work. Lawrence Boadt said it well in a recent review in the *CBQ* of a book by John Barton.[41]

---

36. Feminist and postcolonial literatures are enormous and growing. On *mujerista* interpretation, see especially Ada María Isasi-Díaz, "Communication as Communion: Elements in a Hermeneutic of *lo cotidiano*," in Day and Pressler, *Engaging the Bible in a Gendered World*, 27–36.
37. Nyasha Junior, "Womanist Biblical Interpretation," in Day and Pressler, *Engaging the Bible in a Gendered World*, 37–46.
38. Tat-siong Benny Liew and Gale A. Yee, eds., *The Bible in Asian America*, Semeia 90/91 (Atlanta: Society of Biblical Literature, 2002).
39. See Musa W. Dube, *Postcolonial Feminist Interpretation of the Bible* (St. Louis: Chalice, 2000), esp. 111–24.
40. See the oeuvre of Fernando F. Segovia, including *Decolonizing Biblical Studies: A View from the Margins* (Maryknoll, NY: Orbis, 2000); and Segovia and Mary Ann Tolbert, eds., *Reading from This Place*, 2 vols. (Minneapolis: Fortress, 1995); R. S. Sugirtharajah, *Postcolonial Reconfigurations: An Alternative Way of Reading the Bible and Doing Theology* (St. Louis: Chalice, 2003); and Sugirtharajah, *Voices from the Margin: Interpreting the Bible in the Third World* (Maryknoll, NY: Orbis, 1995); Vincent L. Wimbush, *The Bible and African Americans: A Brief History*, Facets (Minneapolis: Fortress, 2003).
41. Lawrence Boadt, review of John Barton, *The Old Testament: Canon, Literature and Theology: Collected Essays of John Barton*, SOTSMS (Burlington, VT: Ashgate, 2007), *CBQ* 71 (2009): 665–66.

Exegesis has its scientific and critical role of unlocking the historical setting, finding the sense of the text's words in original contexts, and analyzing how the text measures up against the standards by which literature is often measured . . . to enlighten the plain meaning of the text. . . . To prevent ideological kidnapping of the meaning of biblical books, scholarship must preserve rigorous neutrality.[42]

Distance from the text is the goal, of course, but neutrality is not possible. To think so is to be trapped in an ideological argument. Historical-critical studies are essential because they remind us that interpretation of ancient texts is a cross-cultural conversation, that the text is "a stranger," foreign to us, whose meaning is hidden by distances of language, worldview, culture, material realities, and profound gaps in human experience. At the same time, Mikhail Bakhtin, Paul Ricoeur, and other postmodern literary critics, philosophers of language, postcolonialists, and feminists urge us to modify our scientific, dualistic assumptions about texts and interpreters.[43] They have convinced many among us of the culturally situated, linguistically multiple, polyglot nature of all texts and interpretations. The problem for interpreters is the abundance of significance that cannot be exposed by one reader or one cultural approach. Genesis 11, by its own multiplicity of meaning, calls for readings from various cultural perspectives. Although both van Wolde and Hiebert employ an implicit hermeneutics of hunger with their respective themes of ecology and diversity, neither does so with the expressed consciousness of the ways in which cultural

---

42. Boadt, review, 665, 666.
43. See Pam Morris, ed., *The Bakhtin Reader: Selected Writings of Bakhtin, Medvedev, and Voloshinov* (London: Edward Arnold, 1994); Paul Ricoeur, *Figuring the Sacred: Religion, Narrative, and Imagination* (Minneapolis: Fortress, 1995). See further Mark Rathbone, "Unity and Scattering: Toward a Holistic Reading of Genesis 11:1-9 in the South African Context," in *Genesis*, ed. Athalya Brenner, Archie Chi-Chung Lee, and Gale A. Yee, Texts @ Contexts (Minneapolis: Fortress, 2010), 99–106 ; and Solomon Avorti, "Genesis 11:1-9: An African Perspective," in *Return to Babel: Global Perspectives on the Bible*, ed. Priscilla Pope-Levison and John R. Levison (Louisville: Westminster John Knox, 1999), 17–26.

environments contribute to their readings. Interpretations of Genesis 11 from the postcolonial world proceed differently. Here, among others,[44] are three readings from other cultural situations; they exhibit various levels of critical sophistication, but all three engage self-consciously in a hermeneutic of hunger. The late J. Severino Croatto, historical critic from Argentina, agreed that Genesis 11 is a crime-and-punishment tale. The proud sinner, however, is not universal humanity but Babel—the Babylonian empire of the sixth century—with its concentration of power; its oppressive control; and its efforts, in the pattern of empires, to impose a uniform language, normative worldview, and culture.[45] This uniformity imposed by Babylon is the problem that God sees and punishes by destroying the city and tower. José Míguez-Bonino expands Croatto's interpretation in light of Ecuadoran history. Seven years after Pizarro arrived in the new land, the population of native Incans in Ecuador was reduced from seven million to seven hundred thousand.[46] The Spanish conquest imposed a new language and eradicated native tongues. The loss of their languages denied the people everything that gave meaning to life—stories, traditions, songs, words of music, words of family, words of love. Míguez-Bonino sees in Nimrod, the mighty warrior and founder of Babel in the table of nations (Gen. 10:8-12), additional evidence of imperial oppression. But God goes down to thwart the empire's "project of false unity" and to destroy the tyranny of one language, one culture, one economic system.[47] Choan-Seng Song argues something similar from the context of Taiwan.[48] Genesis

---

44. Genesis 11:1-9 was used to support apartheid in South Africa. See Rathbone, "Unity and Scattering"; Avorti, "Genesis 11:1-9: An African Perspective."

45. J. Severino Croatto, "A Reading of the Story of the Tower of Babel from the Perspective of Non-Identity: Gen. 11:1-9 in the Context of Its Production," in Segovia and Tolbert, *Teaching the Bible*, 203–23.

46. José Míguez-Bonino, "Genesis 11:1-9: A Latin American Perspective," in Pope-Levison and Levison, *Return to Babel*, 13–16.

47. Ibid., 15.

11 is not about conflict within God, threatened by human building, but about conflict within the human community, caused by dictators, religious authorities, and the economically powerful, whose towers and cities have created untold miseries. God demolishes this tower because God stands among women and men who suffer and endure hardship under such towers. These interpreters do not have the luxury, as we do in the world's dominant culture, of being ideologically neutral. They understand their work as a living, Spirit-driven process that feeds their communities. All of them push matters of empire, while we who read from within the empire hardly notice it because we live in a different reality.[49]

B. A Roman-Catholic Feminist Interpretation

When I think about a hermeneutic of hunger from my context as an American Catholic laywoman and pew sitter, I note that women and men in the church are hungry for a living word to get them through their days and to join them more fully with Christ's body in the world. Finding such interpretation is like finding a treasure hidden in a field, more rare than a precious jewels. Although there are many institutional reasons for this "famine" of the word of God in the land (Amos 8:11), I lament it mightily and wonder what happened to the biblical renewal movement that helped fuel Vatican II and drew many of us to the joys of this work. I wonder if at least some part of the problem relates to the ways biblical studies conducts its teaching and communicates its research, too often leaving the text in history; accepting the dualisms of the university; excluding aesthetics, imagination, and faith from the enterprise; and skipping over the

---

48. Choan-Seng Song, "Genesis 11:1-9: An Asian Perspective," in Pope-Levison and Levison, *Return to Babel*, 27–36.

49. Since Hiebert ("Tower of Babel," 35) limits himself entirely to the boundaries of this story, he finds it anachronistic to include concerns of empire in its interpretation.

"so what" following upon the rigorous technical work that grounds interpretation. But I have more specific concerns in conversation with this text. Influenced by postcolonial readings, I find Genesis 11 to be a passage that both names the predicament of women and others in the church and reveals a God who creates hope for the excluded. As both source of life and place of oppression, Babel evokes my church. In this passage, Babel is the cradle of civilization, as Hiebert insists, the starting point from which everyone migrates, the source of languages, the place from which Abraham and Sarah's family depart. But Babel is also—for readers of the Priestly version of the Pentateuch, as LaCocque and Croatto remind us—the fierce lion that attacks and destroys Judah, Jeremiah's "foe from the north," the symbol of aggrandizing, oppressive empire. The Roman Catholic Church is surely a source of life; a guardian of justice; and a cradle of faith and intellectual life, religious identity, sacramental teaching, eucharistic practice, and contemplative living that abide thick in my bones. It stands so often with the excluded, the migrant, the hungry, and the burdened. And simultaneously, it is an empire—a city and tower of settled thinking, of uniform planning and acting—that seeks to control languages of praise, that negates women's lives and voices, that prohibits speech about subjects it designates as taboo, that cuts off the words of anyone who disagrees on matters affecting their own most intimate lives. It lives with blindness about sexual bodies and gives room for the repressed to return in monstrous forms. The ecclesial city and the tower operate too often from the desire to control and from fear of the world's multiple tongues of faith and many voices of praise. It seeks to impose one language upon "all the people," squelching the Spirit at work among the laity, and even among clerics and episcopal leaders. The city and tower with its head in the heavens tries to impose false unity, relies on the tongue of authority and submission, and can be deaf to other ways of speaking of the living God. But the theology of Genesis 11 offers a positive vision. This text both hides and reveals God in a baffling glimpse of a divine cohort. It leaves divine motives unnamed behind actions and words. This God acts by coming down among us to see, to look around at the towers and cities of uniform thinking. This God speaks to unsettle, to breed confusion, and to overthrow the dominance of one tongue, one way to speak, one way to understand our neighbors. This is the "unsettled and 'unsettling' God"[50] who removes the shields of protection erected when everyone must think, speak, and act alike. Yet God does not annihilate the builders of city and tower. The baffling God of Genesis 11 acts against fears that muzzle praise. God disperses them over the face of the earth, where they and we become migrants, displaced people who do not know the language of the new place. There we can listen, learn, and meet God anew among the peoples in all their beauteous, blessed, and baffling tongues. Together, perhaps we may create new languages of interpretation and praise, and we may learn that the languages of praise and of interpretation are multiple. This text anticipates the Pentecost scene in Acts 2, where the Spirit comes in tongues of fire. "The crowd gathered and was bewildered [baffled], because each one heard them speaking in the native language of each" (Acts 2:6; NRSV). "All were amazed and perplexed, saying to one another, 'What does this mean?'" (Acts 2:12). I do not think we yet know, but Acts 2 does not reverse Genesis 11;[51] it fulfills it in the glorious profusion of fiery tongues. "Let all the peoples praise you, O God."

50. See Walter Brueggemann, *An Unsettling God: The Heart of the Hebrew Bible* (Minneapolis: Fortress, 2009).
51. Contra Richard I. Pervo (*Acts: A Commentary*, Hermeneia (Minneapolis, Fortress, 2008], 61), who asserts that Acts reverses the "linguistic disunity" of Babel, but that Acts 2 leaves intact the languages of the Jews gathered in Jerusalem from all over the world. The new unity is one of understanding in the midst of multiplicity.

2

———

Feeding the Poor in Isaiah 58:1-9a: A Call to Justice, Mercy, and True Worship

J. L. Manzo

> For the Lord your God is God of gods and Lord of lords, the great God, mighty and awesome, who is not partial and takes no bribe, who executes justice to the orphan and the widow, and who loves the strangers, providing them food and clothing. (Deut. 10:17-18)[1]

Hunger and famine were powerful images to the people of the ancient Near East. In Palestine, an abundant harvest depended on an adequate water surplus. On a land that experienced frequent droughts, hunger and famine meant suffering and loss of life. According to the biblical text, hunger stalked Abraham (Gen. 12:10),

---

1. All scriptural quotations are taken from the NRSV.

Isaac (26:1), Joseph (41:27, 54), David (2 Sam. 21:1), Elijah (1 Kgs. 18:2), and Elisha (2 Kgs. 4:38; 8:1). We also learned that Israel experienced physical hunger in the wilderness (Exod. 16:3) and that hunger was a prominent image in Hebrew poetry (Ps. 107:5, 9, 26; Neh. 9:1). This essay will study the theological meaning of feeding the poor as it is developed with the themes of "fasting and true worship" in Isa. 58:1-9a. Based on a literary analysis of the text, I will consider three fundamental issues—acts of charity as genuine fast and worship, biblical norms dealing with "shared harvest," and spiritual ramifications of caring for the poor. I will treat these topics in the body of the essay under the following titles:

I. A Call to Self-Incrimination;
II. Feeding the Poor: A Call to Share the Abundance of God's Blessing; and
III. Spiritual Rewards to Feeding the Hungry.

The need to care for the hungry in Isaiah is based on the theological conviction that the promised land is a gift from God to the covenant people (Deut. 8:7-10; Lev. 25:23). The land was an image of abundance.[2] The phrase, "land of milk and honey" mentions two agricultural products to represent the fertile condition of the promised land. The Israelites were the beneficiaries of an abundance willed at creation (Gen. 1:22).[3] An abundant harvest produced by the land is in the biblical tradition a sign of divine blessing that must be shared with joy with others, especially the poor. Almsgivings in Isaiah also takes on the meaning of justice. A just man is a kind and charitable person who not only engages on acts of worship, but whose actions mirror God's mercy.

---

2. Passages such as Deut. 8:7-9 and 11:10-12 provide a detailed description of the land's suitability for agriculture. The land given by YHWH yielded abundant water, wheat, barley, fig trees, pomegranates, olive oil, and honey.
3. Walter Brueggemann, *Deuteronomy* (Nashville: Abingdon, 2001), 108.

Isaiah 58 has been identified as a sermon addressed to the returned exiles in Jerusalem by a preacher, teacher, or synagogue leader.[4] The passage deals with the issues of religious observance, social justice, daily relations, and Sabbath observance. Chapter 58:1-9a may be divided into three sections based on its thematic context: vv. 1-2, vv. 3-4, and vv. 5-9a.[5] Verses 1-2 are an exhortation to proclaim the sins of the people. Section two (vv. 3-4) is a communal lament against God for not taking notice of people's fast. The third section explains the reasons for God's failure to acknowledge their fasting (vv. 5-9a). While the penitents are practicing external acts of devotion, their moral behavior does not conform to God's law.

I. A Call to Self-Incrimination

The first section of the text introduces the commissioning of the prophet. Isaiah is called to proclaim a message of condemnation against individuals who considered themselves self-righteous and pious observers of religious tradition:

> Shout out, do not hold back.
> Lift up your voice like a trumpet!
> Announce to my people their rebellion,
> to the house of Jacob their sins
> Yet, day after day they seek me
> and delight to know my ways,

---

4. George A. E. Knight, *The New Israel: A Commentary on the Book of Isaiah 56–66*, ITC (Grand Rapids: Eerdmans, 1985), 22; Michael Thompson, *Isaiah 40–66* (Peterborough: Epworth, 2001), 134; P. Volz, *Jesaja II, Zweite Hälfte: Kapitel 40–66* (Leipzig: Deichert, 1932), 197.

5. In the fourth section (vv. 9b-12), the prophet condemns false righteousness. In the final section (vv. 13-14), he deals with the Sabbath observance. In this study, I will analyze vv. 1-9a as the main focus on the subject of hunger. The last two sections of the text reiterate what is previously mentioned in the passage. See Joseph Blenkinsopp, *Isaiah 56–60: A New Translation with Introduction and Commentary*, AB 19B (New York: Doubleday, 2003), 173–75. For further structural analysis, see also Christopher R. Seitz, "The Book of Isaiah 40–66" in *The New Interpreter's Bible*, 12 vols (Nashville: Abingdon, 1994), 6: 498–99.

> as if they were a nation that practiced righteousness
> and did not forsake the ordinance of their God;
> They ask of me righteous judgments,
> they delight to draw near to God (Isa. 58:1-2)

In verse one, the prophet is commanded to "announce to my people their rebellion, and to the house of Jacob their sin." The prophet is to announce publicly the social sin of the people by raising his voice like a trumpet.[6] Isaiah's action is similar to earlier prophetic announcements. When the people breached the covenant, for example, Hosea is commanded to "put the trumpet to his lips" (8:1), and Ezek. 33:5 speaks of the dangers of ignoring the trumpet blast. In the Old Testament, a trumpet blast signaled the beginning of an attack (Judg. 3:27; 6:34; Jer. 6:1, 17).[7] The metaphor of the trumpet serves to assert the gravity of the people's rebellion and sin. What constituted the people's rebellion and sin? The indictment comes in verse 2. The verse may be divided into three sets of bicola:[8]

a. and yet, day after day they seek me, and delight (חפץ) to know my ways

b. as if they were a nation that practice righteousness (צדקה) and did not forsake the ordinance (משפט) of their God;

c. they ask of me just judgments (משפטי), they delight (חפץ) to draw near to God.

The verb *delight* frames the unit. The attention falls on element b), the abandoning of God's justice. According to Gregory Poland, while

---

6. I interpret social justice within the prophetic tradition to include care for the widow, the orphan, the alien, and the poor (Zech. 7:10; Mal. 3:5; Jer. 22:3; Ezek. 22:7).

7. A trumpet blast also indicated a summons to war (Job 39:24; Jer. 4:19), an end of an attack (2 Sam. 2:28; 18:16; 20:22), a warning of a coming attack (Jer. 6:1, 17; Ezek. 33:3-6; Hos. 5:8; Joel 2:1), or military victory (1 Sam. 13:3).

8. Gregory Polan, *In the Ways of Justice toward Salvation: A Rhetorical Analysis of Isaiah 56–59* (New York: Peter Lang, 1986), 192.

the text speaks of a righteous and just nation, it however suggests that the "inauthentic seeking and knowing of the divinity is a forsaking of God; though a comparison of this people is made with a just nation that does not forsake its God, the point is that when a people claims to seek and know its God and in the end achieves its own pleasures, it strays for its goal, it abandons its God."[9] Thus, while the people display great fervor to know the ways of YHWH so as to be near him, their worship practices are not disinterested. In the midst of the exile crisis, the chosen people desire to know how God will intervene in history to save them; they pray for YHWH's "just decisions," that is, the fulfillment of God's promise to redeem Israel and punish its enemies. The irony of the text is that while they pray for "just decisions" from YHWH, they live unjust lives. The major problem facing this community is that they worship as if they practice righteousness and the justice of God. The phrase צדקה עשה (v. 2) is translated as "doing righteousness." In the prophetic literature, as it is the case here, צדקה (justice, righteousness) is often juxtaposed with משפט (judgment) to describe the responsibilities of the people of the covenant toward each other, including liberation of the oppressed and care for the poor (Amos 5:7, 24; Jer. 22:3, 15; Ezek. 18:5-9).[10]

9. Ibid.
10. John W. Olley, *Righteousness in the Septuagint of Isaiah: A Contextual Study* (Missoula, Montana: Scholars Press, 1979), 110. The Hebrew term צדקה is also used in the Hebrew Bible to speak of God's righteousness as a relationship of responsibility and loyalty with humanity. Some of the words that parallel צדקה (justice, righteousness) include אסת (truth), מירשמי (equity), and חסד (loving kindness). The term refers to judgments made with love and in the pursuit of truth and equality. Such an understanding of God's justice necessitates improving the condition of the poor and afflicted. See Jill Jacobs, *There Shall Be No Needy: Pursuing Social Justice through Jewish Law and Tradition* (Woodstock: Jewish Lights Publishing, 2009), 41–42; Moshe Weinfeld, *Social Justice in the Ancient Israel and in the Ancient Near East* (Minneapolis: Fortress, 1995), 35.

The accusation that the household of Jacob has forsaken YHWH's justice is implicitly expounded in the discussion surrounding true fasting (vv. 3-4). The prophet says,

> "Why do we fast, but you do not see?
> Why humble ourselves, but you do not notice?"
> Look, you serve your own interest on your fast day,
> and oppress all your workers.
> Look, you fast only to quarrel and to fight
> and to strike with a wicked fist.
> Such fasting as you do today
> will not make your voice heard on high.

Fasting is a means of opening oneself to the work of God, expressing profound grief over sin and acknowledging ultimate dependence on YHWH (1 Kgs. 21:27; Lev. 16:29, 31; 23:27, 29, 32; Neh. 9:1-3; 1 Sam. 7:6; 2 Sam. 12:16).[11] By abstaining from food, the penitent shows humility and a sincere desire to be open to God's will. Fasting was meant to be a sign of repentance.[12] Apparently the community was practicing fasting, but nonetheless God does not notice their virtue or piety: Why should we fast, they say, when you take no notice? Why should we afflict ourselves when you do not acknowledge it? (v. 3a). Isaiah explains the reason for God's indifference to the people's fasting (vv. 3-4). The fasting of the Israelites as a religious devotion does not match the behavior toward their neighbor. The people do evil in the sight of YHWH even during the period of fasting. According to the prophet they are engaged in seeking their own interest by oppressing their workers. This could mean that they either physically abuse the workers or they

11. David P. Wright, "Fast," in *Harper's Bible Dictionary*, ed. Paul J. Achtemeier (San Francisco: HarperCollins, 1985), 306–7.
12. Michael L. Barré, "Fasting in Isaiah 58:1-12," *BTB* 15 (1985): 96.

press upon the poor to pay their debts, disregarding Deut. 15:2.[13] In fasting one gets hungry, and as a result, they are also engaged in disputes and quarrels leading to violence against brother. Fasting as a sign of true repentance is inseparable from love of neighbor.[14] The contention implied in these verses is appalling to the covenant community (Amos 5:1-17; Hos. 6:6-10; Isa. 10:1-4; Mic. 6:8; Jer. 5:26-28). A right relationship with God demands that God's people treat others fairly (Isa. 1:21-26). Fasting and religious practices are unacceptable to God if accompanied by neglect and oppression of others: "Such fasting as you do today will not make your voice heard on high" (Isa. 58:4). A genuine fast demands an outreach to those in need.

The prophet then mentions the conventional forms of religious practices. Verse 5 presents the external rituals attached to the people's observance: "Is such the fast that I choose, a day to humble oneself? Is it to bow down the head like a bulrush, and to lie in sackcloth and ashes?" According to Jewish tradition, fasting was accompanied by prayer and acts of self-mortification such as hanging the head, sleeping on the ground, and wearing sackcloth as a sign of penance and mourning (Esth. 4:3; 2 Sam. 31:13; Neh. 9:1; Dan. 9:3; 1 Macc. 3:47).[15] The people fast, not to find favor with God, but to display their holiness to people and gain their admiration. External rituals performed without sincerity and humility affects the relationship between God and humans: Is this what you call a fast, a day acceptable to YHWH? (v. 5b). What are a true fast and a day acceptable to the YHWH? The prophet Zechariah says that a fast

---

13. Jose L. Sicre, *Con los Pobres de la Tierra: La Justicia Social en los Profetas de Israel* (Madrid: Ediciones Cristianas, 1984), 514.

14. Barré, "Fasting," 95.

15. The same actions are described in the New Testament. The Pharisees disfigured their faces so that their fasting may be recognized by men. Jesus exposes their hypocrisy and advises them to anoint their heads and wash their faces so that their devotion may be directed to God alone (Matt. 6:16-17).

acceptable to YHWH is constituted by true judgment (מִשְׁפָּט), kindness, and compassion toward neighbor (7:9). Without these, all pious acts of devotion are nullified.

II. Feeding the Poor: A Call to Share the Abundance of God's Blessing

Following the denunciation of external rituals that are self-serving, YHWH describes what acceptable fasting involves.

> Is not this the fast that I choose:
> to loose the bonds of injustice,
> to undo the thongs of the yoke,
> to let the oppressed go free,
> and to break every yoke?
> Is it not to share your bread with the hungry,
> and to bring the homeless poor into your house;
> when you see the naked, to cover them,
> and not to hide yourself from your own kin?
> (Isa. 58:6-7)

The prophet begins by first stating that a fasting acceptable to YHWH involves seeking freedom for the captive (v. 6). YHWH exhorts the community to loosen the bonds of wickedness by undoing the thongs of the yoke. The Hiphil of the verb פּטח (to loose) is used in the Psalter in the context of setting prisoners free (Pss. 105:20; 146:7).[16] While the reference to feeding is not found here, Deut. 15:12, uses the phrase תְּשַׁלְּחֶנּוּ חָפְשִׁי (to dismiss) to exhort a former slave master to provide a generous provision for a slave being emancipated:[17]

---

16. *Hebrew and Aramaic Lexicon of the Old Testament*, ed. W. Baumgartner, et al. (Leiden: Koninklijke Brill NV, 2001), 1:736.
17. Isaiah 58:6 also uses the phrase, שׁלח חפשים ("to dismiss").

If a member of your community, whether a Hebrew man or Hebrew woman, is sold to you and works for you for six years, in the seventh year you shall set that person free (תשלחנו חפשי). And when you send a male slave out from you a free person, you shall not send him out empty-handed. Provide liberally out of your flock, your threshing floor, and your wine press, thus giving to him some of the bounty with which the Lord your God has blessed you (Deut. 15:12-14).

The freed slave must not be sent away empty handed to ensure basic sustenance. The provisions to be bestowed consist of the produce of the land and in proportion to what they have received from YHWH (v.13). The released slave has the right to receive this blessing.[18] The Deuteronomist expresses here the dignity of the released slave.[19] Every individual, especially the poor, must be afforded the opportunity by the affluent members of the community to alleviate their condition.

Isaiah then stresses YHWH's command to care for the needy neighbor by providing food, shelter, and clothing (v. 7).[20] The exhortation to care for the poor is mentioned in Deuteronomistic law: "Since there will never cease to be some in need on the earth, I therefore command you, 'Open your hand to the poor and needy neighbor in your land'" (Deut. 15:11). The most urgent need for the destitute was survival. Generally this meant having enough food to eat. Lack of food meant no life. In addition to Deut. 15:12-14, the biblical text makes allowances for the care of the poor in the following passages: Lev. 19:9-10, and Deut. 14:28-29; 16:11,14; 23:24-25.[21]

18. J. G. McConville, *Deuteronomy*, AOTC 5 (Downers Grove, IL: InterVarsity, 2002), 263.

19. The Hebrew verb ענק, translated "to provide liberally," comes from the word meaning "garland" or "necklace," a term that expresses honor. Ibid.

20. In this section, I will focus on the importance of feeding the poor. The idea of acts of mercy as elements of justice and authentic religion are also mentioned in the New Testament. Jesus says that feeding the hungry, clothing the naked, and visiting the imprisoned will be considered on judgment day (Matt. 25:31-46).

According to biblical teaching, one way of providing food for the poor is to allow them to glean from fields that have been harvested (Lev. 19:9-10; 23:22).[22] This norm is embedded within the social ethics and holiness practices in Leviticus, and calls for the owner of the field not to harvest entirely the grain, the product of the vine, and the fruits of the trees.[23] This permits the poor to maintain some dignity by working to support themselves (Lev. 23:22; Deut. 24:19-22).[24] The greatest benefit was reaped by the wealthy farmer. In keeping the commandment, a farmer not only manifested love and concern for the poor, but also recognized that the land belongs to YHWH, and its abundant harvest was a divine blessing which needs to be shared with the poor (Lev. 25:23). Walter C. Kaiser summarizes this way:

> If the Lord is the ultimate owner of everything; thus the Land is a gift from the Lord. If the owners are only stewards of the land and all that it produces, there is no reason to be selfish and stingy. Holiness begins with one's treatment of poor people; but grasping, covetous, and stingy personalities are not holy persons.[25]

Another way to ensure that the indigent had enough to eat is the triennial tithes (Deut. 14:28-29; 26:12-13). This norm calls for an offering of grain, wine, and oil, and firstlings to be deposited in storage within their own community every three years. This seems

---

21. David L. Baker, *Tight Fists or Open Hands? Wealth and Poverty in Old Testament Law* (Grand Rapids: Eerdmans, 2009), 223–51; Leslie J. Hoppe, *There Shall Be No Poor Among You: Poverty in the Bible* (Nashville: Abingdon, 2004), 36–39.

22. Lev. 19:9-10 deals the gleaning of fields and vineyards, while Lev. 23:22 mentions only fields.

23. Central to the book of Leviticus is the Holiness Code, as indicated by the phrase, "You shall be holy, for I the Lord your God am holy" (Lev. 19:2). The actions of God in the Bible are the actions of the Holy God. The main meaning of the Hebrew word translated "holiness" (קדשׁ) is separation. Israel as the chosen people became the dominion of God, the priestly people, the holy nation. YHWH's presence conferred a holiness on them that is not simply one of ritual, but a dignity demanding a holy life that must be manifested in social justice.

24. Hoppe, *There Shall Be No Poor Among You*, 37.

25. Walter C. Kaiser, Jr., "Leviticus," in *The New Interpreter's Bible*, 1: 1133.

to imply that the provisions were not distributed immediately, but stored separately and dispensed as needed. This would guarantee that the people would have rations until the next collection.[26] The provisions are to benefit the Levite, widow, orphan, and resident aliens, those who are not property owners.[27] The purpose of the law is to provide an alternative means for the landless to have access to Israel's wealth. Deut. 26:12-13 states that this is a gift from the worshiper to God, just as the land is God's gift to the people.[28] Walter Brueggemann says the following:

> The tithe is an extraordinary characterization of economic reality asserting that the land, its produce, and all its wealth ultimately belong to YHWH, who causes the land to be fruitful. The requirement of such public acknowledgment of YHWH's ownership is in fact a challenge to all ancient and modern theories of the economy that authorize autonomous wealth and that imagine that the production and enjoyment of wealth can be the ultimate goal of one's like.[29]

The law guarantees these people shared the benefits of YHWH's blessings, which they were entitled to as members of the holy people: they "may come and eat their fill" (Deut. 14:29). This same verse closes with an assurance of God's continual blessing upon the farmer who fulfills the command of YHWH: "So that the Lord your God may bless you in all the work that you undertake" (Deut. 14:29).

Beside the triennial tithes, Deuteronomy instructs the Israelites to share the land's bounty with the poor during the Feast of Weeks and Booths (Deut. 16:11, 14). Both of these pilgrimage festivals celebrated YHWH's gift of fertility that ensured the people's well-being. The Deuteronomist commands the Israelite to celebrate these

---

26. Baker, *Tight Fists or Open Hands*, 246.
27. Norbert Lohfink, "Das deuteronomische Gesetz in der Endgestalt: Entwurf einer Gesellschaft ohne marginale Gruppen," *BN* 51 (1990): 25–40.
28. Ibid., 247.
29. Brueggemann, *Deuteronomy*, 162.

festivities not only with their families, but also with their servants, the widows, orphans, aliens, and Levites. As in the previous biblical texts (Lev. 19:9-10; Deut. 14:28-29; 15:12-14), the implication is that the latter do not own land from which to provide the food to celebrate YHWH's blessings upon the nation and to make the wealthy aware of the needs of the poor.[30]

Another text that addresses the social problem of hunger is Deut. 23:24-25. This particular text permits a person to eat of the neighbor's vineyard or cornfield to satisfy hunger but without carrying anything off the field. As in the previous norms, the law here is meant to protect the landless by giving them the right to consume as much food as they need, provided they don't use a sickle or remove it from the property. The law intends to protect the needy.[31] The right of the human person to receive nourishment takes precedent over the rights of the property owner. The law, however, does acknowledge the rights of the landlord by prohibiting the removal of provisions from the field.[32] While all harvest is ultimately a blessing from YHWH, the law also recognizes that the owner has worked the land and had the right not to be deprived of its products by greedy individuals. Thus, the law intends to benefit the whole community.[33]

In this section, the texts mentioned assert that, to practice true fasting, the members of the chosen people must work to undo social corruption and practice works of charity. Feeding the hungry, housing the homeless, and clothing the naked are essential to be in a right relationship with YHWH and to receive spiritual blessings. A true act of worship involves a concern for the destitute (v. 7).[34]

---

30. Hoppe, *There Shall Be No Poor Among You*, 38.
31. Frank Crüsemann, *The Torah: Theology and Social History of Old Testament Law* (Edinburgh: T & T Clark, 1992), 233.
32. Alexander Rofé, "The Tenth Commandments in the Light of Four Deuteronomistic Laws," in *The Ten Commandments in History and Tradition*, ed. Ben-Zion Segal and Gershon Levi (Jerusalem: Magnes, 1990), 60.
33. Baker, *Tight Fists or Open Hands*, 250.

III. Spiritual Rewards to Feeding the Hungry

The section on true fasting concludes with the spiritual benefits of living a righteous life:

> Then your light will break forth like the dawn,
> and your healing shall spring up quickly;
> your vindicator shall go before you,
> the glory of the Lord shall be your rear guard.
> Then you shall call, and the Lord will answer;
> you shall cry for help, and he will say, "Here I am."
> (Isa. 58:8-9a)

These verses contained six promises in three bicola. The first and the second are announcements of a restoration that has eschatological overtones.[35] The first uses the metaphor of light to represent a sanctified life.[36] Isaiah declares that only when one follows YHWH's commandments by acting in favor of the poor would YHWH fulfill their desires: "I will turn the darkness before them into light" (Isa. 42:16). This promise has not been fulfilled because of their indifference to social injustices. The expression *light* (אוֹרְךָ) is explained with the term *justice* (צְדָקָה) which refers to the liberating actions in favor of the destitute (vv. 6b-7.10a).[37] The prophet emphasizes the same point with the image of a restored health. The

---

34. The word translated "kin" comes from the Hebrew בשׂר, meaning "flesh." Some scholars interpret it as an exhortation to assist every individual and not only fellow Israelite. See Sicre, *Con los Pobres de la Tierra*, 416.

35. W. Lau, *Schriftgelehrte Prophetie in Jes 56–66: Eine Untersuchung zu den literarischen Bezügen in den letzten elf Kapiteln des Jesajabuches*, BZAW 225 (Berlin: De Gruyter, 1994), 249.

36. The metaphor of light is associated in the ancient Near East with justice. In the biblical text justice is attributed to YHWH. See F. Vattioni, "Malachia 3,20 e l'origine della giustizia in Oriente," *RivBib* 6 (1958): 353–60.

37. B. Janowski, "JHWY und der Sonnengott: Aspekte der Solarisierung JHWHs in vorexilischer Zeit," in *Pluralismus und Identität*, ed. J. Mehlhausen (Gütersloh: Gütersloher Verlagshaus, 1995), 236–37.

verb צמח ("to spring up") can be interpreted within the historical context to mean the beginning of a new historical event that includes the restoration of the community in the promised land (Isa. 51:5).[38] The verb may be used metaphorically to symbolize prosperity and well-being (Zech. 6:12). This would be in contrast to Isa. 1:5-6, where the prophet speaks of the tragic devastation of Judah after the Assyrian invasion. The images indicate an act of salvation that it is executed on behalf of the poor, and a salvation that is given by YHWH to the just.[39] The third and fourth promises, "your vindication will precede you," and "the glory of YHWH will be your rearguard," were taken from Isa. 6:1, where YHWH exhorts the first exiles returning to the promised land to do what is just in preparation for the revelation of his justice. The phrase "the glory of YHWH will be your rearguard" derives from Isa. 52:12.[40] This is a reference to the return of the exiles from Babylon. Isaiah presents YHWH as walking behind his people, recalling the protecting presence of the angel of YHWH during the crossing of the Red Sea (Exod. 14:19). The return to the promised land is seen also as a benevolent act of the Lord (Isa. 48:20; 55:12).[41] The final two promises respond to the complaint voiced by the people in Isa. 58:3a. YHWH, who provided no response to the prayer of the people, will now answer the petitions of the faithful: "Here I am."

---

38. Blenkinsopp, *Isaiah*, 180.
39. W. Lau (*Schriftgelehrte Prophetie in Jes 56–66*, 252n231) says, "Man kann vielleicht sagen, daß nach der Auffasung des Verfassers das eschatologische Handeln der Gemeinde einen soteriologischen Prozeß in Gang setzt, den Jahwe mit heilvollem Tun belgleiten wird." My translation: One can perhaps say that in the eschatological view of the author, the action of the community puts in motion a soteriological process in which the healing power of God will be manifested fully.
40. Ibid.
41. Louis Stulmann and Hyun Chul Paul Kim, *You Are My People: An Introduction to Prophetic Literature* (Nashville: Abingdon, 2010), 81–82.

Conclusion

Isaiah advocates the Old Covenant traditions regarding the care of the poor. The need to feed the hungry, in particular, is based on the theological belief that the promised land is a gratuitous gift to the covenant people. An abundance of harvest symbolizes God's blessings, signs of divine care and concern for the covenant people. Thus, the wealthy landowners must reciprocate to God's generosity by given thanks to the Creator and by showing the same concern for the needy. The community should seek not only their own well-being but the greater good. Providing for the poor is explained in terms of "rendering justice." This is the biblical vision of egalitarianism. It does not mean, however, that everyone is economically level, but that individual gifts and interest ought to be considered to create a community of inclusion, humility, and generosity. The biblical text has also shown how God's response to the prayers of the covenant people depend on the faithful's own response to God's call to justice.

3

———

From Drought to Starvation (Jeremiah 14:1-9): A National Experience, a Global Reality

Carol J. Dempsey, OP

Repeatedly, the prophets proclaim the foreboding message that people, animals, and the land will be made to suffer by God because of the iniquities committed by some members within the human community. One of the divine chastisements to be suffered is drought, which will inevitably lead to hunger and starvation for all communities of life, most of whom will suffer the direct consequences of a few who have misused and abused their power and have violated right relationship. This essay explores Jeremiah 14:1-9, "The Great Drought," in its own context and then in the context of contemporary times, where the single greatest crisis on the planet right now is the depletion of water sources and the availability of water due to climate change related to the environmental and ecological devastation of the planet, caused by the emission of greenhouse gases, and by some minds and powerful enterprises unwilling to address this critical issue. The droughts being experienced today and in recent years past are one of the leading causes of hunger, starvation, and death, which have taken the lives of countless people and other life species—the most vulnerable—because they do not have choices or economic means available to them to survive.

Although the theological spin that the prophet Jeremiah puts on his threatening message is not to be taken literally and, in effect, is perhaps part of the political and religious agenda of the prophet or later editors and redactors, the central point of the prophet's message remains clear and timeless: communities of life are and will be negatively impacted by the failure at right relationship and concern for the common good by those who have it within their power to make a difference. Hunger is not only a social problem; it is also an ecological one, and this essay will attempt to make those links that will allow Jeremiah's ancient message to resound in the ears of contemporary listeners, calling us all to critical change rooted in political, social, and religious responsibility.

I. Droughts in the Ancient Near Eastern and Biblical World

In the ancient Near Eastern and biblical world, droughts were common. Abraham, Isaac, and Jacob and their families were forced to leave their homelands and relocate because of drought-related famines (see Genesis 12; 26; and 41, respectively). In Egypt, Joseph was looked upon with favor by the pharaoh of the land because Joseph was able to manage the nation's food supply during drought conditions (Genesis 41). Elijah took care of a widow in Zarephath who was expected to die because of a famine caused by a drought (1 Kgs. 17:7-24). Droughts that caused famines also plagued the Israelites in the days of David (2 Sam. 21:1), Elisha (2 Kgs. 4:38), Haggai (Hag. 1:11), and Nehemiah (Neh. 5:3). At times the coming of droughts and famines was predicted by prophets (2 Kgs. 8:1; Isa. 3:1). The famines caused by the droughts were often severe, with some famines lasting for many years (see, e.g., Gen. 12:10; 41:27). During famines, those who were starving sometimes ate such things as wild vines, heads of animals, garbage, dung, and even human flesh (2 Kgs. 4:39; 6:25; Lam. 4:4-10) just so they could try to survive.

In ancient Israel, droughts were sometimes seen as God's judgment and as a covenant curse.[1] For example, in Deut. 28:23-24, the people hear that God will change the rain of their land into powder and only dust will fall from the sky until all the inhabitants are destroyed. In 1 Kgs. 17:1, Elijah announces God's judgment on Israel and declares that there will be neither dew nor rain for a while. Thus, in ancient times, droughts were associated with God's punishment in response to the people's violation of covenant. The same remains true for the account of the drought in Jer. 14:1-9.

II. Drought in Jeremiah 14:1-9

With vivid images that capture the plight of both human beings and the natural world, the poet of Jer. 14:1-9 features Jeremiah receiving a word from God. Jeremiah delivers this word, which is a description of the effects of a horrific drought that plagues the entire land of Judah, from its major capital city Jerusalem to its countryside and farmlands. No consensus exists among scholars as to setting or time frame for this drought, and in fact, the drought may have been a

---

1. For further discussion on drought, divine judgment, and the transgressions of the community, see Robert P. Carroll, *The Book of Jeremiah*, OTL (Philadelphia: Westminster, 1986), 308–9.

metaphor for the imminent end of covenant relationship with God, as Ahida Pilarski suggests.[2] Whether or not the drought was actual or was metaphorical, a suggestion that seems quite plausible in light of the poetics of the book of Jeremiah as a whole, this drought that the prophet Jeremiah describes poetically is a terrible disaster that ushers in a time of mourning, a time of lament.

The passage can be divided into three units: v. 1, a superscription; vv. 2-6, a lament; and vv. 7-9, a confession. The poem is part of a longer section (Jer. 14:1—15:4) that not only describes the drought conditions of Judah but also details Judah's iniquities. The dryness of the land and its inability to bear food to sustain the people and the animals alike parallels the relationship that some of the Judahites now have with their God—a lifeless, dry relationship, and one that will lead to death because some among the Judahites are guilty of apostasy and other iniquities (vv. 7-9; see also Jer. 14:10—15:4)—and thus, all in the land will be made to suffer.

Jeremiah's poem, a story about the drought, opens with a superscription (v. 1), a secondary addition meant to lend authority to the words that follow. This superscription is not unusual and is found elsewhere in the book of Jeremiah (see Jer. 46:1; 47:1; 49:34).

After the superscription comes the lament (vv. 2-6). The first part of the lament is in relation to Jerusalem and urban life (vv. 2-4a); the second part is in relation to the farmers and life in the countryside (vv. 4b-6). Hence, all of Judah mourns, and her gates languish and are blackened (v. 2). Here, the poet's use of personification captures the devastated state of the land, a land personified as female. Judah, once fertile and lush, is now unable to feed her families who reside in her; Judah is unable to care for her own, and her own are suffering. When

---

2. For a clear and detailed discussion on the proposals surrounding the setting and timeframe for the drought in the Jeremiah text, and for the suggestion that the drought may, in fact, be a metaphor, see the dissertation by Ahida Pilarski, *A Textual and Literary Analysis of the References to 'iššâ and nāšîm in the Book of the Prophet Jeremiah* (Ann Arbor: ProQuest LLC, 2008), 284–89.

the nobles send out their servants in search of water, the servants discover that the cisterns are dry. With empty vessels, the servants return to their nobles. The drought makes no distinction between classes of people. All are made to suffer, and thus they cover their heads, which is a sign of grief (see 2 Sam. 15:30; Esth. 6:12).

Besides the empty cisterns, another indication of the severity of the drought exists: the cracks in the ground (vv. 4a-b). Even the ground suffers for lack of rain that would have kept the earth moist, softened, and fertile. Such land conditions cause distress to the farmers, the next group of people who suffer because of the drought. They too join in the mourning ritual—they cover their heads just like the servants had done (v. 4; cf. v. 3). The farmers mourn because they are unable to produce any crops for their own families and for the marketplace. Like the servants, the farmers are part of the lower class of society. The drought causes them personal pain and robs them of their livelihood.

Not only do the people and the ground suffer because of the drought, but also the animals and the herbage suffer (vv. 5-6). Jeremiah's description of such suffering is heart-wrenching:

> Even the doe in the field forsakes her newborn fawn
>> because there is no grass.
> The wild asses stand on bare heights,
>> they pant for air like jackals;
> Their eyes fail
>> because there is no herbage. (Jer. 14:5-6)

Ordinarily deer give birth to their young deep in the woods, where they also nurture them in their early days of life (see Job 39:1). This mother doe, however, is out in the open field, presumably searching for food for herself and her newborn fawn. Grass plays an important role in the sustenance of both doe and fawn. The consumption of grass by a mother deer enables her to produce the milk she needs in order to feed her babies. Here the mother deer is forced to abandon her newborn so that she can search for food for herself and her baby, but because no grass can be found, both mother and child will starve and meet an unnecessary fate: death (cf. Joel 1:19, 20).

The wild asses also suffer because of the drought. Jack R. Lundbom notes that the wild ass is regarded as the hardiest of wild animals and is not normally seen on the heights panting for air, like jackals. Its habitat is the semi-wilderness where it wanders alone (Jer. 48:6; Hos. 8:8; Job 39:5-8).[3] Wild asses, like many other animals, sniff the wind for moisture. Here the wild asses are panting, which could also be an indication of being overheated and in need of water, or as J. Kinnier Wilson suggests, the need for the wild asses to depend on their sense of smell because they have gone blind.[4] In v. 6 the prophet declares that the eyes of the wild asses are failing because there is no herbage. Lundbom attributes the failing eyesight to a deficiency in vitamin A: "A deficiency in vitamin A is known to cause blindness, and grass contains 'carotene' that is converted into vitamin A. Wild animals can therefore go blind without grass."[5] Thus, the drought has caused the earth to become infertile. No longer is grass or herbage able to come forth from earth's soil, which lies cracked for lack of rain.

In sum, the order and cycles of creation have come to an abrupt halt. Humans and nonhumans now share a common experience—the threat of death. Even the nobles, a privileged class who would normally have access to additional resources, such as water, that the lower classes and the poor would not ordinarily have access to, are

3. Jack R. Lundbom, *Jeremiah 1–20*, AB 21A (New York: Doubleday, 1999), 697.
4. See J. Kinnier Wilson, "Medicine in the Land and Times of the Old Testament," in *Studies in the Period of David and Solomon and Other Essays*, ed. Tomoo Ishida (Winona Lake: Eisenbrauns, 1982), 361–62.
5. Lundbom, *Jeremiah*; see also Wilson, "Medicine in the Land," 361–62.

suffering and living under this common threat. Of note, the animals, fauna, and land are being made to suffer because of the iniquities done by some human beings in the community, which now results in the suffering of the entire community.

Verses 7-9 are a confession. The confession also contains two petitions directed to God. In v. 7, Jeremiah gives voice to the cause of divine chastisement that has resulted in the drought, and at the same time he calls upon God to act. Here Jeremiah speaks on behalf of the community:[6]

> Though our iniquities testify against us
>   act, O Lord, for your name's sake;
> our apostasies are many,
>   and we have sinned against you.

Curiously, the community acknowledges its wrongdoings but offers no amends or change of heart. The request is simply for God to act, and in other words, for God to relieve them of the drought.[7] Here the community appeals to God's own honor and reputation but gives no hint at what it will do to change its ways, other than admitting to having committed transgressions and apostasy. The people recognize that they are the problem but offer no solutions to rectify the situation.

In v. 8a, the community confesses to God as being the hope of Israel (cf. Jer. 50:7; Ps. 71:5; Joel 3:16) and savior in time of

---

6. Terence Fretheim sees God as the speaker of vv. 7-9, since no textual marker exists to indicate a change of speaker from vv. 1-6 (God speaking through Jeremiah) and vv. 7-9. The commonly held view, however, is that Jeremiah is the speaker in vv. 7-9 where he speaks on behalf of the community (see Fretheim, *Jeremiah*, Smyth & Helwys Bible Commentary (Macon: Smyth & Helwys, 2002], 219). I accept the latter position in favor of a dialogue between God and the community that has now received foreboding news that points to a drought, one that could symbolize, metaphorically, the drying up of the relationship between God and the people.

7. Amos 4:7-8 give evidence that droughts have not been successful in bringing the people back to God and to right relationship with one another.

trouble (cf. 2 Sam. 22:3; Ps. 106:21; Isa. 43:3, 11; 45:15; 49:26; 60:16; Hos. 13:4). Israel's God is known to the people as the one who acts on their behalf in times of trouble and distress. Two rhetorical questions follow this double acknowledgment (vv. 8b–9a). These two rhetorical questions, which take the form of complaints, indicate how the community now perceives God who, once intimately involved in the life of the community, has now become like a stranger, a transient traveler, a mighty warrior unable to save. Israel's God has become distant to the people and has taken a back seat because the people have committed iniquities (v. 7). Verse 9b closes this segment of the poem. The first part of the verse is ironic. On the one hand, the people feel God's distance; on the other hand, they do realize that God is in their midst. They also confess to the reality that they are a people called by God's name. Their confession indirectly answers their rhetorical questions and leads them to voice one last plea: "Do not forsake us!"[8]

In sum, Jer. 14:1-9 is a poem that describes a drought and the terrible suffering that will result from this disaster, which the people of Jeremiah's day believed to be a divine chastisement cast upon them on account of their own transgressions. They themselves are the ones responsible for the suffering they now have to endure, and this suffering will extend to the nonhuman communities of life as well. The drought will cause all the communities of life to die of both hunger and thirst. Hence, Jeremiah, speaking on behalf of the community, pushes the community to acknowledge its wrongdoings and thus take responsibility for its actions. Although the drought of which Jeremiah speaks may be metaphorical or may, in fact, have occurred during his lifetime, his vision remains an unsettling beacon of light for life on planet earth in the twenty-first century. Jeremiah's drought may have been a national experience, but today, it is a

8. Cf. Josh. 7:8; Pss. 23:3; 25:11; 31:3-4; 79:9; 106:8; 109:21; 143:11; Isa. 48:9-11; Ezek. 20:9, 14, 22, 44, among other passages.

global reality due in large part to global climate change. Furthermore, because of the lack of water needed for agriculture, food prices are soaring and the poor among us are dying of hunger, not to mention the loss of life to nonhuman communities also affected adversely by the lack of water, and consequently, the lack of food.

III. Drought in the Twenty-First Century

The global food crisis and its connections to the unavailability of water because of drought conditions related to climate change is ominous. These drought conditions have adversely affected agriculture, resulting in skyrocketing food prices and dwindling reserves.

A. The Global Situation

In their study entitled "A New Era of World Hunger? The Global Food Crisis Analyzed," James A. Paul and Katarina Wahlberg observe that

> While grain harvests reached record levels, prices of corn increased 131% between January 2005 and February 2008, while wheat prices increased 171% in the same period and rice increased 62%. Similarly, from December 2005 to March 2008, soybean oil rose 175%, coconut oil 153% and palm oil 137%. These are the highest price increases in 30 years and some of the highest on record.[9]

The increase in food prices is directly related to the need for and use of fresh water. Paul and Wahlberg continue to note that

> Food production requires a lot of fresh water. World-wide about 70% of fresh water use is for agriculture. But water is getting scarcer in all

9. See James A. Paul and Katarina Wahlberg, "A New Era of World Hunger? The Global Food Crisis Analyzed," *Friedrich Ebert Stiftung Briefing Paper* (July 2008): 2.

world regions, as demand soars for drinking water, industry, recreation, and other uses, as well as more intensive farming methods.[10]

One of the main reasons why the fresh water supply is becoming scarcer is because of climate change, which is already harming agriculture negatively by droughts, desertification, intense rainfalls, and floods.[11] Unfortunately, agriculture itself plays a negative role in climate change because agriculture, as practiced today, is heavily dependent on fossil fuels used to power machinery, for irrigation systems, to create fertilizers and pesticides, and to process and transport the foods being produced. Agriculture also contributes to the release of two gases, namely, methane and nitrous oxide. These gases are released especially in the cases of rice farming and livestock production. Paul and Wahlberg note that

> These gases have a much more potent greenhouse effect than carbon dioxide. Some experts estimate that the agricultural system contributes a third of all climate changing gas releases—progressively reducing long-term food productivity in the process.[12]

Hence, climate change, droughts, the production of food, and rising food prices are all interrelated.

B. Climate Change, Droughts, and Food Price Increases

Climate change contributes most definitely to water shortages that are the results of droughts. Since the mid-1990s, prolonged droughts have intensified chronic water shortages. Currently, the Colorado River basin, a key watershed in the United States, is experiencing a serious drought. In China, the lower course of the Yellow River

10. Ibid., 6–7.
11. Ibid., 6.
12. Ibid.

is now dry for many months during the year, which is having a negative impact on agriculture.

In a recent study that focuses on the arid Americas, Christopher A. Scott and colleagues lay out one scenario, among several, that involves the impact of droughts on indigent goat herders, their livelihood, and their ability to feed themselves and their families:

> Indigent goat herders—most of them descendants of indigenous Huarpes—depend on rainfall for their grazing lands. When there is drought, they are forced to migrate with their herds; they simply do not gain access to water from the irrigation system. . . . Today, scattered in nonirrigated locations downstream of the irrigated oases, either these groups rely on the meager and erratic 3 inches (8 mm) per year average rainfall and leftover agricultural runoff or they have settled and work for agribusinesses. As herders, they depended on rainfall; as wage earners, their livelihood now hinges on the river-based supply of water coming from remote regions. But river flows have been diminishing due to upstream consumption and are now threatened by climate change.[13]

More locally, in 2012, the United States experienced and continues to experience the worst drought in fifty years. This drought engulfed some 60 percent of the country and dealt the harshest blow to the corn crop, which is the most abundant source of grain in the world and for the world. The disruption in the corn stocks had and continues to have a negative impact on the food supply for the world's population, since the US is the world leader in exporting corn, and many countries depend on receiving a healthy corn harvest from the US. Corn is the primary component in livestock beef and is part of the food chain in a myriad of other ways. This great drought of 2012 caused an increase in food prices domestically and abroad, because not only was the corn crop affected, but other crops and

---

13. Christopher A. Scott, Robert G. Varady, Francisco Meza, et al., "Science-Policy Dialogues for Water Security: Addressing Vulnerability and Adaptation to Global Change in the Arid Americas," *Environment: Science and Policy for Sustainable Development* (May–June 2012): 9.

staples were as well. Those affected the worst by the increase in food prices were low-income American families, and more drastically, poor people and their families around the world. Thus, poverty increased and hunger prevailed.[14]

C. Droughts, Poverty, and Hunger: A Global Reality

On August 30, 2012, the World Bank issued a press release entitled "Severe Droughts Drive Food Prices Higher, Threatening the Poor." In this release, the following statements were made that link droughts to global poverty and nutrition.

> Droughts have severe economic, poverty and nutritional effects. In Malawi, for instance, it is projected that future droughts observed once in 25 years could increase poverty by 17 percent, hitting especially hard rural poor communities. And in India, dismal losses from droughts occurred between 1970 and 2002 to have reduced [sic] 60–80 percent of the households' normal yearly incomes in the affected communities.[15]]

Furthermore, in their study on water insecurity and the right to water, Andrea K. Gerlak and Margaret Wilder make these observations:

> The global South—especially Sub-Saharan Africa and Southeast Asia—lacks access to clean potable water and sanitation relative to other world regions. Indigenous communities worldwide also disproportionally lack access to clean water. Climate change projections indicate future challenges related to water could make our current problems even worse, as already-vulnerable regions experience drought and desertification, loss of traditional crops and other anticipated impacts. Often women and children are hit the hardest.[16]

14. Elsewhere in 2010 to 2011 droughts associated with climate change also affected Russia's wheat harvest and hurt China's grain harvest. In Australia, floods destroyed much of the country's wheat crop. Both the drought and the floods sent the price of grain skyrocketing and increased the cost of most food staples.
15. See "Severe Droughts Drive Food Prices Higher, Threatening the Poor," a press release by the World Bank (August 30, 2012), 1.

Roger Pulwarty, Gary Eilerts, and James Verdin push the issues further and make a stark projection: "By 2080 the effects of climate change—on heat waves, floods, sea level rise, and drought—could push an additional 600 million people into malnutrition and increase the number of people facing water scarcity by 1.8 billion."[17]

Hence, the connections that exist between climate change, droughts, rising food prices, poverty, and hunger seem quite clear. The planet's ecosystems directly and indirectly support food security. With the effects of climate change that has manifested itself through droughts, those who will be most affected by the breakdown of the ecosystem will be the poor, which will leave many communities without any food security. This devastating situation, in turn, will lead to malnutrition and ultimately, to hunger and starvation, either because people will be unable to grow crops on cracked, desertified soil, or because they lack the funds to buy imported food, or both.

IV. Where the Rubber Hits the Road

The divine word that the prophet Jeremiah proclaims to his community concerning a great drought is as timely today as it was for the people of the prophet's day. Unlike the drought as it is portrayed by in the biblical text, however, today's droughts are not the result of divine chastisement. They are, though, the result of humankind's transgressions flowing from greed, the inordinate use of power, the need to dominate and control, and a failure to care for the common good in a way that is genuine, life giving, and life sustaining. Just as the innocent mother doe and her newborn fawn are made to suffer because some human beings have transgressed, so

16. See Andrea K. Gerlak and Margaret Wilder, "Exploring the Textured Landscape of Water Insecurity and the Human Right to Water," *Environment: Science and Policy for Sustainable Development* (March–April 2012): 1.

17. See Roger Pulwarty, Gary Eilerts, and James Verdin, "Food Security in a Changing Climate," *Solutions: For a Sustainable and Desirable Future* 3, no. 1 (Feb. 2012): 31.

also many people today, and in particular women, children, and the most vulnerable found among human and nonhuman communities alike, are being made to suffer because some people fail to take climate change seriously, while others make no effort to adjust their lifestyles and choices so that others may have a chance at a good and wholesome life.

Jeremiah 14:1-9 and Climate Change

Without a sustained global response to global climate change, the situation of droughts will only become more dire and will eventually have an impact, both directly and indirectly, on the earth and on all people in all places on the globe. Failure to slow the increase of atmospheric greenhouse gases only adds to the warming effect. Failure on the part of everyone to lessen the carbon emissions footprint stifles attempts at the rehabilitation of the fragile ecosystem, and failing to work toward the ecosystem's rehabilitation is, perhaps, humanity's gravest sin, because the ecosystem supports not only human life but all life forms on the planet. This sin—this failure to help rehabilitate the ecosystem—will eventually lead to death, not through God's actions, as suggested in Jer. 14:1-9, but through humankind's own doings. Failure to act on behalf of the common good for all communities that share life on the planet is no longer a choice. If we want to continue living, then we have no other option but to act ethically and interdependently, especially on behalf of the poor and disenfranchised.

Hence, drought, poverty, and hunger are all connected. What may have been metaphorical in Jeremiah's day with respect to a national drought is a global reality today. Jeremiah's message is addressed not only to the commonfolk but also to the social, political, and religious leaders of his day—the powerbrokers of his community. Today, his message also needs to be addressed to the commonfolk and to today's powerbrokers, particularly those who legislate or fail to legislate environment policies, and especially to those who have seized control of the world's land, agriculture, food and water supplies, natural resources, and ecosystems. Jeremiah's message needs to go out to the Nestles, Coca-Colas, Monsantos, ConAgras, and Archer Daniels Midlands of the world, among others. The divine vision that Jeremiah is given, as recorded in Jer. 14:1-9, foreshadows what is already occurring in many parts of the world today, a situation that is leaving people, fauna, and animals dying from thirst and hunger.

Would that we humans all come to realize and acknowledge what we have consciously and unconsciously done and continue to do to our planet. Would that we acknowledge our iniquities and work more diligently for the common good of all. If such a realization and acknowledgment is not possible, then would there be more prophets among us like Jeremiah to expose, to sound the death knell, to lament, and to beg the God who dwells in our midst not to forsake us (Jer. 14:9). As long as the prophets among us continue preaching in an effort to motivate the people to change, hope exists. Hunger, a byproduct of droughts and climate change, can be alleviated once God's people make the necessary choices for the good of all. Such choices involve not only personal lifestyle changes, but also a willingness to be a prophetic presence in the soup kitchens and in the corporate board rooms where some powerbrokers often make self-serving decisions behind closed doors that sometimes have negative global effects for life on the planet.

In closing, when the hunger for justice and righteousness is as strong and searing as the hunger for food, then and only then will people be motivated to act on behalf of the two-thirds of the world's population—not counting non-human life—that is starving and dying of hunger today. If that hunger for righteousness and justice on behalf of the starving is not felt deeply enough today to motivate us to act more decisively for the common good than we have been doing, then perhaps many of us, like many of Jeremiah's hearers, have failed to grasp the full purport of the drought that already exists in our midst—a drought that is not only physical but also spiritual and ethical. This drought, then, about which Jeremiah speaks, can also exist spiritually and ethically inside of human beings, causing people's eyes to fail and blinding them to the reality of suffering in our world today.

My hope is this: that one day we, together with creation, be restored to our balance so that with creation, we can participate in the noble and divine task of sustaining life by working together to make Jeremiah's message more of an ancient metaphor of things past and less of a contemporary reality of a prophecy unfolding.

4

War, Famine, and Baby Stew: A Recipe for Disaster in the Book of Lamentations

Lauress L. Wilkins

The Israelite prophets frequently use the paired metaphors of "famine and the sword" to describe weapons wielded by the Divine Warrior to punish sinful nations.[1] These prophetic references function either to motivate the Israelites to repent in order to avert YHWH's judgment, or to justify a disaster that had occurred and is interpreted by the prophets as divine retribution. Metaphorical references to war and hunger, however, play a very different role in the book of

---

1. For example, see Jer. 5:12, 14:12-18, 16:4, and 44:18 and 27. The prophets often list "sword" and "famine" along with "pestilence" as a triad of weapons in judgment oracles. See, for example, Jer. 21:7 and 9, 24:10, and 27:8 and 13. Similar references appear in Ezek. 6:11-12, 7:15 and 12:16, and in Isa. 51:19.

Lamentations. The poems' references to war-related hunger evoke sympathy for the city's population, especially women and children, and call into question the appropriateness of God's aggression that is mediated through an enemy nation. No other texts in the Hebrew Bible depict more graphically the destructive power of siege warfare, especially the impact of hunger used as a weapon of war against Israel's vulnerable civilians. From the opening chapter that speaks of Jerusalem's siege victims begging for food "just to stay alive" (Lam. 1:11, 19), to the last chapter where survivors are burning with fever from the long-term effects of war-related famine (5:10), the theme of hunger lends literary coherence, but also raises theological ambiguity in the book of Lamentations.

In this essay, I argue that the rhetoric of war-related hunger in Lamentations suggests that starvation is intentionally used against the besieged city both to decimate Zion's people and to demoralize the city's leaders and defenders. This rhetoric, furthermore, challenges the moral authority of YHWH the Divine Warrior, who leads the offensive by "devouring" the starving inhabitants of Jerusalem in a way that is unprecedented in the Hebrew Bible. The essay begins with a brief description of how famine and siege warfare are portrayed in a similar Mesopotamian city-lament, followed by a chapter-by-chapter examination of the rhetorical function of references to war-related hunger in Lamentations, especially its impact on women and children. I am mindful of Kathleen O'Connor's caution against "historical-critical analysis that leaves the text in the past as if its meaning for today were self-evident or, more likely, outside the scope of scholarly work." Many Lamentations scholars (O'Connor excluded), in fact, have limited their inquiry to structural or text-critical approaches that strip Lamentations of any relevance to general audiences today.[2] When these poems are read with a "hermeneutics of hunger," however, the powerful rhetoric describing real-life starving victims of war in Lamentations presents an enormous challenge to readers in a world where women and children still pay the human price for military actions by warring nations.

The essay concludes with brief remarks about implications of this study for the church today. I suggest that just as the coupling of "famine and the sword" in ancient siege warfare is not by accident, so also today's military strategies utilize food deprivation as a weapon against vulnerable civilians. The book of Lamentations offers chilling reminders of the suffering of war victims and strong support for the church's continued demand for social justice, human rights, and the dignity of all people, which should be a frequent subject of Catholic preaching in our war-torn world.

Famine and War in the Ancient Near East

Starvation is an important element in any successful siege operation in the ancient Near East because of its debilitating effect on those trapped inside the city. During times of peace, fresh foods such as grain, wine, and oil are available from surrounding farmlands and can be stored as reserves in private dwellings inside the city. Farm produce and livestock that are collected as taxes and temple offerings are kept in public storage facilities, and in years when crops failed, the city's reserves provide a safety net for both the urban population and the rural peasants. When a city is besieged, however, its defensive walls are transformed into a death trap: access to fresh food, water, and other necessities outside the city is cut off, while food reserves inside the city dwindle, leaving its inhabitants with a frightening sentence of slow and painful death by starvation and disease.

2. Kathleen M. O'Connor, "Let All the Peoples Praise You: Biblical Studies and a Hermeneutics of Hunger," *CBQ* 72 (2010): 1–14; here 1.

Famine and hunger, therefore, are common motifs in the laments of besieged Mesopotamian cities. The closest parallels to the biblical city-laments appear in the "Lamentation over the Destruction of Sumer and Ur" (*LSUr*) that contains complaints such as the following:

> Enlil made Famine, who brings nothing but harm, dwell in the city . . .
> In his palace there was no bread to eat . . .
> In the granaries of Nanna there was no grain . . .[3]

> Famine bends low their faces, it swells their sinews,
> Its people were filled with thirst, short is (their) breath.[4]

> Ur—inside it is death, outside it is death.
> Inside we die of famine,
> Outside we are killed by the weapons of the Elamites.[5]

Starvation occurs because the invading army raids and plunders after victory; they burn the remaining crops and make the fields unusable, leaving the survivors with enormous challenges of immediate and long-term recovery.

> In all its storehouses which abounded in the land,
> fires were kindled.[6]

> In the fields there was (neither) grain (nor) vegetation,
> the people had nothing to eat.

3. *LSUr* 297, 308, 310; in James B. Pritchard, *Ancient Near Eastern Texts Relating to the Old Testament (ANET)*, 3rd ed. with supplement (Princeton: Princeton University Press, 1969), 616.
4. *LSUr* 394–395; *ANET*, 618.
5. *LSUr* 402–4; *ANET*, 618.
6. "Lamentation over the Destruction of Ur," 240 (henceforth *LU*); in *ANET*, 459.

Its orchards (and) gardens were parched like an oven,

their *produce perished*.[7]

The starvation of women and children is described in poignant detail:

The young lying on their mothers' laps, like fish were carried off by the waters.[8]

[The mother abandoned her child] she said not 'Oh my child.'[9]

These examples demonstrate the power of the rhetoric of hunger associated with warfare in the ancient world. The loss of access to basic needs takes its toll on siege victims on multiple levels: psychologically, rationing of limited resources prompts a fear of hunger when food runs out; socially, neighbors are tempted to horde food at the expense of others; and physically, malnutrition gives way to starvation and disease, rendering the city's inhabitants too weak to defend themselves. Within this literary and social context, the biblical laments over the destruction of Jerusalem will be examined.

---

7. *LSUr* 132–33; *ANET*, 614. The scenes described in Mesopotamian city-laments are consistent with references to siege warfare in other literary genres as well as visual depictions in iconography from the ancient Near East. For example, Sennacherib boasts in a conquest account of his use of fear and famine as weapons against Shuzubu the Chaldean. See Daniel D. Luckenbill, *The Annals of Sennacherib* (Chicago: University of Chicago Press, 1924), 42. Yigael Yadin (*Art of Warfare in Biblical Lands in the Light of Archaeological Discovery* [London: Weidenfeld and Nicolson, 1963]) presents numerous iconographic depictions of conquered peoples and their livestock being carried off as plunder following a battle. James B. Pritchard, *The Ancient Near East in Pictures Relating to the Old Testament*, 2nd ed. with supplement (Princeton: Princeton University Press, 1969), 51, includes a reproduction of an Assyrian relief (fig. 168) portraying Elamite captives being led on their journey into exile.

8. *LU* 239; *ANET*, 459.

9. *LSUr* 99; *ANET*, 613.

II. Women, Children, and War-Related Famine in the Rhetoric of Lamentations

Like other ancient Near Eastern city-laments, the book of Lamentations expresses the severity of famine that civilian victims of war suffer. Eight of the sixteen verses that refer to war-related hunger focus specifically on its impact on women, children, or both. Lamentations 1 and 2 depict the desperation of besieged Jerusalemites for whom hunger is the first stage of their fatal ordeal. Starving, weakened by disease, then stricken by the sword, the people of Zion become deprived and depraved under the stress of the siege. The setting of Lamentations 4 and 5 seems to shift to a time, years after the war has ended, when the war-weary people of Judah are struggling to survive in their war-weary land. Lamentations 3, which is anomalous in several respects, is the only poem without any direct reference to hunger, although the poet bemoans the "poverty and destitution" which he has endured in Lam. 3:19.

A. Lamentations 1

Jerusalem is personified as "Daughter Zion" in Lamentations 1, a disquieting and ambiguous metaphor from a feminist perspective. On the one hand, "she" is likened to a woman of questionable virtue and of notable shame, raising doubt as to whether she and, by extension, the inhabitants of Jerusalem, are worthy of YHWH's compassion. Her lovers (treaty partners?) have abandoned her and have become her enemies (v. 2). She who had been "princess among the provinces" (שרתי במדינות, v. 1) has plummeted to poverty and destitution (v. 7). She has been hunted and raped (vv. 3 and 9), and her nakedness has been exposed (v. 8). Once full of splendor (v. 6), she is now "bitterly sad" (מר, v. 4). And as if Zion's condition is not already too appalling to imagine, the poet reports that it is YHWH the

Divine Warrior who has inflicted this suffering upon her "because of her many transgressions" (v. 5). Jerusalem has become "an object of scorn" (נידה, v. 8), and YHWH's refusal to intervene on her behalf appears to be justified.

On the other hand, many of the female metaphors and images associated with besieged Jerusalem, lonely widow (v. 1), grieving mother (v. 5), precious daughter (v. 6), and mourning maiden (v. 4), draw sympathy for the city in crisis and challenge the notion that she is culpable. The poet calls on YHWH to look upon her piteous state and to respond with compassion to her suffering.

All of her people are groaning, pleading for bread.

They trade their treasures for food just to stay alive.

"Look, YHWH, and see what a nobody I have become!" (Lam. 1:11)

The rhetorical effect of Lam. 1:11 is to divert the reader's attention away from references to Zion's sin and humiliation and to call attention to the enormous human suffering that causes people to sell "their treasures [מחמודיהם] . . . just to stay alive." The poignancy of the verse is intensified by the poet's reticence in identifying the "treasures" in 1:11b. Are they personal property that the Jerusalemites attempt to barter for food, as Johan Renkema proposes?[10] Or are they something far more precious, perhaps children, whose desperate parents are selling in order to survive? If the reader imagines this latter case, then it becomes even more difficult to blame "Mother Zion" without at least a twinge of compassion or to accept YHWH's brutal treatment exacted on her as justified.

---

10. See his commentary for this verse in *Lamentations,* Historical Commentary on the Old Testament (Leuven [Belgium]: Peeters, 1998).

The ambiguity introduced in Lam. 1:5 and 1:8 regarding Zion's culpability for her own calamity returns in verses 18-22. Again, reference is made to the desperate measures that Jerusalemites must take "just to stay alive:"

> I cried out to my lovers, but they deceived me.
>
> My priests and elders perish in the city
>
> while they beg for food just to stay alive. (Lam. 1:19)

Priests and elders who are now begging for food are condemned elsewhere in the book for their corruption and failed leadership. Lamentations 1:19 restrains the sympathy for the starving Jerusalemites as evoked in 1:11. If Lamentations 1 were the only example of a biblical lament over Jerusalem, one might concede that the Divine Warrior is justified in wielding the weapon of hunger as punishment for the city-woman's rebelliousness and sin! The severity of the famine and YHWH's aggression against Daughter Zion become even more compelling in subsequent poems in the book.

B. Lamentations 2

The rhetoric of hunger is intensified in Lamentations 2. Two general observations provide a framework for this discussion. First, a shift occurs in the way the city is personified. In the first lament, Zion "herself" is presented as an unnamed "mother" grieving over the plight of "her people." In the second poem, that personification is broadened to refer to the city's inhabitants, especially mothers and their children who elucidate the human faces of siege victims. A second observation is the chilling contrast between the starvation of Zion's people and the excessive consumption of her attackers, including the Divine Warrior who voraciously devours (בלע) and consumes (אכל) the Israelites. Consider this litany:

> The Lord *devoured* without compassion the whole countryside of Jacob. (Lam. 2:2a)

> He stormed against Jacob like a flaming fire, *consuming* everything around. (Lam. 2:3c)

> The Lord has become like an enemy. He has *devoured* Israel, *devoured* all of its strongholds, demolished its fortresses.(Lam. 2:5a and b)

> He stretched out a line; he would not refrain from *devouring*. (Lam. 2:8b)

It is no accident that verbs related to eating are used to describe the offensive measures of the attackers. YHWH consumes Daughter Zion and empowers her enemies to devour her (v. 16) while "her little ones" (עולליך) perish in the streets (v. 19). In addition, YHWH destroys his own shrine and its ritual feasts (מועד in v. 6); he "slaughters" (הרג) and "butchers" (טבח) Zion's people, the ones whom Daughter Zion had nurtured, and has summoned "terrors" as on a feast day (מועד) to "finish them off" (vv. 21-22). The only "meal" being eaten in Lamentations 2 is the Divine Warrior's relentless consumption of starving Jerusalemites, whom he devours "without compassion."

Lamentations 2:1-10 describes the Divine Warrior's attack on the city's physical structures: its fortress, sanctuary, strongholds, wall, rampart, and gates; and on Jerusalem's ruling class: its king and rulers, priests and prophets. The poet refrains from accusing YHWH of directly attacking the women and children of the city, who seem to be among the unnamed "collateral damage" in a male Deity's war against his own people. Zion's civilians, nevertheless, do come into focus in 2:11-12, where the mother's breast, a primal symbol of nourishment, is described as depleted and empty.

> My eyes are consumed with tears, my insides writhe . . . as infants faint at the breast in the open streets of the town.

> To their mothers they plead, "Where are grain and wine?" as they faint away like one mortally wounded in the open streets of the city; as their life spills out at their mothers' breast. (Lam. 2:11-12)

This image elicits grief and sympathy in the reader. Infants, Jerusalem's most vulnerable inhabitants, are faint with hunger and the children of Zion plead with their mothers (v.12a), as if pleading could result in the food they so desperately need. The city's reserves of grain and wine have been exhausted in the relentless months of the siege, and, because of their own state of malnourishment and dehydration, Zion's mothers are unable to nurse their children. They who have spilled out their own lives to birth these infants watch helplessly as their young lay lifeless at the breast.

Upon close examination, it becomes apparent that these civilians are not unintended victims at all; they are deliberate targets whose suffering demoralizes and debilitates the city's leaders and defenders who have failed to secure their survival.

The closing verses of Lamentations 2 urge "Mother Zion" to advocate on behalf of her children:

> Arise! Cry out at night at the start of the watches!

> Pour out your heart like water in the presence of the Lord!

> Lift up your hands to him for the sake of your little ones,
>
> fainting from hunger on every street corner. (Lam. 2:19)

The grieving city-mother is unable to take up the cause, so the poet indignantly challenges the silent Deity with two rhetorical questions concerning Judah's devastated condition:

> Look, YHWH, and consider whom you have treated so harshly!
>
> Should a woman eat her offspring, the children whom she has carried?
>
> Should priest and prophet be slain in the sanctuary of the Lord? (Lam. 2:20)

The revolting image of mothers eating their children in Lam. 2:20b is juxtaposed to their inability to nurse their infants in 2:19. Should a mother who is drained of her ability to nurse her young be driven by desperation to consume them? The rhetorical question is directed to YHWH and intends to elicit an emphatic and negative response. Such an action is as reprehensible as YHWH's voracious devouring of Zion's little ones! Surely, the Deity will cease from consuming the people and provide them with "grain and wine" again.

Lamentations 2:20b sets the tone for the next rhetorical question, which is much more ambivalent. "Should priest and prophet be slain in the sanctuary of the Lord?" (2:20c). Because of their failed leadership in Jerusalem, the response to this question could well be "Yes, they deserve death." The coupling of 2:20b with 2:20c, however, infers that the slaughtering of Zion's priests and prophets in YHWH's sanctuary is as unthinkable as a woman cannibalizing her own offspring.

The poet insinuates in Lam. 2:20-22 that YHWH himself bears the blame for Zion's plight. The accusation in Lam. 2:2 that YHWH has butchered "without compassion" is repeated in verse 21; and the fact that YHWH has not prevented Zion's enemy from destroying those whom she has "carried and nurtured" (v. 22) rouses even greater sympathy for the siege victims. The rhetoric in these closing verses seems to be an attempt to persuade YHWH to alleviate Zion's anguish, and the anomalously optimistic tone of Lamentations 3 even hints that some Jerusalemite survivors persist in their hope for an eventual reprieve. Sadly, however, as Lamentations 4 suggests, conditions only worsen in the aftermath of the siege. The long-term effects of the famine are as devastating as the initial eighteen-month crisis had been, and Jerusalem's women and children continue to bear the brunt of famine's attack.

C. Lamentations 4

Lamentations 4 depicts a Jerusalemite society that is in complete disarray: those who had been raised in luxury wallow in squalor (v. 5), defiled priests have been ousted from the land (vv.13-15), and desperate mothers resort to cannibalism in order to survive (v.10). While the personification of Jerusalem is a significant rhetorical feature of Lamentations 1 and 2, the fourth lament focuses on the people of Jerusalem as they plead for help that tragically never comes (vv.17-20).

The physical and psychosocial effects of famine permeate the first half of this chapter. Jerusalem's children, once "worth their weight in gold," have been reduced to the value of common pottery (v. 2). They suffer from symptoms typical of famine victims: thirst and dehydration (v. 4), skin discoloration and desiccation (v. 8), drastic weight loss and skeletal deformity (v. 8), and the relentless pangs of hunger (vv. 4, 5, 9, and 10). References to the special plight of mothers and their children awaken a sense of horror and indignation in the reader, but the images reflect the tragic reality of starving war victims throughout history. The physical symptoms of famine tend to be more acute in children than in adults, and mothers who are widowed or abandoned by their husbands during war time frequently faced the impossible task of nourishing their starving offspring.

The rhetorical force of Lamentations 4 lies in the poem's suggestion of cause and effect between the physical experience of starvation and the subsequent psychosocial dehumanization of Jerusalem's survivors. References to mothers and children epitomize this tragedy:

> Even jackals offer their teats and nurse their young.
>
>> But my precious people became cruel, like ostriches in the wilderness.
>
> The suckling's tongue clung to his palate from thirst.
>
>> Children begged for food; they had no one to share with them.
>
> Those who had dined on delicacies starved in the streets.
>
>> Those raised in purple grasped at trash heaps. (Lam. 4:3-5)

While Lam. 2:11-12 expresses undeniable pathos for the starving mothers and children, Lam. 4:3 diminishes such pity for them by stating that these women have forsook their maternal responsibility to nurture and suckle their children, an act so cruel that even wild animals instinctively would not do. The images of languishing infants and mendicant children illustrate how the city's entire population is devoid of any sense of social commitment, moral responsibility, or compassion; none of the city's starving people is willing to share with the youngest and most vulnerable among them (v. 4). Human degradation is augmented by the reference to Zion's formerly privileged class now reduced to scavengers, hunting for food in piles of garbage even as they perish in the streets (v. 5). Lamentations 4:7-8 provides a stark contrast between the pre- and postwar appearance of Jerusalem's nobility.

Her princes were brighter than snow, whiter than milk.

Their bodies were redder than coral, sapphire their physique.

Their form became darker than black; they were unrecognizable in the streets.

Their skin shriveled upon their bones; it became dry as wood. (Lam. 4:7-8)

If the strongest members of Jerusalem's society were reduced to such a pitiable state, what then is to be said of the weakest? The poet declares,

Better were those pierced by the sword than those pierced by hunger

who, wounded, wasted away for lack of fruits of the field.

The hands of loving mothers boiled their children.

They became food for them, in the destruction of my precious people. (Lam. 4:9-10)

Lamentations 4:10 appears to be an indictment against the mothers who have become so inhumane that they are devouring their own offspring. A feminist reading of Lam. 4:10, however, suggests a different message. The poet insists with tragic irony that these women are compassionate and loving mothers, thus affirming the women's fundamental and unshakable humanity, but the conditions in which they struggle to survive have become so deplorable that they are no longer free to make morally acceptable choices. As repulsive as this scene is, the rhetoric of verses 9-10 suggests that some compassionate but desperate mothers might have taken their children's lives as quickly and painlessly as possible in order to end their slow death from starvation (v. 9) and to provide for those remaining one more bitter meal (v. 10).

D. Lamentations 5

The final poem in Lamentations functions rhetorically as a synopsis of the central message of the book: the enormous suffering inflicted on Zion and her people is complete and permanent; she received no help from human allies or from YHWH to ease the burden of her survivors. Lamentations 5 indicates that the Jerusalemites experienced severe social disorientation: family bonds have been severed (v. 3), property expropriated (v. 2), and social roles of privilege and servitude reversed (v. 8), leaving the people of Zion in grief and despair (v. 16), with only the faintest hope of restoration (v. 21). In this postwar desolation, famine is one of the few constants. Like the other complaints rehearsed in Lamentations 5, references to hunger are not elaborated; the rhetoric of the whole chapter, in fact, is quite terse, with only a single colon per verse, as if the survivors' ability to express emotion has been exhausted along with their food supply. The poet only has one brief reference to women and children in a stark declarative statement that the adult male defenders are no more:

> We have become orphans, fatherless; our mothers like widows. (Lam. 5:3)

In the war-torn world of postsiege Jerusalem, all is awry and survival is barely possible. The poet complains that life's necessities that once could be taken for granted have become costly and precious commodities:

> Our water we drink for a fee; our wood comes with a price.

> With a yoke upon our necks, we are oppressed. We are weary, but we have no rest. (Lam. 5:4-5)

One can imagine the strength that Zion's women and children had to summon in order to survive such conditions. In agrarian societies, gathering water and wood for fuel is typically "women's work." The elite urban communities have servants to perform such tasks under the supervision of the (woman) manager of the household, the "mistress of the house." The razing of Zion's fortresses, however, leveled "her" social class structure so that the formerly privileged women are left to do the grueling manual labor of peasants in order to provide basic needs for their families.

Lamentations 5:6 indicates that food is so scarce that Jerusalem's survivors are forced to seek aid from Egypt and Assyria in order to have enough bread, a reference that illustrates the disastrous effect of YHWH's abandonment. Implicit in Lam. 5:6, too, is an accusation that YHWH has not heard or has not responded to the community's supplications. Their appeal for help to former enemies and oppressors counters the admonitions by prophets such as Isaiah and Jeremiah not to rely on the nations for strength, but on YHWH alone. This proves to be an ineffective option because of the Deity's prolonged silence.

Lamentations 5:9-10 alludes to the difficulty of growing crops in a parched and ravished land:

> At the risk of our lives we gather our food because of the desert heat.

> Our skin is scorched like an oven because of the raging fever of famine. (Lam. 5:9-10)

Judah's postwar recovery demands strenuous physical labor in often precarious conditions. Fields damaged in war have to be cleared, plowed, reseeded, and cultivated before hope of a harvest could be realized. This daunting task is exacerbated by periodic droughts in the Syria-Palestine area three out of every ten years. Judah's survivors are at the mercy of nature that, like YHWH, often seems to show "no compassion." Abandoned by their God and ravaged by famine, Jerusalem's survivors languish beneath the long-term effects of war, perhaps even decades after Zion has been razed.

III. Summary

The rhetoric of war-related hunger in the book of Lamentations evokes sympathy for the siege victims, especially the women and children, and raises questions as to whether the extent of YHWH's aggression is proportionate to Zion's transgressions. Lamentations 1 introduces a sense of ambiguity about the justification of YHWH's attack. The early portions of the poem cast doubt about Daughter Zion's virtue and pronounce judgment on "her" inept and vanquished leaders. Her people are so desperate that they trade their treasures, even their children, for food (Lam. 1:11). This description effectively diverts the readers' attention from the disparaging remarks about Zion's character and prompts a response of compassion for the suffering of Zion and her people. The rhetoric of famine intensifies in Lamentations 2 with images of starving mothers with infants perishing at their breasts (2:11-12); this calls forth not only grief and sympathy but also feelings of moral indignation. It becomes clear in Lamentations 2 that the suffering of the weak is not by accident; Jerusalem's mothers and children are not "collateral damage" but rather intended casualties, whose deaths are meant to demoralize and debilitate the besieged city's defenders. Again, YHWH's moral authority is questioned as the Deity fails to take notice of this travesty. The poet challenges the Deity's judgment, insinuating that YHWH's relentless "devouring" of Zion's people is as reprehensible as it would be for a mother to devour her young (2:19-20).

Lamentations 4 presents alarming portrayals of women who seem to have plunged into subbestial cruelty. Verses 3-5 begin with a suggestion that starving mothers, like all of Zion's "precious people," are withholding food from their dying children. The text suggests causality, so that the survivors' deprivation reduces them to depravity. The rhetoric of the dehumanizing effects of hunger grows even more morbid in the description of Jerusalem's nobility (v. 8). If Jerusalem's strongest could not withstand the harsh conditions of postsiege survival, then what hope is there for the weak? The most shocking reference to hunger, however, appears in Lam. 4:9-10, where cannibalizing mothers, noted as "compassionate women," boil their children for food. Do these mothers want to spare their young a slow and painful death by starvation, or is it to provide food for themselves and give their remaining children one more chance to survive? The fact that the poet can call these mothers "compassionate" reinforces the dehumanizing impact of siege warfare upon its victims.

Lamentations 5:3 has the only direct reference to women and children in the final lament, but the effects of long-term famine among Jerusalem's survivors are as palpable as in the other poems.

In the years after the war, "women's work" of collecting fuel (wood) and water becomes an oppressive burden for members of Jerusalem's former ruling class (5:4). In the absence of help from allies, human or divine, the struggling survivors are forced to seek aid from foreign nations (v. 6). The challenge of food production and procurement, nevertheless, is a life-threatening venture (vv. 9-10), leading to one unavoidable conclusion: of all the weapons in the arsenal that YHWH wields against Jerusalem, famine proves to be the cruelest for the women and children of Zion.

IV. Implications for Catholic Social Teaching and Preaching on Modern Warfare

The crisis of war-related famine is as relevant to contemporary Catholic social teaching as it was to the authors of Lamentations. Principles such as the dignity of the human person, the common good, and special concern for the poor are at the heart of the Church's social doctrine. Post–World War II popes have consistently and unequivocally condemned the persistence of poverty and oppression caused by warfare that produces conditions similar to those described in the book of Lamentations. Two themes in particular have appeared frequently in recent papal documents. First is the recognition that military programs drain resources from local and national economies, with a disproportionately high negative impact on the poor. Pope John XXIII, in his 1961 encyclical *Peace on Earth*, linked famine and the sword, just as Judah's prophets have done. He noted that the arms race requires "a vast outlay of intellectual and material resources, with the result that the people of these countries are saddled with a great burden, while other countries lack the help they need for their economic and social development."[11] The pope asserted that

---

11. John XXIII, *Pacem in terris* [*Peace on Earth*] 109; http://www.vatican.va/holy_father/john_xxiii/encyclicals/documents/hf_j-xxiii_enc_11041963_pacem_en.html.

"justice, right reason, and the recognition of [human] dignity cry out insistently for a cessation to the arms race."[12]

A second papal argument against modern forms of warfare is that, in a nuclear age, it is virtually impossible to avoid striking civilian populations. According to the Vatican II document *On the Church in the Modern World* (1965), "Any act of war aimed indiscriminately at the destruction of entire cities or of extensive areas along with their population is a crime against God and man [*sic*] himself. It merits unequivocal and unhesitating condemnation."[13] Twenty years later, Pope John Paul II continued the denunciation of modern warfare, noting that war inevitably results in the displacement, disenfranchisement, and despair of the world's most vulnerable citizens.

Despite the Church's condemnation of the conditions under which modern warfare is conducted, and the poverty, turmoil, and suffering that war inevitably inflicts on civilian populations, the biblical texts that speak most clearly to that problem, namely Lamentations 1–2 and 4–5, rarely are preached from Catholic pulpits. The only Lamentations texts that are included in the Roman Catholic Lectionary for Sundays or Holy Day liturgies are taken from Lamentations 3, the one chapter that makes no reference to war-related hunger.[14] This oversight practically guarantees that the laments that would most strongly challenge those who promote aggressive military operations in the name of patriotism and national security are muted in Catholic preaching. The Church's instruction

12. John XXIII, *Pacem in terris*, 112.

13. Vatican II, *The Pastoral Constitution* Gaudium et spes, *On the Church in the Modern World*, 80; http://www.vatican.va/archive/hist_councils/ ii_vatican_council/documents/vat-ii_cons_ 19651207_gaudium-et-spes_en.html.

14. See the list of lections in United States Conference of Catholic Bishops Committee on Divine Worship. *Liturgical Calendar for the Dioceses of the United States of America* (Washington, DC: United States Conference of Catholic Bishops, 2012), http://www.usccb.org/about/divine-worship/liturgical-calendar/.

that Catholics should refuse to engage in war that debilitates civilian populations fails to reach the ears of most Catholics who engage in such activity. As a result, "Daughter Zion," wherever she struggles to survive today, still mourns "without a comforter" and is forced to consider taking desperate measures "just to stay alive."

The Church is God's presence and a prophetic voice in the world today. If she is going to be faithful to the "ethical imperative . . . of her Founder, the Lord Jesus," then all of the Lamentations of ancient Jerusalem's survivors must be proclaimed in the communities founded in his name. The bishops must provide leadership in this effort, by instructing Catholics in every nation to listen to the voices of ancient Zion's starving women and children that are echoed by victims of war today. As Pope Benedict XVI declared, "Elimination of world hunger has . . . in the global era, become a requirement for safeguarding the peace and stability of the planet. . . , whether due to natural causes or political irresponsibility, nationally and internationally."[15] Only by ending the use of famine as a weapon against the world's most vulnerable citizens will the human family create a true recipe for peace.

15. Benedict XVI, *Caritas in veritate* 27; http://www.vatican.va/holy_father/benedict_xvi/encyclicals/documents/hf_ben-xvi_enc_20090629_caritas-in-veritate_en.html.

5

———

Social and Theological Aspects of Hunger in Sirach

Bradley C. Gregory

Ben Sira was a scribe who lived and worked in Jerusalem in the late third and early second centuries BCE, when Judea was under the rule first of the Ptolemies and then the Seleucids. While his primary mode of instruction was oral, near the end of his life, perhaps around 180 BCE, he set his teachings into written form.[1] Ben Sira's work is characteristic of "traditional wisdom" and he was deeply influenced

---

1. See James Crenshaw, "The Primacy of Listening in Ben Sira's Pedagogy," in *Wisdom You Are My Sister: Studies in Honor of Roland E. Murphy, O.Carm., on the Occasion of His Eightieth Birthday*, ed. M. L. Barré, CBQMS 29 (Washington: Catholic Biblical Association of America, 1997), 172–87. Evidence within Sirach suggests that the book may have been composed by Ben Sira in stages. See Jeremy Corley, "Searching for Structure and Redaction in Ben Sira: An Investigation of Beginnings and Endings" in *The Wisdom of Ben Sira: Studies on Tradition, Redaction, and Theology*, ed. Angelo Passaro & Giuseppe Bellia, DCLS 1 (Berlin: Walter de Gruyter, 2008), 21–48.

by the book of Proverbs in both form and content. While the focus here will be on the role of hunger in Ben Sira's thought, it will be most illuminating to explore his treatment of the topic with reference to similarities and differences to Proverbs. It will be argued that while Ben Sira's high social standing has deeply shaped his view of food and hunger, it does not lead to a characterization of the problem of hunger in terms that are elitist and self-serving. Rather, earlier biblical traditions on God's love for the poor and the necessity of social justice are the more dominant influence on how he addresses the social reality of hunger and poverty.

I. The Relationship between Social Location and Food

As a sage and professional scribe, Ben Sira trained young men in his "house of instruction" (Sir. 51:23) for their future roles in Judean society.[2] The ability of Ben Sira and his students to read and to write signals a high social setting, since Seleucid Judea was basically an agrarian society. According to Gerhard Lenski's model of agrarian societies, there is a very large lower class, comprised mainly of peasants and farmers, and a very small upper class with a large economic and social gap between the two. The small upper class is comprised of rulers, governmental officials, priests, and the retainer class.[3] Many scholars working on Second Temple Judaism and Christian origins have found Lenski's model of agrarian societies to be a useful paradigm with one major adjustment: since Judea in the late Second Temple period was essentially a temple-state, Lenski's

2. The most exhaustive treatment of Ben Sira's education program is Frank Ueberschaer, *Weisheit aus der Begegnung: Bildung nach dem Buch Ben Sira*, BZAW 379 (Berlin: Walter de Gruyter, 2007). Also see Robert Doran, "Jewish Education in the Seleucid Period," in *Second Temple Studies III: Studies in Politics, Class, and Material Culture*, ed. Philip R. Davies & John M. Halligan; JSOTSup 340 (London: Sheffield, 2002), 116–32.

3. Gerhard Lenski, *Power and Privilege: A Theory of Social Stratification* (New York: McGraw-Hill, 1966), 189–296.

separation of rulers, priests, and the retainer class is not applicable. Rather, in Second Temple Judea these three had considerable overlap.[4] Thus, the high priest was the central political figure and high-ranking priests were part of the aristocracy and the retainer class.[5] It is likely that in Seleucid Judea approximately 90 percent of the total population consisted of the lower class.[6] Most of these were poor subsistence farmers who frequently stood on the brink of financial ruin and had only minimal possessions, such as basic food and shelter (cf. Sir. 29:22; 31:4; 34:24). At the very bottom of the social hierarchy there were slaves and destitute beggars (cf. Sir. 33:25-33; 40:28-30).

The statements about Ben Sira's society presented in Sir. 38:24—39:11 conform quite well to this picture. The scribe, such as Ben Sira, is considered socially superior to the farmers and various craftsmen, and while artisans are held in high regard, they are still held to be inferior to the scribe. This is because the scribe studies and transmits the law of God (38:31-34) and dispenses counsel. In addition, it was not unusual for scribes to participate in legal proceedings, and they had the prestige to appear before rulers,

---

4. See Richard Horsley, *Scribes, Visionaries, and the Politics of Second Temple Judea* (Louisville: Westminster John Knox, 2007), 53–70; Richard Horsley & Patrick Tiller, "Ben Sira and the Sociology of the Second Temple" in Davies & Halligan, *Second Temple Studies III*, 74–107; Benjamin G. Wright, "'Fear the Lord and Honor the Priest': Ben Sira as Defender of the Jerusalem Priesthood" in *The Book of Ben Sira in Modern Research: Proceedings of the First International Ben Sira Conference 28–31 July 1996, Soesterberg, Netherlands*, ed. Pancratius C. Beentjes, BZAW 255 (Berlin: Walter de Gruyter, 1997), 189–222.

5. Some have suggested that Ben Sira himself was a priest, most notably Helge Stadelmann, *Ben Sira als Schriftgelehrter: Eine Untersuchung zum Berufsbild dees vor-makkabäischen Sofēr unter Berücksichtigung seines Verhältnisses zu Priester-, Propheten-, und Weisheitslehrertum*, WUNT 2/6 (Tübingen: Mohr Siebeck, 1980); and Saul Olyan, "Ben Sira's Relationship to the Priesthood," *HTR* 80 (1987): 261–272. However, I agree with Beentjes and Wright that there is insufficient evidence as to whether or not Ben Sira was a priest. See Pancratius C. Beentjes, "Recent Publications on the Wisdom of Jesus Ben Sira (Ecclesiasticus)," *Bijdr* 43 (1982): 191–94; Wright, "Fear the Lord and Honor the Priest," 196; cf. Bradley C. Gregory, *Like an Everlasting Signet Ring: Generosity in the Book of Sirach*, DCLS 2 (Berlin: Walter de Gruyter, 2010), 231–32.

6. Horsley, *Scribes, Visionaries, and the Politics of Second Temple Judea*, 66.

perhaps even traveling to foreign lands as ambassadors (39:4). The upshot of this discussion of sociological models is that it indicates that Ben Sira was part of the retainer class and thus a member of the socially and economically elite.

As is to be expected, Ben Sira's social location substantially shapes his view of food and hunger. In a pericope on "the good life," Ben Sira encourages his students to be generous with themselves as well as with others:

Do not deprive (yourself) of daily delights (מטובת יום)

and let no desirable portion pass you by.

Will you not leave your wealth to another

and your earnings to those who cast lots?

Use your money how you want and gratify yourself

for in Sheol there is no seeking luxury. (14:14-16)[7]

Ben Sira's argument in this passage approximates the Hellenistic notion of *carpe diem*: in light of the unpredictability and finality of death one should enjoy one's wealth *daily*. The social presupposition here is that Ben Sira and his students have the means to enjoy the finer things in life and that hunger is not a serious threat for them. This is even clearer later in the book when Ben Sira delivers an extensive

---

7. For a fuller discussion, including text-criticism of this passage, see my *Like an Everlasting Signet Ring*, 104–20. The first part of v. 16 is usually rendered "give and take", but in light of other ancient Near Eastern and Mishnaic texts, the phrase likely has the sense of being able to use wealth however one wishes. See Jonas Greenfield, "Two Proverbs of Ahiqar" in *Lingering over Words: Studies in the Ancient Near Eastern Literature in Honor of William L. Moran*, ed. T. Abusch, J. Huehnergard, & P. Steinkeller, HSS 37 (Atlanta: Scholars Press, 1990), 198. In my book I translate it as "engage in commerce" (*Like an Everlasting Signet Ring*, 107), but I have changed it here to "use your money how you want," which I now think is truer to the sense of the idiom.

discourse on proper behavior at a banquet.[8] The beginning of this long lesson is telling:

> Are you seated at the table of the great?

> Do not be greedy and say "How much there is here!" (31:12)[9]

Among the elite, the sign of a good host was his provision of an abundance of food and wine, as is clear later when Ben Sira describes a host's reputation in the city as dependent upon his generosity or stinginess in the context of dinner parties (31:23-24). For this reason, the dominant theme of Ben Sira's lesson is the need for moderation. He warns against greediness and gluttony and lists in graphic detail the consequences of eating or drinking to excess. Ben Sira even says that if the student finds himself in the situation of having overeaten he should excuse himself, vomit, and then he will have relief (31:21).

From passages such as these, a clear picture emerges that those who shared Ben Sira's social standing did not face any serious threat of going hungry unless circumstances changed radically (see below). Further, because in agrarian societies like those modeled by Lenski significant *upward* social mobility was relatively rare, it is likely most of them never had previously. Yet, Ben Sira's view of food goes beyond a simple dichotomy between hunger and satiation. Ben Sira and his students are regularly in situations where they face both quantitative and qualitative excess, which is why Ben Sira's statements concerning table etiquette are dominated by calls for moderation. The elite regularly enjoyed food that was plentiful *and*

---

8. Ben Sira's description of the banquet his students might attend basically conforms to characteristics of banquets elsewhere in the Hellenistic world. See Dennis E. Smith, *From Symposium to Eucharist: The Banquet in the Early Christian World* (Minneapolis: Fortress, 2003), 133–44; cf. Hans-Volker Kieweler, "Benehmen bei Tisch" in *Der Einzelne und seine Gemeinschaft bei Ben Sira*, ed. R. Egger-Wenzel & I. Krammer, BZAW 270 (Berlin: Walter de Gruyter, 1998), 191–215.

9. Idiomatic for Greek: πολλά γε τὰ ἐπ'αὐτῆς; Hebrew: ספוק עליו.

delicious. Interestingly, later in his book Ben Sira draws a direct analogy between the discerning mind and the discerning palate:

> The gullet can swallow any food; yet some foods are more agreeable than others.
>
> The palate is the judge of delicacies put forward as gifts; so it is with the discriminating mind and deceitful tidbits. (36:23-24)[10]

In this passage, social location among the educated mirrors the ability to enjoy fine foods. Unlike the lower classes, who often needed food of any kind just to survive, Ben Sira here assumes that those of his own social standing have enjoyed fine, expensive foods enough to have developed a well-trained palate.

On the other hand, while hunger was not a daily threat to those in Ben Sira's social class, he was also aware that circumstances can change quite quickly. Compared to some other sages, Ben Sira has a remarkably candid view of the future's uncertainty. Kings and rulers can fall with astonishing speed (10:14; 11:1-6). Ben Sira was personally aware of "many" whose financial miscalculations brought them to complete ruin and he warns his students to avoid a similar fall (29:7, 18, 21-28; cf. 40:28-30). Keeping this in mind, his students should be cautious and not take their present situation for granted:

> Remember the time of hunger in the time of plenty, poverty and deprivation in the days of wealth.
>
> From morning to evening things change and all things are swift before the Lord. (18:25-26)[11]

---

10. I have adopted the translation of Patrick Skehan & Alexander Di Lella, *The Wisdom of Ben Sira: A New Translation with Notes, Introduction and Commentary*, AB 39 (New York: Doubleday, 1987), 424.
11. There is no Hebrew extant for this passage; my translation follows the Greek.

The parallelism in v. 25 suggests that one of the most acute characteristics of falling into poverty was the experience of hunger. In fact, Ben Sira seems to treat hunger as a *pars pro toto* for poverty in general. While Ben Sira and his colleagues did not face serious threats of going hungry in the normal course of events, Ben Sira advised his audience not to allow this state of affairs to anesthetize one to the tragic possibility of a sudden, catastrophic fall into poverty, exemplified by the experience of hunger.

II. Social and Theological Dimensions of Hunger

As the passage just cited shows, Ben Sira believes that hunger, poverty, and deprivation are closely associated and that no one is *completely* insulated from this threat. The seriousness with which Ben Sira takes hunger is reflected not only in the number of references to food and hunger, but in the way the concepts appear in his book. In short, because Ben Sira affirms that food is one of the most basic needs of humans for survival, its presence in society is a serious, concrete problem that makes unavoidable demands on those of high social standing. Let us consider these two related themes in turn.

In multiple places Ben Sira indicates how essential the provision of food is. As mentioned above, slaves and destitute beggars were at the very bottom of the social ladder. In his description of how one should treat a slave, Ben Sira draws an analogy with the treatment of a donkey:

> Fodder, rod, and burden for a donkey;
>
> bread,[12] discipline, and labor for a slave. (33:25)

---

12. "Bread" is missing from manuscript E, but is attested in both Greek and Syriac (though Syriac has it transposed with the following term). In all likelihood, it has dropped out of the Hebrew due to parablepsis since the first stich ends with לחמור ("for a donkey"), which is similar to לחם ("bread"). So Skehan & Di Lella, *The Wisdom of Ben Sira*, 403.

The parallelism between the donkey and the slave is obvious. Both are used for hard manual labor and despite needing to be disciplined to do it, they need a bare minimum of fuel (fodder or bread) to power this work.[13] Moving up the social hierarchy, Ben Sira views sufficient food as a basic need of a respectable existence for the poor. After his discourse on loans, alms, and surety in 29:1-20, Ben Sira accents how important it is not to fall into poverty through crushing debt, especially through going surety for a neighbor:[14]

> The basic needs of life are water, bread, clothing, and a house for privacy.
>
> Better is the life of the poor under the shelter of his roof than splendid delicacies among strangers.
>
> Whether you have little or much, be content with what you have so that you will not hear the reproach of being a sojourner.
>
> It is a terrible life (to go) from house to house; the one who is a sojourner should not open his mouth.

13. Despite slaves being at the bottom of the social hierarchy, it is clear that Ben Sira did not view them as somehow subhuman entities. While his description of the treatment of slaves strikes modern readers as quite harsh, he does counsel empathy towards them at the end of the passage, even if for merely utilitarian ends: "If you have but one slave, treat him like yourself, because you have bought him with blood. If you have but one slave, treat him like a brother, for you will need him as you need your life. If you ill-treat him and he leaves you and runs away, which way will you go to seek him?" (33:31-33 NRSV)

14. The description in 29:21-28 is interpreted by Norbert Peters (*Das Buch Jesus Sirach oder Ecclesiasticus übersetzt und erklärt*, EHAT 25 [Münster: Aschendorffsche, 1913], 240–42) and Andreas Eberharter (*Das Buch Jesus Sirach oder Ecclesiasticus* [Bonn: Hanstein, 1925], 105–6) to refer to a merchant who travels abroad in pursuit of wealth. However, the reference to the creditor in v. 28 and the common motif of wandering through foreign lands in 29:18 and 29:22-24 suggest that the person described in 29:21-28 is the person who has come to financial ruin through surety. This is the majority opinion. See, for example, Maurice Gilbert, "Prêt, aumône et caution" in Egger-Wenzel & Krammer, *Der Einzelne und seine Gemeinschaft bei Ben Sira*, 184; Georg Sauer, *Jesus Sirach/Ben Sira: Übersetzt und erklärt*, ATD 1 (Göttingen: Vandenhoeck & Ruprecht, 2000), 211; Skehan & Di Lella, *The Wisdom of Ben Sira*, 376.

You will play the host and will thanklessly serve drinks and you will hear bitter words like these:

"Come here sojourner, set the table; if something is in your hand, feed it to me.

Leave, sojourner, for one of higher status is here, my brother is visiting and I need the room."

These things are burdensome to a sensible man, criticism at home and the reproach of the creditor. (29:21-28)[15]

For our purposes a couple of points can be highlighted. First, food is a basic necessity for life along with water, clothing, and shelter. This, as we will see below, points to the seriousness of hunger as a social problem. Second, while Ben Sira has a discerning palate and enjoys the finer things in life, he also recognizes that self-sufficiency and financial stability are more important that the enjoyment of quality foods. The poor person is better off with basic sustenance than the sojourner who may enjoy some fine foods, but only from the position of an expendable servant. Thus, while food is a good thing and should be enjoyed, it should never come at the expense of financial and social instability (cf. 14:11!). Ben Sira revisits this perspective later in the book, when he warns,

When one looks to the table of a stranger,

One's life cannot be considered a life.

Its delicacies are loathsome to the soul,[16]

and to the knowledgeable person, agony. (40:29)[17]

---

15. The Hebrew is not extant for this passage. My translation is from the Greek.
16. So the marginal reading of manuscript B (= Greek).

Thus, passages like 29:21-28 and 40:29 highlight that while quality food is a good thing, one should keep priorities in order and eat only as well as possible within one's means.

Because Ben Sira views food as part of the minimal necessities for life in 29:21 and 33:25, it follows from this that the presence of hunger is a threat to human life itself. In one of his most pointed discussions of social justice Ben Sira draws out the blunt implications of this:

> The bread of the needy[18] is the life of the poor; whoever deprives them of it is a murderer.

> The one who takes away his living executes his neighbor; the one who withholds a laborer's wages is a shedder of blood. (34:25-27)

Since peasants were mostly subsistence workers and normally stood on the brink of destitution, to treat them unjustly imperils their lives. For Ben Sira, then, unaddressed hunger is quite literally a matter of life and death.[19] His conviction in this regard has little precedent

---

17. So the marginal reading of manuscript B, which is supported by the fragmentary Masada Scroll.

18. This verse is not extant in Hebrew. The Greek reads "the bread of the needy", presupposing לחם חסר. The Syriac reads "the bread of charity", presupposing לחם חסד. Either is explainable as a misreading of the other, but the overall context of 34:21-27 seems to me to favor the Greek reading, since the passage is about the exploitation of the poor, and so a reference to charity seems slightly intrusive. So also G. H. Box & W. O. E. Oesterley, "The Book of Sirach" in *The Apocrypha and Pseudepigrapha of the Old Testament in English, with Introductions and Critical and Explanatory Notes to the Several Books*, ed. R. H. Charles, 2 vols. (Oxford: Clarendon, 1913), 1:436; Mosheh Z. Segal, ספר בן־סירא השלם 4th ed. (Jerusalem: Bialik, 1997), 221; contra Skehan & Di Lella, *The Wisdom of Ben Sira*, 414.

19. Although space does not allow a full discussion, it is worth noting that Ben Sira employs the phenomenon of hunger as a primal urge for survival as a metaphor for capturing the need to pursue Wisdom. In 15:2-3 Ben Sira claims that the one who seeks God's law will obtain Wisdom because "She will come to meet him like a mother, and like a young bride she will welcome him. She will feed him with the bread of learning, and give him the water of wisdom to drink." (NRSV) The connection of Wisdom to the sustenance of food and drink can be seen in Prov. 9:5, and the further connection to the Torah is found in numerous places in rabbinic literature. For the references see Box & Oesterley, "Sirach," 369. In the famous poem about

in Proverbs, but is in strong continuity with the social vision of Deuteronomy, as is typical for Ben Sira's understanding of aspects of social justice.[20] In Deut. 24:14-15 it is legislated,

> You shall not withhold the wages of poor and needy laborers, whether other Israelites or aliens who reside in your land in one of your towns. You shall pay them their wages daily before sunset, because they are poor and their livelihood depends on them; otherwise they might cry to the Lord against you, and you would incur guilt.[21]

This is a distinctly Deuteronomic expansion of the Covenant Code (Exod. 22:24-26; cf. Lev. 19:13),[22] but Ben Sira draws out the implication further than does Deuteronomy by equating such injustice with murder. Ben Sira's statements in 34:25-27 highlight both the essential role of food in survival and the seriousness of hunger inducing injustice. This raises the question of how Ben Sira assesses and addresses the presence of impoverished hunger within his own society.[23]

III. Hunger as a Concrete Social Problem and Its Remedy

To this point, I have tried to show the different ways that Ben Sira's view of food and hunger is related to his social location within

Wisdom in chapter 24, the idea of hunger is used in a paradoxical way:Come to me, you who desire me,and eat your fill of my fruits.For the memory of me is sweeter than honey,and the possession of me sweeter than the honeycomb.Those who eat of me will hunger for more,and those who drink of me will thirst for more. (24:19-21 NRSV)The "consumption" of Wisdom (or her fruits) brings both satisfaction and yet also amplifies the student's hunger for more. Since Wisdom is the highest good, hunger here is good since it functions almost as an addiction that drives the student to continue imbibing her.

20. On this, see generally my *Like An Everlasting Signet Ring*. Note also the broad assessment of Di Lella that "[Ben Sira's] pervading theological outlook is Deuteronomic" (*The Wisdom of Ben Sira*, 75).

21. All quotations from the Bible, outside of Sirach, are from the NRSV.

22. On this see J. David Pleins, *The Social Visions of the Hebrew Bible: A Theological Introduction* (Louisville: Westminster John Knox, 2001), 58–61.

23. Horsley observes, "'Poor,' 'hungry,' 'needy,' 'desperate,' and other such terms in his speeches apparently refer not to exceptional cases, but to a large proportion of the population (e.g., 4:1-10)" (*Scribes, Visionaries, and the Politics of Second Temple Judea*, 66). On 4:1-10 see below.

the context of Seleucid Judea. Because Ben Sira and his students were among the elite minority, the possibility of experiencing grave hunger was quite small, and they moved in circles that had not only enough food, but a high quality of food. Social norms required banquet hosts to provide plenty of good food, such that a considerable concern for Ben Sira is inculcating the virtue of moderation in his students. Overeating was a more common risk for his students than starving. On the other hand, Ben Sira views hunger as a real and serious social ill that threatens human life. This is especially clear when he argues that the withholding of the basic necessities of survival is tantamount to murder in 34:25-27.

In light of these socioeconomic realities and Ben Sira's own social location among the elite, it is especially striking that he *never* traces the origin of hunger, or poverty in general, to a fault on the part of the hungry/poor. For the sake of comparison, consider these examples from the book of Proverbs (and note how *many* such statements there are!).

> Anyone who tills the land will have plenty of bread,
> but one who follows worthless pursuits will have plenty of poverty. (28:19 ≈12:11)

> Do not love sleep, or else you will come to poverty;
> open your eyes, and you will have plenty of bread. (20:13)

> Laziness brings on deep sleep;
> an idle person will suffer hunger. (19:15)

> The righteous have enough to satisfy their appetite,
> but the belly of the wicked is empty. (13:25)

> The lazy do not roast their game,
> but the diligent obtain precious wealth (12:27)

> The Lord does not let the righteous go hungry,
> but he thwarts the craving of the wicked.
> A slack hand causes poverty,
> but the hand of the diligent makes rich. (10:3-4)

In these verses it is laziness and wickedness that lead to hunger and poverty. The intention of the sages, of course, is to encourage their students to be diligent by pointing to the consequences of different behaviors. Thus, when hunger serves as motivation for hard work it is viewed positively:

> The appetite of workers works for them;
>
> their hunger urges them on. (16:26; cf. Qoh. 6:7)

Although these statements are sometimes interpreted to be merely self-serving justifications for the status quo, I think Timothy Sandoval is right when he argues that "the lazy/diligent sayings are likely not in the first place concerned with offering quasi-sociological observations about how social groups (or "classes") come to be constituted. They are not designed to answer the question of why the poor are poor or the rich are rich."[24] In other words, these proverbs are pedagogical, not abstractly descriptive, in nature. Their purpose is to motivate the students toward diligence and away from laziness by calling attention to the normal (relative) consequences of such character traits. This interpretation is confirmed by a surprising number of statements in Proverbs that view the poor and those who help them in a more positive light (e.g. Prov. 14:31; 17:5; 19:17), as Bruce Malchow has noted.[25]

---

24. Timothy J. Sandoval, *The Discourse of Wealth and Poverty in the Book of Proverbs*, BINS 77 (Leiden: Brill, 2006), 137.
25. Bruce V. Malchow, "Social Justice in the Wisdom Literature" *BTB* 12 (1982): 120–24.

However, with this caveat in mind, it is not difficult to see how these kinds of aphorisms could be employed to underwrite the status quo and essentially blame those who are suffering for their own condition. Job's interlocutors, however much they might be literary constructs, represent just this sort of theologizing.[26] Ben Sira actually seems to refer to this type of thinking in 13:24 when he says,

> Wealth is good if there is no sin,
>
> but poverty is evil in the opinion of the arrogant.

The idea is that the arrogant (זדון) infer someone's quality of character from his socioeconomic status. For them, poverty is "evil" because it is always the consequence of the poor person's failings. Rather than "the opinion [lit. 'according to the mouth'] of the arrogant," it might be possible to read the Hebrew in a more explicitly sapiential sense of "in the sayings of the arrogant." In contrast, Ben Sira believes that wealth is not necessarily a sign of God's blessing; rather, it is a good thing only if it has been acquired righteously. It is striking in this regard that Ben Sira does not blame the poor/hungry for their own condition. In fact, his discussion of the social situation in Seleucid Judea in the passage leading up to this statement (13:2-24) comes quite close to prophetic-style critique of those in power who exploit the poor.[27] In addition, while laziness is a major theme in Proverbs, it appears relatively infrequently in Sirach.

26. This is particularly clear in the discussion of Gustavo Gutiérrez, *On Job: God Talk and the Suffering of the Innocent*, trans. Matthew J. O'Connell (Maryknoll: Orbis, 1987), especially 21–30.
27. Given the way hunger can function as a *pars pro toto* for poverty in general, it is particularly striking that in this critique Ben Sira chillingly describes the peasants as "the feeding grounds of a rich person" (13:19). This graphic description of exploitation capitalizes on the dynamics of hunger and satiation as a difference between the poor and the rich. While in Sir. 13:19 it is on analogy with a predatory lion, cannibalistic imagery is used for social injustice in Mic. 3:3, for persecution in Ps. 27:2 (cf. Dan. 3:8; 6:25), and for self-destruction in Isa. 49:26 and Qoh. 4:5.

Where it does appear, Ben Sira links it with shame and dishonor rather than hunger or poverty (22:1-2; cf. 2:12; 4:29; 37:11).[28]

In short, Ben Sira does not adopt positions regarding the hungry and poor that would be most self-serving to himself and those whom he served among the Jerusalem elite. Instead, it needs to be emphasized that he consistently defends the poor and advocates on their behalf, even when it dangerously implicates in sin those who held sociopolitical power over him. This interesting aspect of Ben Sira's thought might be somewhat unexpected, but an examination of 4:1-10, in which he advocates for proactive actions to help the poor/hungry, can help to shed light on why he approaches hunger and poverty in this way.[29] Although this passage treats the poor more broadly, the manner of assisting them would naturally include the feeding of the hungry (made explicit in the Greek rendering of v. 2). In his first major discussion of social justice Ben Sira says,

My son, do not mock the life of the poor

and do not make the eyes of an embittered person weary.

Do not deride a needy person[30]

and do not hide from one who is crushed.

Do not inflict pain on the heart of the poor

and do not withhold a gift from the needy.

---

28. On honor and shame as an important dimension of Ben Sira's thought, see David A. deSilva, "The Wisdom of Ben Sira: Honor, Shame, and the Maintenance of the Values of a Minority Culture," *CBQ* 58 (1996): 433–55. For how it affects Ben Sira's understanding of retributive justice, particularly in connection to wealth and poverty, see my *Like an Everlasting Signet Ring*, 85–88.

29. The discussion of Sir. 4:1-10 that follows is adapted from my *Like an Everlasting Signet Ring*, 261–70.

30. So Hebrew; Greek: "a hungry person."

Do not despise the requests of a peasant

and do not give him an occasion to curse you.

When an embittered person cries out in the anguish of his soul

then his Maker will heed the sound of his cry.

Endear yourself to the assembly

and bow your head to the ruler of the city.

Incline your ear to the poor person

and return his greeting with humility.

Save the oppressed from his oppressors

and do not let your spirit be repulsed by just judgment.

Become as a father to orphans

and in the place of a husband to widows.

Then God will call you a son

and will be gracious to you and deliver you from the pit.
(4:1–10)[31]

This passage is a collage of themes prominent in the Hebrew Bible. The reference to mocking the poor in v. 1 echoes Prov. 17:5, "Those who mock the poor insult their Maker," which operates on the assumption that one's treatment of the poor is simultaneously an action directed toward God. The references to mocking, deriding,

31. The text-criticism of this passage is very difficult. See my discussion in *Like an Everlasting Signet Ring*, 295–303.

and "inflicting pain on the heart of the poor" probably refer to the tendency to blame the poor for their own condition. However, the sapiential principle of retributive justice cannot always be applied in reverse.[32] While those who sin can expect to encounter poverty, poverty is not always the result of sin. Those who assume that the poor are always to blame for their condition fail to account for the complexity of social reality.

Most commentators are agreed that vv. 1-3 appear to evoke Prov. 3:27-28, which reads:

> Do not withhold good from those to whom it is due,
>
>   when it is in your power to do it.
>
> Do not say to your neighbor, "Go, and come again,
>
>   tomorrow I will give it"—when you have it with you.

What is important to recognize about this allusion is that, in context, Prov. 3:27-28 is not addressing charity, but social obligations. As Michael Fox comments, "Verse 27, like [the passage] as a whole, preaches fairness and honesty, not charity or kindness."[33] Yet, Ben Sira has adapted this text to refer to generosity to the poor, which makes sense given that elsewhere the idea of doing good [טובה] refers to generosity (14:3-19). He was not alone in reading Prov. 3:27 in this way. The LXX renders the verse as, "Do not refrain from doing good to the needy whenever your hand is able to help." Thus, instead of "to whom it is due" (literally in the MT, "from its owners"), the Greek translator has rendered it as "to the needy." The implication of this adaptation is that giving to the poor is not optional

---

32. Josef Schreiner, *Sirach 1–24*, NEchtB 38 (Würzburg: Echter, 2002), 31.
33. Michael V. Fox, *Proverbs 1–9: A New Translation with Introduction and Commentary*, AB 18A (New York: Doubleday, 2000), 165.

because the extra money of the wealthy is understood to belong to the poor *by right*. They are the rightful owners, the ones to whom it is due. This is consistent with Ben Sira's teaching that generosity to the poor is an obligation of the Torah (29:9), and that many of the wealthy had obtained their wealth through the exploitation of the poor (13:2-23; 34:21-27).

The development of themes from the Hebrew Bible continues in vv. 4-6, where Ben Sira assumes a complex theological relationship between God, the poor, and the sage. In v. 5, Ben Sira asserts that the student should not give the poor person an occasion to curse (קלל) him. Clearly from v. 4, the occasion of the curse is a refusal to aid the poor person, which comports with the view that the poor have a right to financial assistance. The implication of the phrasing is that the poor person's complaint is legitimate and, therefore, will be heeded by God (v. 6). As Jonathan Ben-Dov has shown, the efficacy of the poor's curse is a common motif in the ancient world and can be found ranging from Mesopotamian literature to Homer.[34] The motif can be found in the Hebrew Bible as well, in passages such as Exod. 22:21-23 and Deut. 24:13-15 (which was noted in connection to Sir. 34:25-27).

In Ben Sira, it is evident that the poor person's curse carries a power similar to that in other ancient sources. As with the use of Prov. 17:5 in v. 1, the unstated theological premise behind Ben Sira's argument is that the poor have a special relationship with God such that treating them poorly is considered an offense toward God and will result in divine punishment. In v. 6. Ben Sira draws on Exod. 22:21-23 for the occasion of the curse: "When an embittered person cries out in the anguish of his soul." As with the Covenant Code in Exodus, Ben Sira promises that God will heed their cry. He does not state the result of

---

34. See Jonathan Ben-Dov, "The Poor's Curse: Exodus XXII 20–26 and Curse Literature in the Ancient World," *VT* 56 (2006): 431–51.

this heeding, which is explicit in the Covenant Code, but the reader who is aware of the antecedent text can fill in the picture with the idea of the divine avenger.

At this point, it should be observed that Ben Sira places no qualifications on assistance to the needy. He focuses on the requirement to help and the possible curse incurred for refusing. The moral quality of the poor person does not come into view. As Friedrich V. Reiterer notes, "Whether people should be helped does not depend on the seriousness of their difficulties, nor on the cause of the situation; rather, they should simply be helped because they are suffering."[35] This same perspective is found a few chapters later, when Ben Sira exhorts his students to "give a gift to anyone alive and even from the dead do not withhold kindness" (7:33).[36] The reason for this, of course, is that in this passage the operative paradigm has been the solidarity of God with the poor. From this angle, the poor are worthy of help insofar as they function as proxies for God. How one treats the poor qua poor has a correlation with the treatment of the deity.

Yet, this theological paradigm takes on an added dimension when vv. 4-6 are read in light of another common motif that is reflected in Ps. 22:25. In that verse, it is stated that God does not despise the cry of the afflicted; rather God hears and does not turn away. Alexander Di Lella observes that in his application of this verse to the conduct of the pious, "Ben Sira in effect is urging his readers to imitate YHWH in his love and care for the poor."[37] This connection is strengthened in v. 8 with the exhortation to incline the ear toward the poor, a common psalmic motif regarding God's dealings with the poor (including Ps.

35. Friedrich V. Reiterer, "The Influence of the Book of Exodus on Ben Sira," in *Intertextual Studies in Ben Sira and Tobit: Essays in Honor of Alexander A. Di Lella, O.F.M*, ed. Jeremy Corley & Vincent Skemp, CBQMS 38 (Washington D.C.: Catholic Biblical Association of America, 2005), 106.

36. On this passage and its relationship to other passages regarding the recipients of assistance, see the discussion in my *Like an Everlasting Signet Ring*, 245–90, especially 270–76.

37. Skehan & Di Lella, *The Wisdom of Ben Sira*, 166.

22:25). Therefore, in addition to the relationship between God and the poor, there is also a subtle connection between God and the sage in how they treat the poor. By caring for the poor, the sage enacts God's own special care for the poor as an instance of *imitatio Dei*. This same relationship continues to function in the following verses in calling the students to imitate God's dealings with the poor, especially as portrayed in the Psalms. God inclines an ear to the needy (e.g. Ps. 31:3), responds to their pleas (e.g. Ps. 28:6), and seeks justice for the oppressed (e.g. Ps. 103:6).

The idea of *imitatio Dei* is especially prominent in the last four stichs of this passage. In 4:10a-b, Ben Sira advocates becoming like a father to orphans and a husband to widows. In the ancient Near East, the protection and assistance of orphans and widows was a standard requirement of justice since they represented the most vulnerable members of society. But notably, while the defense of the orphan and the widow is a common theme in the Bible, the idea of becoming a *father* to the orphan and *husband* to the widow is peculiar.[38] Many commentators have identified Ben Sira's statement in v. 10a-b as an adaptation of Ps. 68:5, which reads:

> Father of orphans and protector of widows
>
> is God in his holy habitation

Here the notion of being a father to orphans is present, but that of being a husband to a widow is not.[39] Yet, the similarity in phrasing between this psalm and Sir. 4:10a suggests that Ben Sira may well

---

38. A very near parallel can be found in *The Eloquent Peasant*, an Egyptian story from the Middle Kingdom. In the peasant's first petition he says, "For you are father to the orphan, husband to the widow, brother to the rejected woman, apron to the motherless." Miriam Lichtheim, *Ancient Egyptian Literature*, vol. 1: *The Old and Middle Kingdoms* (Berkeley: University of California Press, 1973), 172.

39. Intertextually, this motif could be derived from Deutero-Isaiah's appropriation of Lamentations, but it cannot be ascertained whether this stands behind Ben Sira's thought.

have this text in mind. If Ben Sira is alluding to Psalm 68, then he is applying a description of God to the moral requirements of his students, again, through the model of *imitatio Dei*.[40] This results in a reciprocal action on the part of God in Sir. 4:10c-d: "Then God will call you a son and will be gracious to you and deliver you from the pit." The symmetry is evident in that the one who acts as a father to orphans will enjoy the parental favor of God.[41]

To sum up: Sir. 4:1-10 employs the idea of *imitatio Dei* in connection with the conviction that there is a special relationship between God and the poor. As a result of this configuration of the idea of *imitatio Dei*, there is no thought as to the worthiness of a potential recipient. Since the poor in this passage are functioning in their role as proxies for God (4:6), the language of these verses is unequivocal, such that those in need should be helped simply *because* they are in need. Those who do not help the needy risk being cursed with the vengeance of God (vv. 1-6), while those who do help can expect an analogous treatment from God (vv. 8-10).

IV. Conclusion

We are now in a position to draw the various threads of the preceding discussion together. As is always the case, one's views on social issues are a function of one's particular social location. For Ben Sira, his location among the social and intellectual elite of his day profoundly shapes his understanding of the nature and social role of food. He views its consumption in terms of social graces and the acquisition of a refined palate. For those in his circles, overeating is a

---

40. It is worth pointing out that there is an antecedent for this move already in the wisdom literature in Job 31:16-18.

41. The Greek introduces maternal imagery into the repayment by glossing 4:10c-d under the influence of Isa. 49:15 and 66:13: "Then you will be as a son of the Most High and [the Most High] will love you more than your mother [does]." The Hebrew reading is favored by most commentators; see Gregory, *Like an Everlasting Signet Ring*, 302–3.

more pressing danger than starvation, and for his students who must navigate this social world his advice is to enjoy the finer things in life (14:3-10), but in moderation. This exhortation of moderation is tellingly framed in terms of social acceptability and proper etiquette rather than an awareness of the socioeconomic imbalance in his own culture.

Yet, while Ben Sira's view of food is shaped by his social location, it is not completely determined by it. He is not simply tone-deaf to the reality and seriousness of hunger and he never blames the needy for their condition. Rather, he takes hunger seriously as a matter of life and death and shows a greater concern for issues of social justice than does Proverbs. He completely decouples issues of hunger and poverty from the standard sapiential retributive rhetoric concerning laziness and diligence, and instead aligns it with the strong social justice concern of the Torah, especially Deuteronomy. This leads Ben Sira to exhort his students to alleviate hunger and poverty, rather than to write the hungry and poor off as simply getting what they deserve. In 4:1-10, we can see how Ben Sira draws on other biblical themes in order to motivate his students to aid the needy/hungry. He builds his instruction on the conviction that there is a special relationship between God and the poor, such that how one treats the poor involves a corresponding treatment of God. Since God loves the needy, so the student ought to imitate God in assisting them. In its most elemental forms this includes ensuring that they have at least the basic necessities of life. Thus, for Ben Sira feeding the hungry, regardless of the circumstances that led to that hunger, stands near the center of what it means to love and serve God.

6

"You Give Them Something to Eat" (Mark 6:37): Beyond a Hermeneutic of Hunger

Mary Ann Beavis

In her 2009 presidential address to the Catholic Biblical Association, Kathleen O'Connor called for a "hermeneutics of hunger."[1] The phrase is borrowed from the German feminist theologian Dorothee Sölle, who argued that theology needed to move beyond a hermeneutic of suspicion to an "interpretive religious stance that engages the religious content of Christian traditions and feeds the world's physical and spiritual hungers."[2] O'Connor recognizes the

1. Kathleen M. O'Connor, "Let All the Peoples Praise You: Biblical Studies and a Hermeneutics of Hunger," *Catholic Biblical Quarterly* 72 (2010): 1–14.
2. Dorothee Sölle, *The Silent Cry: Mysticism and Resistance*, trans. Barbara Rumscheidt and Martin Rumscheidt (Minneapolis: Fortress Press, 2001), 45–49.

utility of historical-critical biblical studies in that they "remind us that interpretation of ancient texts is a cross-cultural conversation, that the text is 'a stranger,' foreign to us, whose meaning is hidden by distances of language, worldview, culture, material realities, and profound gaps in human experience."[3] However, she reminds us that exegesis is a starting point, not an end in itself; the Scriptures, like all texts and interpretations, are "culturally situated, linguistically multiple, polyglot," and amenable to readings from multiple global and cultural contexts.[4]

The Feminist Biblical Hermeneutics Task Force of the Catholic Biblical Association has taken up the challenge to apply a hermeneutic of hunger to the Scriptures. This essay originated in a communal exegesis on Mark 6:34-44—the "feeding of the five thousand men (*pentakischilioi andres*)"—that I was asked to facilitate subsequent to an initial presentation by Kathleen O'Connor and Tatha Wiley. Task Force members discussed the pericope in the context of their own locations, communities, and cultural contexts. I introduced the discussion with a description of my own local context in relation to the hermeneutic of hunger and the Marcan feeding narrative. The following pages will expand on my introductory remarks, which focused on an inner-city food-security initiative in the city where I live. As I write, I am aware of the multiple global and local contexts in which the scriptural mandate to share bread with the hungry (e.g., Ps. 146:7; Prov. 25:21; Isa. 58:7, 10; Ezek. 18:7, 16; Matt. 25:37; Luke 6:21; Rom. 12:20[5]) resonates urgently, from

---

3. O'Connor, "Hermeneutics of Hunger," 11.
4. Ibid.
5. A related strand of biblical tradition is the Sabbath and Jubilee laws of the Hebrew Bible (Exod. 21:2-6; 23:10-11; Deut. 15:1-18; Lev. 25:1-55; Jer. 34:8-22; Isa. 61:1-2); similar traditions are found in the records of ancient non-Israelite nations: "In these traditions liberty is presented in economic, social, and political terms: freedom for slaves, release for captive peoples, cancellation of debts, redistribution of land, care for the poor, food for the hungry, and healing of physical ailments. The language is primarily the language of ethics, dealing with values, social relationships, and the establishment or restoration of justice" (Sharon H. Ringe, *Jesus,*

daily news reports of drought, war, and famine driving thousands of Somalian refugees to seek sanctuary in Kenya, to warnings that food production must double if the growing world population is to be fed,[6] to a morning phone call from a former student who had run out of food and money for herself and her child.

The essay will be constructed (appropriately enough in the light of the topic) in the form of a "Marcan sandwich," in which two narratives—in this case the contemporary, real-life story of Station 20 West in Saskatoon and Mark's feeding narratives (6:34-44; 8:1-9)—are intercalated, signaling that the two stories are interrelated in some way (e.g., 3:20-35; 4:1-20; 5:21-43; 6:7-30; 11:12-21; 14:1-11; 14:17-31; 14:53-72; 15:40—16:8).[7] Unlike the evangelist, who leaves it to the reader/audience to discern the relationship between the two stories, I will conclude by attempting to connect the ancient and contemporary narratives through the lens of the hermeneutic of hunger.

The Local Context: Station 20 West

Saskatoon, SK is a small Canadian prairie city with a population of about 225,000. In North American terms, the province of Saskatchewan has fared well in the wake of the financial crash of 2008 and the subsequent recession, and has enjoyed economic and population growth thanks to its abundant resource industries (potash, oil, uranium). Although citizens have access to social services, including publicly funded medicare, that much of the world's population would find enviable, there are sharp economic disparities within the populations of Saskatchewan cities, especially Saskatoon

Liberation, and the Biblical Jubilee: Images for Ethics and Christology [Philadelphia: Fortress, 1985], xiv).

6. Charles Siebert, "Food Ark," *National Geographic*, July 2011, 108–31.

7. See Mary Ann Beavis, *Mark*, Paideia Commentaries on the New Testament (Grand Rapids: Baker Academic, 2011), 19.

and Regina (the provincial capital), which share similar populations and demographics.

In Saskatoon, residents of the "west end" core neighborhoods of Riversdale, King George, Pleasant Hill, Caswell Hill, and Westmount experience economic, health, and nutritional deficits relative to the averages in other parts of the city.[8] Since 1997, there have been no grocery stores to serve the west end, although in more affluent areas of Saskatoon, multiple supermarket chains are easily accessible. In contrast, carless inner-city residents, including a disproportionate number of First Nations people and low-income single mothers, must make do with expensive convenience stores or rely on the municipal bus service to access the suburban supermarkets, in a climate where winter temperatures often dip below minus thirty degrees Celsius for up to five months of the year. For the past two years, the Salvation Army has run a summer brown-bag lunch program serving the core area parks to address the needs of local children who were going hungry in July and August in the absence of the school lunch program.[9] The lack of convenient, affordable grocery stores in the city's core led the authors of the Community Food Access report compiled by the Saskatoon Health Region (2010) to define the area as a "food desert": "When people have trouble accessing healthy foods because of where they live and because of money problems, they are said to live in a 'food desert.' Saskatoon has a primary food desert in Saskatoon's core and surrounding neighborhoods."[10]

8. See Station 20 West Community Enterprise Centre, http://station20west.org/.
9. Jeanette Stewart, "Summer Lunch Program Feeds Children in Need," *Saskatoon Star Phoenix*, (Wednesday, August 24, 2011). http://www2.canada.com/saskatoonstarphoenix/news/local/story.html?id=d4c8caaa-852f-4d16-9ee7-af1a1918528a.
10. Quoted in Anne-Marie Hughes, "Marchers Walk Saskatoon's Food Desert," *Prairie Messenger*, October 26, 2011, 7.

In order to address the nutritional and related needs of the west end communities, a community development project called Station 20 West (after 20th Street West, running through the city's core neighborhoods) was planned over five years ago, supported by substantial funding from the social democratic provincial government of the time. The proposed community center would accommodate a grocery store, community services, and medical and dental clinics. However, in 2008, the politically conservative Saskatchewan Party replaced the New Democratic (NDP) government, and the eight-million dollar grant earmarked for the project was withdrawn on the excuse that the government was not in the business of building supermarkets.[11] Station 20 West was left in limbo, and the core area still remains without a nearby grocery store. Nonetheless, on Wednesday, July 20, 2011, a groundbreaking ceremony for the center took place, with an expected completion date in July 2012, looking forward to a practical feeding miracle on the Canadian prairies.

Strange Texts: The Marcan Feeding Narratives (6:34-44; 8:1-9)

As Kathleen O'Connor reminds us, the biblical text is "a 'stranger,' foreign to us, whose meaning is hidden by distances of languages, worldview, culture, material realities, and profound gaps in human experience."[12] Religion should be added to this list, particularly with reference to the Gospels, since they relate stories about Jews written by proto-Christians that function as Scriptures for a wide range of Christian denominations.[13] Although Mark's stories of the feedings of the five thousand and of the four thousand seem familiar after

---

11. Jeanette Stewart, "Shovels in the Ground at Station 20 West," *Saskatoon Star Phoenix* (July 20, 2011), http://www2.canada.com/saskatoonstarphoenix/news/local/story.html?id=5bb0c6f7 -eec9-49a0-8929-d1b8fc18e04b.
12. O'Connor, "Hermeneutics of Hunger," 11.
13. The exegesis in this section is adapted from Beavis, *Mark*, 105–7, 127–28.

two millennia of Christian reception, they share in the "strangeness" of all biblical narratives. They are also amenable to the "abundance of significance" that opens the Scriptures to multiple interpretations from diverse cultural perspectives.[14]

The first "strangeness" to note with respect to the feeding narratives is that there are two of them, situated in distinctive sections of the Gospel, exemplifying a distinctively Marcan compositional technique: the use of two similar stories in different parts of the Gospel (e.g., 4:35-41 and 6:45-52 [two boat narratives]; 7:31-37 and 9:9-29 [two healings of deaf-mutes]; 8:22-26 and 10:46-52 [two healings of blind men]). These doublets underline the themes of the respective stories, challenging the reader/audience to "see, see, and perceive," "hear, hear, and understand" their significance (Mark 4:12; cf. Isa. 6:9-10), contrary to the obtuseness of the literary characters of the disciples (see Mark 4:10, 41; 6:52; 7:18; 8:17-21). Moreover, as David Beckman observes, in canonical context, stories of Jesus feeding a hungry crowd are repeated more often than any other miracle story: six times in all (cf. Matt. 14:13-21; 15:32-38; Luke 9:12-17; John 6:1-14),[15] signifying the importance of the feeding stories to the early churches.

The feeding of the five thousand (6:34-44) takes place in Galilee, from whence Jesus sends the twelve on a mission of teaching, preaching, and healing (6:7-13, 30). The disciples return to report on "all they had done and taught" (6:30), and the feeding story begins. The account of the disciples' mission is interrupted by the tale of the death of John the Baptist, plotted during Herod's birthday banquet (6:14-29). As Kathleen Corley has noted, Mark's first feeding narrative stands in an inverted typological relationship to Herod's

14. Ibid.
15. David Beckman, *Exodus from Hunger: We Are Called to Change the Politics of Hunger* (Louisville: Westminster John Knox, 2010), 72. Beckman counts five, but there are in fact six.

banquet, contrasting the life-giving abundance of God's provision of bread in the wilderness with the gruesome royal feast where the murdered prophet's head is served on a platter:

> Herod's guests form . . . groups (6:21), as do Jesus' (6:39-40), and only men attend both meals (6:21-22, 44). Both Jesus and Herod send out emissaries (6:7, 17, 27, 30), but for entirely different tasks. Furthermore, both utilize serving dishes, but again for different purposes (6:28, 43). Thus, the meals of Jesus and Herod serve as bold contrasts.[16]

The Jewish setting of the initial feeding story is underlined by the exodus imagery that pervades it. Jesus, like Moses, has compassion on the crowd because they resemble "sheep without a shepherd" (cf. Num. 27:17). The scriptural phrase recalls the story of the appointment of Joshua (in Greek, _Iēsous_) to be Moses' successor, foreshadowing the _Iēsous_ of the Gospel: "Who shall go out before them and come in before them, . . . and at his word they shall go out, and at his word they shall come in, both he and all the Israelites with him, the whole congregation" (Num. 27:17a, 21b). The shepherd imagery is enhanced by the notice that the people were instructed to recline on the "green grass" (Mark 6:39). More than mere local color, this detail recalls the "green pastures" of Psalm 23 and the blossoming wilderness in the "way of the Lord," a new exodus (Isa. 35:1; 40:3; 51:3).[17] In the context of the feeding miracle, it echoes the creation of the "green plants" for food in Genesis (1:30; 9:3). Most prominently, the provision of bread for a hungry crowd in the desert recalls Exodus 16; similarly to the Israelites who complain to Moses and Aaron over lack of food (Exod. 16:2-3), the disciples

---

16. Kathleen Corley, _Private Women, Public Meals: Social Conflict in the Synoptic Tradition_ (Peabody, MA: Hendrickson, 1993), 94; cf. Robert M. Fowler, _Loaves and Fishes: The Function of the Feeding Stories in the Gospel of Mark_, SBLDS 54 (Chico, CA: Scholars Press, 1981), 85–86, 199–227.

17. M. Eugene Boring, _Mark: A Commentary_, New Testament Library (Minneapolis: Fortress, 2006), 186.

urge Jesus to send the people away to buy something to eat and respond incredulously when he replies that they should feed the crowd themselves: "Are we to go and buy two hundred denarii worth of bread, and give it to them to eat?" (Mark 6:36-37).[18] In both the Exodus and Marcan stories, two foodstuffs (manna and quails, bread and fish) are provided, the hungry are satisfied, and there are leftovers (Exod. 16:18; Mark 6:42-43). The statement that five thousand men (*andres*) were fed (6:44) does not necessarily mean that only males were there, but echoes enumerations of Israelites in the wilderness (Exod. 12:37; Num. 11:21; Matthew's version of the story specifies that women and children partook in the meal along with the five thousand men [14:21]).[19] The feeding takes place in the context of Jesus' teaching (6:34b), recalling the scriptural use of bread as a symbol of divine wisdom/word (e.g., Deut. 8:3; Prov. 9:5; Job 23:12; Sir. 15:3; cf. Philo, *Names* 259–60). The term used for "basket" in Mark 6:43 (*kophinos*) is mentioned by the Roman author Juvenal (*Sat.* 3.14; 6.452) as associated with poor Jews in Rome. The number of baskets of fragments left over is twelve, possibly contrasting the twelve tribes of Israel and the seven (or seventy) Gentile nations of the world (cf. Mark 8:8; *Genesis Rabbah* 37).[20]

The feeding narrative also resonates with the Elijah-Elisha typology that informs Mark's Christology. When the widow of Zarephath shares her scanty bread and water with Elijah during a famine, God multiplies the remaining flour and bread until the drought ends (1 Kgs. 17:7-16; cf. 2 Kgs. 4:1-7). Elisha miraculously multiplies twenty loaves to feed a hundred men (LXX: *andrōn*); as

18. A denarius would amount to a day's pay for a male laborer, two days' pay for a woman (Luise Schottroff, *Lydia's Impatient Sisters: A Feminist Social History of Early Christianity* [Louisville: Westminster John Knox, 1995], 92–95).

19. John R. Donahue and Daniel J. Harrington, *The Gospel of Mark*, Sacra Pagina 2 (Collegeville, MN: Liturgical Press, 2002), 207.

20. Donahue and Harrington, *Mark*, 207.

in Mark, there is bread left over (2 Kgs. 4:42-44). The feeding anticipates the biblical theme of the eschatological banquet, where "the Lord of hosts will make for all peoples a feast of rich food, a feast of well-aged wines, of rich food filled with marrow, of well-aged wines strained clear" (Isa. 25:6; cf. *1 Enoch* 62.12-16; *2 Baruch* 29.1-8); similarly Mark 14:25 portrays the Last Supper as foreshadowing a banquet in the realm of God (*basileia tou theou*).[21] The account of the sharing of the loaves (6:41) is full of liturgical terms —"took," "gave thanks," "broke," and "gave" (cf. 8:6; Matt. 14:19; 15.36; 26:26; Luke 9.16; 22.19; John 6.11; 1 Cor. 11:23-24)—that would remind the Markan audience of their own sacred meals (Mark 14:22).[22]

The feeding of the four thousand (Mark 8:1-10) is obviously very much like 6:30-44: both involve a miraculous feeding; in both, the disciples initially regard the task of providing bread for the crowd as impossible; both echo the manna in the wilderness of Exodus; both evoke Elijah/Elisha; both foreshadow the eschatological banquet; in both, Jesus ritually takes, gives thanks, breaks and shares the bread. One major difference is that the first feeding takes place in Jewish territory (cf. 6:1-45), while the second takes place in a Gentile region, the Decapolis (7:31). The narrative has several features that highlight the Gentile context: Jesus remarks that some have come from far away (8:3), elsewhere in Scripture, a description often applied to non-Israelite nations (e.g., Deut. 28:49; 29:22; Josh. 9:6, 9; 1 Kgs. 8:41; Isa. 40:4-5; Ezek. 23:40; Joel 3:8). The term used for baskets in 8:8 is *spyrides*, a word that lacks the specifically Jewish connotations of *kophinos* (Mark 6:43). The first feeding evokes the biblical imagery

---

21. See J. Priest, "A Note on the Messianic Banquet," in *The Messiah: Developments in Earliest Judaism and Christianity*, ed. James H. Charlesworth, First Princeton Symposium on Judaism and Christian Origins (Minneapolis: Fortress, 1992), 222–38; Damien Casey, "The 'Fractio Panis' and the Eucharist as Eschatological Banquet," *McAuley University Electronic Journal* (August 18, 2002). http://www.womenpriests.org/theology/casey_02.asp.

22. C. S. Mann, *Mark: A New Translation and Introduction*, AB 27 (Garden City, NY: Doubleday, 1986), 300.

of shepherd and sheep (6:34; cf. Psalm 23; Ezekiel 34), whereas here, Jesus is concerned about the crowd for the practical reason that they haven't eaten for three days (Mark 8:1-2).

Some interpreters see the seven loaves and seven baskets (8:5, 8; cf. 6:38, 43) as symbolizing the Gentile nations; according to Rudolph Pesch, Jewish tradition divided the non-Israelite world into seventy nations (e.g., *1 Enoch* 83–90); he further notes that the "seven commandments of Noah" were believed to be binding on Gentiles (*b. Sanh.* 56a; cf. Acts 15:19, 28-29).[23] Joel Marcus argues that the number seven symbolizes eschatological completeness,[24] a theme that could include the recognition of the true God by all nations (e.g., Isa. 11:10; 42:6; 49:6; 60:3, 5; 62:2; Jer. 16:19; Mal. 1:11; cf. Luke 13:29).

Scholars are divided as to why Mark includes two feeding narratives. One possibility is that they are pre-Markan variations on the same story, simply taken over by the evangelist. Robert Fowler argues that 8:1-10 is the earlier story, and that Mark deliberately composed 6:30-44 in order to emphasize the theme of the disciples' incomprehension of the meaning of Jesus' ministry.[25] In contrast, Karl P. Donfried argues that 8:1-10 was modeled on the feeding of the five thousand,[26] on the basis of several Markan duplicate expressions.[27] Whatever the redaction history of the two narratives may be, it is obvious that Mark's repetition of feeding stories is intentional; 8:1 notes that in those days "again" (*palin*) there was

23. Rudolph Pesch, *Das Markusevangelium*, vol. 1, HTKNT (Freiburg: Herder, 1976–77), 404. The Noachide laws prohibit idolatry, murder, theft, sexual promiscuity, blasphemy, eating the flesh from a living animal, and require the nations to have an adequate justice system.
24. Joel Marcus, *Mark 1–8: A New Translation with Introduction and Commentary*, AB 27 (New York: Doubleday, 2000), 489.
25. Fowler, *Loaves and Fishes*, 43–90, 95–96.
26. Karl P. Donfried, "The Feeding Narratives and the Marcan Community: Mark 6,30–45 and 8,1–10," in *Kirche: Festschrift für Günther Bornkamm zum 75. Geburtstag*, ed. D. Lührmann and G. Strecker (Tübingen: Mohr Siebeck, 1980), 95–103.
27. For a list of parallels, see Marcus, *Mark*, 493–95.

a great crowd with nothing to eat. The placement of the second feeding after two miracles performed in Gentile territory (7:24-30, 31-37) deliberately reinforces the theme that Jesus proclaims the good news to both Jews and Gentiles, who can expect more than the "crumbs" begged for by the (Gentile) Syro-Phoenician woman (7:28).

Another effect of the doublet of stories is indeed to underline the obtuseness of the disciples. In the second feeding narrative, the disciples, whom the audience knows have already witnessed a multiplication of loaves in the desert (6:31-32, 35), ask Jesus how he can feed so many people with bread in the wilderness (8:4). This time, the disciples don't even have to seek out food, since they immediately inform Jesus that they have seven loaves with them (v. 5; and, as in the first feeding, a few fish [v. 7; cf. 6:38]). Ironically, they have literally "seen and seen" two almost identical situations and "not perceived," "heard and heard" and "not understood" (Mark 4:11; Isa. 6:9-10). They still fail to comprehend the significance of Jesus' words and deeds (cf. Mark 4:12; 7:18). The reader/audience is implicitly challenged to a deeper level of perception than that of the disciples when the crowd eats, is satisfied, and seven basketsful are left over (8:8).

In the nineteenth and early twentieth centuries, naturalistic explanations of miracles like the Marcan feedings were popular, such as the surmise that the evangelist may have exaggerated the numbers of people fed, or that the meal was eucharistic, and so everyone received only a small fragment of bread.[28] Some scholars continue to question whether the feedings are meant to be interpreted supernaturally. For instance, in his political interpretation of Mark, Ched Myers insists that the feeding of the five thousand reports

28. Dennis E. Nineham, *St. Mark* (Harmondsworth: Penguin, 1963), 179.

nothing supernatural; the true miracle is in the ascendancy of an economics of sharing in community over the ethos of autonomous consumption in an impersonal marketplace.[29] Megan McKenna takes the story in a feminist homiletical direction, suggesting that the women in the crowd brought food along with them and shared with those around them, possibly following Jesus' example of sharing his own supplies.[30] Nonetheless, in the context of Mark 4:36—6:56 and 7:24-37 with their exorcisms, healings, and demonstrations of divine power over the wind and the sea, it is unlikely that the feedings can or should be read purely rationalistically. For Mark, faith in God gives believers the power to work miracles (9:23-24; 11:22-23). At another level, the feedings and other miracle stories convey a christological message: Jesus is a prophet with powers that echo and surpass those of the prophets of old, a holy man with an unprecedented relationship with God.

The Local Context II: Back to Station 20 West

Despite their apparent familiarity, the Markan feeding narratives, with their miraculous worldview and multiple layers of scriptural resonances, seem worlds away from 21st century Saskatoon. However, in addition to their theological and christological layers of meaning, these stories bear an explicit and obvious ethical message: the God who sends Jesus is concerned about both the spiritual and *physical* hunger of the shepherdless flock (6:34), whom he both teaches *and* feeds with real, nourishing bread and fish. Jesus' command to the disciples—"*You* give them something to eat" (6:37)—reverberates to this day as challenge to people of faith to

29. Ched Myers, *Binding the Strong Man: A Political Reading of Mark's Story of Jesus* (Maryknoll, NY: Orbis, 1988), 206.
30. Megan McKenna, *Not Counting Women and Children: Neglected Stories from the Bible* (Maryknoll, NY: Orbis, 1994), 15–16.

address both spiritual and physical hunger; to stand in solidarity with "the excluded, the migrant, the hungry, and the burdened."[31] The scriptural mandate to feed the literally hungry reaches beyond the Gospel to each generation; as Sharon Ringe observes with respect to the Jubilee,

> *each generation* must take responsibility for responding to God's decree of liberty, and for doing justice, in its own circumstances and for its children. We cannot, from our human perspective, design structures and social organizations that will be eternally appropriate, and that will always and everywhere support concerns of justice and liberation. . . . But we are called to respond to that larger vision as it breaks into the institutions, systems, and world views that characterize life in our own time and place.[32]

This brings us back to the year 2011, and the story of Saskatoon's Station 20 West.

When government funding for Station 20 West was cancelled, the need for an affordable and accessible grocery store remained. A coalition of local residents and members of the broader community organized to plan and fundraise the millions of dollars required for the community center to materialize. The City of Saskatoon cooperated by selling the land for the project to the group for a dollar and granted them several deadline extensions as the board of directors laboriously sought funding from private donors, businesses, and service clubs, supplemented by proceeds from bake sales, school projects, and cultural and social events. A local construction company agreed to provide project management services free of charge. Fundraising is still not complete, but, as noted above, building is underway with a projected completion date of summer 2012. The completed project will include "a neighborhood grocery store, food,

---

31. O'Connor, "Hermeneutics of Hunger," 13.
32. Ringe, *Jubilee*, 98. The italics are Ringe's.

housing, employment, and health services to the city's core neighborhoods. Programs will include collective cooking, community gardens and nutrition education programs."[33]

Although it is not a church-led initiative, on November 24, 2010, a coalition of ten Christian denominations lent their public support to the effort to bring Station 20 West, and especially the Good Food Junction, the project's grocery store, to realization. Their joint statement read:

> This Christmas season many churches in Saskatoon seek to enhance the momentum of a vital project—the community-owned Good Food Junction cooperative store located at Station 20 West. It is a community project that the churches seek to support as a concrete expression of God's love.

Christians share the conviction that in Jesus Christ God has drawn near to us. The Advent and Christmas seasons remind us that when God in Christ came to dwell among us he was born and lived in poverty and simplicity. In Jesus' ministry, we see his profound concern for those who were in need. He gave dignity to those who were poor, suffering or oppressed. He identified himself with those who were hungry or thirsty, saying that whatever we do for those most in need, we do for him (Matthew 25:31-40). As his disciples we have a moral imperative to follow his example.

Church groups serve in many projects which support the people of the core neighborhoods, such as the Food Bank, the Bridge, the Salvation Army and Friendship Inn, among others.

Saskatoon's core neighborhoods are the heart of the city. For our city to be healthy, it needs a healthy heart. Maintaining good health is a challenge for many in the area whose needs are high and whose resources are limited. Access to healthy food is vital for wellness and

33. Stewart, "Shovels in the Ground."

self-reliance. Since 1997, no full-service grocery store has operated in our core neighborhoods. Many residents have no cars and thus have little access to healthy, affordable food.

The Good Food Junction, at 20th St. and Ave. L, will provide in-store nutrition education and offer healthy food at reasonable prices, close to home. Equipping the store will cost approximately $650,000. Being able to accomplish this without going into debt is crucial to the store's success.

Together we can bring this essential service to the people of our core neighborhoods. This is not specifically a church initiative: neither is it the project of a single political party, nor should we as Christian communities allow it to be so. The potential for good is immense.

As church leaders and as individuals we commit ourselves to making the Good Food Junction a priority for the weeks leading up to Christmas. We will express support through our prayers, practical assistance, and where appropriate through fundraising to equip the store. We do this in the name of Jesus Christ who is Emmanuel, God-with-us.

Signatories:

- Most Rev. Bryan Bayda, C.Ss.R., Bishop, Ukrainian Catholic Eparchy of Saskatoon

- Most Rev. Donald Bolen, Bishop, Roman Catholic Diocese of Saskatoon

- Rev. Jeremiah Buhler, Area Church Minister, Mennonite Church Saskatchewan

- Jay Cowsell, Saskatoon Monthly Meeting, Religious Society of Friends (Quakers)

- Rev. Amanda Currie, Minister, Presbytery of Northern Saskatchewan, Presbyterian Church in Canada

- Rev. Claire Ewert-Fisher, Executive Director, Mennonite Central Committee

- Rev. Cynthia Halmarson, Bishop, Saskatchewan Synod, Evangelical Lutheran Church in Canada

- Rt. Rev. David Irving, Bishop, Anglican Diocese of Saskatoon

- Rev. Ron McConnell, Chair, Riverbend Presbytery, United Church of Canada

- Rev. Harry Strauss, Chair, Saskatoon Evangelical Ministers Fellowship[34]

A clearer endorsement of the command to "give them something to eat" in response to the real needs of a disadvantaged community would be difficult to find, pointing to the realization that a hermeneutic of hunger is incomplete and ineffectual without concrete efforts to feed the hungry.

The moral of this story could be taken to be that the withdrawal of government funding was actually a good thing that challenged the community to pull together to provide the money and resources to make Station 20 West a reality. However, if the government had honored its predecessor's commitment, the project would already have been completed, and residents of west end Saskatoon would already have access to the grocery co-op and other much-needed services it will provide. Moreover, since the eight million dollars pledged by the NDP amounted to half the projected cost, no doubt substantial community effort would have been required to raise

---

34. Churches Together: Supporting Station 20 West. http://ecumenism.net/archive/2010/11/ churches_together_supporting_station_20_west.html. This website includes a 10-minute video about the Advent Initiative for the Good Food Junction.

additional funds. As it happened, the volunteer effort to realize the project has been extraordinary and laudable, and the interchurch cooperation it sparked is an example of ecumenism at its best in the light of the scriptural imperative to "give them something to eat." However, the community-service benefits the center will generate go far beyond building a grocery store:

For Saskatoon

- Social and economic revitalization
- Additional business opportunities
- Polluted land converted into usable space
- Showcase for community program integration and for green building

For the Core Neighborhoods

- Business development, jobs, training and housing
- Food security—access to healthy food
- Improved nutrition for long term health
- Multi-purpose room for community gatherings
- Outreach health and educational services

For the Partner Organizations

- Partners collaborating on service delivery
- Reduced overhead from sharing facilities and equipment[35]

35. Station 20 West Benefits for All; http://station20west.org/benefits.html.

This is a viable model of community development that surely deserves government support (i.e., taxpayers' money), and that illustrates that the hermeneutic of hunger—and of its remediation—extends far beyond the realms of theology and biblical exegesis.[36]

36. Note from the editors: Station 20 West opened its doors in 2012. For more information visit the following link: http://www.chep.org.

7

The Friend at Midnight (Luke 11:1-10)

Linda Maloney

The most common reading of the parable of the Friend at Midnight (Luke 11:1-10) holds that it is about generosity, the requirement to give to those who ask, and the trust that God will supply one's own needs. Social-science commentary, as exemplified by Bruce Malina and Richard Rohrbaugh, adds the further dimensions of patronage and hospitality in the context of honor and shame: "Thus the petitioner threatens to expose the potential shamelessness of the sleeper. By morning the entire village would know of his refusal to provide hospitality. He thus gives in to avoid public exposure as a shameless person."[1] This is correct procedure for parables interpretation.

---

1. Bruce J. Malina and Richard L. Rohrbaugh, *Social Science Commentary on the Synoptic Gospels*, 2d ed. (Minneapolis: Fortress Press, 2003), 273.

But I am interested in the material of the parable, the physical and social substratum—the "scenery" that makes the parable plausible. To "work," a parable—and especially a similitude-type parable like this one, depicting a scene from daily life—has to be drawn against a background that is instantly recognizable to the audience.

So my first questions of this text are about the backdrop. In particular: since the whole thing revolves around bread, I want to bring into the picture the person responsible for bread in the household. Who mills the flour, kneads the dough, and takes it to the bake oven? The three loaves that are requested would be the entire family's ration. If the householder (assuming, as the Greek text does, that this is an exchange between men) gives away the household's bread, how will they be fed? And who will be shamed if they are not?

According to Malina and Rohrbaugh, "milling was done at night and would require three hours of work to provide 3 kg (assuming a ½ kg daily ration) for a family of five or six. . . . Prosperous families might have their own outdoor ovens, but ordinary women arose in the morning to take their bread dough to a common village oven . . . or, less usually, to the village baker."[2] So we can assume this housewife has milled her flour for the next day in the hours before midnight. She will probably rise before light to mix and knead the dough and set it to rise, so that she can take it to the oven later in the morning. But until the fire has been kindled in the oven—even if she has an oven of her own, it would only be fired once a day, in all likelihood—and until the oven has grown hot enough, she cannot bake her dough. Her family will have no bread for the morning.

So the householder can salvage his honor by giving away the family's bread. But he does so at the expense of his wife's shame; for either his "shamelessness" will be known throughout the village if he

2. Ibid., 333.

does not give what is asked, or her "shame" will be spread abroad because she has not provided for her household (cf. Prov. 31:15).

As Malina and Rohrbaugh note, the petitioner is also "shameless," though they, like most commentators, seem to think more of the disruption of the family's sleep than of the demand for their whole breakfast. What does it mean that one person, who has not provided for his own household, may ask that his neighbor give him an entire meal at the expense of the neighbor's family, and expect to have the request honored as a matter of social convention? If we take Luke's moral at face value, what is the implication in our own not-very-post-colonial society, in which rich nations expect, as a matter of course, to take from poor countries whatever they, the "First World," desire, and return a pittance?

We assume this is a poor household, since father and children sleep in one bed (v.7a). But what about the wife/mother? Note that nothing is said of the woman of the house at any point; there is only the householder, the friend, and the children. Perhaps she is still awake, milling, and has not gone to bed at all. But why is she absent from the story altogether, when it is her work that is key to the availability of bread, the central object, in the first place? Is she "consumed" in the bread?

(When, later, Jesus gives himself as bread, is he identified with the householder who gives the bread someone else has made, or with the one who has put *herself* into it?)

In the preceding pericope Jesus has instructed his disciples to pray to the Abba for their *epiousion* bread—the bread for tomorrow (v.3). In the parable we see the *epiousion* bread being given away. The disciple ("one of you") has asked that bread of the friend, and the friend has given it. So where does the friend (and the friend's family) get *epiousion* bread? Presumably they will have to ask for it from someone else.

This parable is as radical in its demands as any part of the Gospel: sell, give, don't worry about tomorrow. It is as much about the reign of God as any passage. But that means we cannot see it in terms of rescuing honor or incurring shame. We have to be open-eyed about the cost, and the relatively different costs, of living the Gospel in a world whose values are so contrary to it. We may have lost the notion that it is shameful not to give to those who ask (just consult any member of Congress!), but we are all the more judgmental toward those who do not provide for their families, or who are "profligate" with what they have (unless, of course, they are very rich).

Luke interprets the parable in terms of the moral he appends ("Ask and you shall receive . . . "). Was that Jesus' original intention, if it was he who told the story? Was he as much embroiled in his own social situation as the Gospel author, and unable to see where the burden falls heaviest here?—and in fact, that the person on whose actions everything else depends is completely absent from the narrative itself?

In terms of Luke's reading, the parable pairs with that of the widow and the unjust judge in chapter 18, which Luke also interprets as being about constant petitioning, this time for justice rather than for food. (We thus have another of Luke's parallel pairs of narratives with a male and a female protagonist, respectively.) The widow in that story behaves shamelessly, like the friend at midnight, and she threatens shame for the judge if he does not respond to her badgering. Again one partner in the marriage is missing: in this case he is dead. The reluctant giver's motive is the same in both stories: to save face. But the widow seeks something to which she is entitled in justice, not a favor. Therefore the perspectives on property and justice are different in the two stories. Or are they?

Ultimately the parable of the Friend at Midnight calls us to question all our notions of property and generosity and even justice. When I give something away—my clothes to the church rummage sale, for example—who is the real giver? I, who paid a small price for those clothes and have more than exhausted that payment in the wearing of them, or the women who put their days and nights into making them and were paid scarcely anything for their labor?

More generally, in how many ways do I gain honor and respectability in society through the work of others who receive no acknowledgment for their contributions, who may even have received less in order that I may have more?

At the pastoral level, what good does it do me to know these things? If I preach them to an American congregation, they will "go away grieving, because they have many possessions." The message would resonate among those who are helpless to change their situation; will it ever be heard by those who have the power to effect change? I have asked of God, and God has given me this *epiousion* bread of knowledge, through the gifts and generosity and companionship of others, but will it be sawdust in my mouth?

8

An Empty Jar and a Starving Woman: *Gospel of Thomas* Logion 97 and a Hermeneutics of Hunger

Susan M. (Elli) Elliott

Jesus said, "The [Father's] imperial rule[1] is like a woman who was carrying a [jar] full of meal. While she was walking along [a] distant road, the handle of the jar broke and the meal spilled behind her [along] the road. She didn't know it; she hadn't noticed a problem.[2] When she

1. Greek, *basileia tou theou*. Translation from Robert J. Miller, *The Complete Gospels: Annotated Scholars Version*, 4th ed. (Salem, OR: Polebridge, 2010), 301–20. Miller uses the expression "Father's imperial rule" to minimize the androcentrism of the Greek expression, which usually is translated "kingdom of God." In the *Gospel of Thomas*, one often finds the similar expression, "kingdom of the Father." In this article "kingdom" (in quotation marks) will be used to translate *basileia*; the expression has the advantage of familiarity since it has been the customary translation.
2. Verse 97:3: "She hadn't noticed a problem" or "She had not understood how to toil." See ibid.,320.

reached her house, she put the jar down and discovered that it was empty."[3]

A woman returns from a long journey to discover that the jar of meal she had walked so far to obtain is empty. Surely this parable cries out for a feminist hermeneutics of hunger. The parable draws us to look into an empty food jar with a hungry woman. What will we see? The first task is deceptively simple. The first task is to look. To join this woman and look into her empty jar, however, appears to be a difficult task for interpreters. To look into the empty jar is to approach the text with a hermeneutic of hunger.

Origins of the *Gospel of Thomas*

The parable of the Woman and the Empty Jar is found only in the *Gospel of Thomas*. A noncanonical gospel, *Gospel of Thomas* was mentioned unfavorably by early orthodox Christian writers.[4] The text had been lost to scholars until recently (1945), when a copy was discovered as part of the find at Nag Hammadi in Egypt. A Coptic version of an ancient Greek text of the *Gospel of Thomas* was preserved with other texts in a jar that had been buried since antiquity. With this nearly complete Coptic version, Greek papyri fragments found earlier in Egypt at Oxyrynchus reliably could be identified as sayings from the *Gospel of Thomas*.[5]

3. Ibid.
4. Marvin W. Meyer, *Secret Gospels: Essays on Thomas and the Secret Gospel of Mark* (Harrisburg, PA: Trinity Press International, 2003), 52–73; Petr Pokorný, *A Commentary on the Gospel of Thomas: From Interpretations to the Interpreted*, Jewish and Christian Texts in Contexts and Related Studies 5 (New York: T & T Clark, 2009), 3–5.
5. For general introductions to the discovery and significance of the *Gospel of Thomas*, see Meyer, *Secret Gospels*, 76–84; Pokorný, *Gospel of Thomas*, 1–3; Stephen J. Patterson, *The Gospel of Thomas and Jesus* (Santa Rosa, CA: Polebridge, 1993), 33–74; Richard Valantasis, *The Gospel of Thomas*, New Testament Readings (New York: Routledge, 1997), 1–3; April D. DeConick, *The Original Gospel of Thomas in Translation with A Commentary and New English Translation of the Complete Gospel*, LNTS 287 (New York: T & T Clark, 2007), 13–15; and other commentaries.

Sometimes known as a "sayings gospel," the *Gospel of Thomas* is composed entirely of sayings of Jesus with no intervening narrative. The *Gospel of Thomas* has been of interest to those attempting to retrieve and connect to a suppressed tradition of early Christianity to work toward a more liberating contemporary faith. Dorothee Sölle labels this a hermeneutic of hunger. She asks, "What it is that women and men are looking for in their cry for a different spirituality."[6] Her work, interpreting through the lens of this hunger, links the physical hunger and oppression of the third world addressed in liberation theology to spiritual hunger in the first world, where there are people yearning to live a different kind of life.

Scholars have differing opinions about the dating of the *Gospel of Thomas*.[7] William Arnal places the first layer of the *Gospel of Thomas* in a period and context corresponding to the first layer of Q.[8] This is consistent with April DeConick's dating of the kernel to 50 CE or before.[9] Both scholars have discerned at least two layers of development in the document.[10] In the earliest layer, Jesus emerges as "a strong advocate for the reversal of normalcy."[11] Arnal includes

6. Dorothee Sölle, *The Silent Cry: Mysticism and Resistance*, trans. Barbara Rumscheidt and Martin Rumscheidt (Minneapolis: Fortress, 2001), 48.
7. For a discussion of the problem of dating the *Gospel of Thomas*, see Valantasis, *Gospel of Thomas*, 12–21. See references in section below on stratification.
8. William E. Arnal, "The Rhetoric of Marginality: Apocalypticism, Gnosticism and Sayings Gospels," *HTR* 88 (1995): 471–94, here 489–92.
9. April D. DeConick, *Original Gospel of Thomas*, 153. See also Pokorný, *Gospel of Thomas*, 20–25 for additional comments on dating.
10. According to a review of his work, Thomas Zöckler also proposes a stratification based on themes. He views the focus of the *Gospel of Thomas* as "self-discovery." Zöckler's work is not available to me at this writing. A reference to his work can be found in Michael Allen Williams, *Rethinking "Gnosticism": An Argument for Dismantling a Dubious Category* (Princeton, NJ: Princeton University Press, 2001), 458. Richard Valantasis also comments on a proposal for seven layers of development made by Edward Relowinski in a private communication to Valantasis in 1996 (Valantasis, *Gospel of Thomas*, 4–5); Valantasis himself proposes a stratification based on John Dominic Crossan's more general stratification of the Jesus material (ibid., 16–21); He cites John Dominic Crossan, *The Historical Jesus: The Life of a Mediterranean Jewish Peasant* (New York: HarperCollins, 1992), 427–34.
11. DeConick, *Original Gospel of Thomas*, 140.

Logion 97 in this first layer of sayings that emphasize a "wise or penetrating discernment" that "serves as a basis for implicit claims that things are not as they appear to be."[12] Logion 97 thus can be considered a parable from a very early tradition, which will prove significant for interpreting the saying with a hermeneutic of hunger.

Logion 97: A Problem-Posing Parable

Many scholars indicate a significant probability that this parable originates in the teaching of the historical Jesus. Scholars of the Jesus Seminar, for example, evaluated the saying in their "pink" category, as a saying that is probably a saying of Jesus, although they did not include it among the "red" sayings rated to be most likely authentic.[13] However, another scholar, A. J. B. Higgins, comments, "In the absence of compelling reasons to the contrary, it may be added to the parables of Jesus."[14] If it is not an authentic saying of Jesus, it is probably quite early, as has been seen in the discussion of compositional layers in the *Gospel of Thomas* above.

The parable itself indicates a rural setting, not a city, since it pictures a woman traveling a long way on a road to obtain meal. While this is consistent with the location of Jesus' teaching ministry, it hardly eliminates other possible settings. The setting does offer a useful image for a puzzling detail in the parable. Petr Pokorný pictures how the meal leaked from the jar in a dusty, dry environment. If the jar were a small hand-carried jar for a daily supply of flour, the handle could have extended from the lip to the bottom of the jar. In a dry environment, the flour could have gradually leaked from a crack where the handle attached at the

12. Arnal, "Rhetoric," 476.
13. Robert W. Funk and Roy W. Hoover, eds., *The Five Gospels: The Search for the Authentic Words of Jesus* (New York: MacMillan, 1993), 523–24.
14. A. J. B. Higgins, *The Historicity of the Fourth Gospel* (London: Lutterworth, 1960), 304.

bottom without the woman noticing it.[15]While a village setting is not ruled out, no neighbors or other people appear in the parable, and the woman may live in an outlying location or hut. The setting would thus be one that Jesus' audience, or an early audience in the Thomas community, could readily imagine.

As an early saying, the parable can be read as one used as a problem-posing narrative in what was likely to have been Jesus' teaching method.[16]

Parables as Problem-Posing Stories

William Herzog offers perhaps the most plausible understanding of the character of Jesus' parables, depicting them as pedagogical narratives.[17] He contends that a relevant analogy for Jesus' teaching mission can be found in the work of the twentieth-century Brazilian educator Paulo Freire, who developed a literacy campaign among the Brazilian underclasses using pictures called "codifications" to spark group discussion and analysis of their social situation.[18] Herzog proposes that Jesus used parables as problem-posing narratives in the same way that Freire used pictures as codifications. Herzog's interpretations of well-known parables from the canonical Gospels reveal vital and overlooked perspectives, although he tends to propose

15. Pokorný, *Gospel of Thomas*, 140. He also mentions a gnostic interpretation that "applied the parable to the celestial Adam, who is being kept in the earth in the body of clay," but this description is not readily apparent in the passage he cites in Hippolytus, *Philosophumena* (5.7.36).

16. Stephen Patterson also comments on the parable, "There is no reason to consider this parable particularly late." Patterson, *Gospel of Thomas and Jesus*, 90. William Morrice comments, "It could be authentic. It cannot be dismissed as a gnostic fabrication since it would be difficult to imagine Gnostics making up a story whose subject was a woman." William G. Morrice, *Hidden Sayings of Jesus: Words Attributed to Jesus Outside of the Four Gospels* (London: SPCK, 1997), 81. He attributes this position to Quispel as well. See Morrice, *Hidden Sayings*, 225n22.

17. William R. Herzog II, *Parables as Subversive Speech: Jesus as Pedagogue of the Oppressed* (Louisville, KY: Westminster John Knox, 1994), 9–29.

18. For a description of his work, see Paulo Freire, *Pedagogy of the Oppressed*, trans. Myra Bergman Ramos (New York: Seabury, 1974).

his own social analysis as a singular decoding of each parable. For the kind of social analysis by group discussion that Paulo Freire stimulated, we need to envision the parables as problem-posing narratives that provoked discussion among multiple interpretations. Most of the familiar parables from the synoptic Gospels are difficult to hear without assumed interpretations. Logion 97, however, offers what is quite possibly a parable from Jesus that has not already been interpreted for centuries. We can imagine Jesus using this parable creatively to pose an unusual situation as a parable for discussion. An uninterpreted parable has power to excite hearts and minds, evoking a rich variety of possible meanings.

A Vision of the "Kingdom"

April DeConick has categorized the early strata of Thomas as "apocalyptic," expecting an imminent arrival of the kingdom of God to displace the world's contemporary rulers, while later developments take a "gnostic" turn when the kingdom has not arrived as quickly as expected.[19] Her reading is that the initial layer or "kernel" of sayings contains a critique of the "world as it is," although the *Gospel of Thomas* does not necessarily proclaim a futuristic apocalyptic vision of the "kingdom." If we picture an oral culture in a community that was discussing and critiquing the "world as it is," a variety of eschatological assumptions may have been present. Arnal characterizes this initial layer as "inversionary," an encompassing term that can include apocalyptic tendencies.

Stevan Davies refines this characterization in a discussion of the "protology" of the *Gospel of Thomas*.[20] He discerns in the *Gospel of*

19. DeConick, *Original Gospel of Thomas*, 3; DeConick, *Recovering the Original Gospel of Thomas: A History of the Gospel and Its Growth* (New York: T&T Clark, 2005), 53, 159–61.
20. Stevan L. Davies, "The Christology and Protology of the Gospel of Thomas," *JBL* 111 (1992): 663–82.

Thomas the assumption of an exegesis of the first story of creation in Genesis similar to other Hellenistic Jewish interpretations. According to this "protology," the light of the original creation "persists in the world and in people" and those "who actualize their light perceive the world and themselves to be at the condition of the beginning seven days."[21] The "inversionary" wisdom would thus have the authority of the original creation, and the inversionary critique of the "world as it is" is grounded in a perception of the "world as it is meant to be."[22]

The *Gospel of Thomas* conceptualizes the "kingdom of God" as timeless and spaceless, located in experience;[23] "a primordial time, a time that persists in the present";[24] or referring to "those who belong to the kingdom rather than to the spatial or temporal connotations."[25] As *Gospel of Thomas* Logion 113 describes it: "His disciples said to him, 'When will the <Father's> empire come?' 'It won't come by watching for it. It won't be said, "Look, here!" or "Look, there!" Rather, the Father's empire is spread out upon the earth, and people don't see it.'"[26]

The "kingdom" is also not only perception but action grounded in "the world as it was created to be," a way of life that differentiates the Thomas community. Richard Valantasis characterizes the theology of the *Gospel of Thomas* as a "performative theology whose mode of discourse and whose method of theology revolves about effecting a change in thought and understanding in the readers and hearers."[27]

21. Davies, "Christology and Protology," 679.
22. An aspect of this protology is the image of the original human as an androgyne. This can be seen in many sayings about male and female that have been read as misogynist. For more extensive discussion of this issue, see Meyer, *Secret Gospels.* As will be seen below, some interpreters read the woman with the jar as a negative figure due to her gender.
23. B. F. Miller, "Study of the Theme of 'Kingdom,' The Gospel According to Thomas: Logion 18," *NovT* 9 (1967): 52–60, here 52.
24. Davis, "Christology and Protology," 674.
25. Karen King, "Kingdom in the Gospel of Thomas," *Forum, Foundations and Facts* 3 (1987): 48–97, at 55.
26. Meyer, *Secret Gospels,* 303.

He dates the completion of the *Gospel of Thomas* to the first decade of the second century, when the focus of the change in thought was a form of asceticism as a means to create a new individual identity or "subjectivity."[28] This asceticism performs a cultural critique by individual withdrawal from the prevailing culture. The critique implies a social and cultural context, a context that changed over the course of the development of the *Gospel of Thomas*.

Social Context: the Cluelessness of Privilege

The envisioned social context of the *Gospel of Thomas* included impoverished people. The audience may have been radical itinerant charismatics[29] or "a lower-level scribal group" settled in marginalized rural villages.[30]

Without defining the context too precisely, we can assume that the audience of the early composition of Thomas did not comprise the privileged elites. Instead they fit in a marginal and countercultural setting.[31] Even if we cannot distinguish their social position with precision, we can assume that they were familiar with oppressive debt and food insecurity. Their "inversionary" perspective perceives the world with the "wise eyes" that Sandra Schneiders points out that the powerless bring to the interpretation of Scripture: "The 'hermeneutical advantage' of the oppressed is precisely this ability to see, from the margins of social reality, what is second nature to those who are the beneficiaries of the social system."[32] This inversionary

---

27. Valantasis, *Gospel of Thomas*, 7.
28. Valantasis, *Gospel of Thomas*, 21–27.
29. Patterson, *Gospel of Thomas and Jesus*, 159–63; see also chapters 5 and 6.
30. Arnal, "Rhetoric," 489–90.
31. DeConick, *Recovering*, 140–41. See also DeConick, *Original Gospel of Thomas*.
32. Sandra Schneiders, *The Revelatory Text: Interpreting the New Testament as Sacred Scripture* (Collegeville, MN: Michael Glazier, 1999), 183.

wisdom identifies the foolishness of the elites' perception of the "way things are," revealing the "cluelessness" of privilege.

Logion 97: Previous Interpretations

Scholars have treated the question of Logion 97's authenticity as one of Jesus' own sayings or as a saying from an early tradition, or used Logion 97 as evidence that the *Gospel of Thomas* is an independent source of Jesus' sayings.[33] The content of Logion 97 has not received much attention in scholarly literature, and some scholars even dismiss it as too perplexing to be taken seriously.[34] The scholars who have attempted an interpretation have settled on two themes: a cautionary tale that blames the woman, and a parable of the "kingdom."

A Cautionary Tale

Some interpreters read Logion 97 as a cautionary tale about the consequences of inattention or lack of knowledge.[35] Joachim Jeremias labels the parable "the careless woman,"[36] and considers it a "warning

---

33. Meyer, *Secret Gospels*, 198–200. See also Stephen J. Patterson, James M. Robinson, and Hans-Gerhard Bethge, *The Fifth Gospel: The Gospel of Thomas Comes of Age*, new ed. (New York: T & T Clark, 2011), Kindle locations 1544–1554.

34. Dale P. Martin, "The Gospel of Thomas," CosmoLearning (video lecture, Feb. 4, 2009), http://www.cosmolearning.com/video-lectures/the-gospel-of-thomas-6802/. Dale Martin, for example, reads the parable in a lecture for undergraduates to illustrate that some sayings are "just inscrutable," and provokes giggles from the class with his sarcastic comment, "How profound, Jesus. She lost her meal, and she found her jar empty when she got home."

35. Following Joachim Jeremias, Stephen Patterson also offers a tentative and minimal interpretation of this parable as a cautionary tale: "If, as Jeremias argues, it warns against false security, in that one is enjoined to remain attentive lest the kingdom slip away, one might consider it comparable to Luke 11:24-26//Matthew 12:43-45, Q." These references are to a passage on the "Return of the Unclean Spirit," and the connection is not readily apparent. Patterson, *Gospel of Thomas and Jesus*, 90. He cites Joachim Jeremias, *New Testament Theology* (London: SCM, 1984), 175. Patterson also mentions interpretations of the parable as Gnostic and Naasene in his footnote 356. In addition to the interpretations discussed here, Thomas Zöckler assumes this interpretation. According to a review of his work, he characterizes the parable as one of several cautions to the "the seeker" who "must not let opportunity irreversibly slip away, like the meal from the cracked jar carried by the woman through whose own fault all was lost (Logion 97)." (Williams, *Rethinking Gnosticism*, 458).

against false security."[37] Gilles Quispel assumes an apocalyptic reading: "At the eschatological moment some may turn out to have empty vessels owing to their own negligence."[38] Morrice concurs with Quispel's "warning against Christian self-assurance and lack of watchfulness," adding that the woman's failure lies in not relying on divine guidance. [39]

Although Robert Doran points out that "there is no hint of negligence on the part of the woman," he ultimately contrasts the woman's "failure" in the middle parable to the "successes" of the woman with the yeast in Logion 96 and the assassin who practices with the knife in Logion 98.[40] The failure, he proposes, is the woman's "self-enclosed existence."[41] Allen Callahan points to the word "ear" as a connection between the conclusion of Logion 96, "The one who has an ear, let him hear," and the broken "ear" of the jar in Logion 97. He comments, "The woman had unknowingly wasted the precious sustenance for which she had worked so hard and traveled so far. She comes to this sad state of affairs because she does not have an ear . . . to hear."[42] Karen King reads Logion 97 together with Logion 109 and characterizes the central figures in these parables as ignorant and foolish.[43]

---

36. Joachim Jeremias, *The Parables of Jesus* (Upper Saddle River, NJ: Prentice Hall, 1972) 92; 102n52.
37. Jeremias, *The Parables of Jesus*, 175n12.
38. Gilles Quispel, "The Gospel of Thomas and the New Testament," *VC* 11 (1957): 189–207, here 205.
39. Morrice, *Hidden Sayings*, 81–82.
40. Robert Doran, *Hellenistiches Judentum in römischer Zeit, ausgenommen Philon und Josephus*, ANRW 2.20.1 (New York: Walter De Gruyter, 1987), 350, 351–52.
41. Doran, *Hellenistiches Judentum*, 352. Doran also includes some examples of the theme of a vessel with holes from tradition literature, a Hawaiian folk tale, and a Greek myth of the Danaids, but he does not make any precise connections with these stories or indicate how they inform his reading of Logion 97 except to demonstrate that realism is unnecessary in parables and folk tales.
42. A. Callahan, "'No Rhyme or Reason': The Hidden Logia of the *Gospel of Thomas*," *HTR* 90 (1997): 411–26, here 423–24.
43. King, "Kingdom in the Gospel of Thomas," 56–57.

Petr Pokorný's cautionary reading may be attributed to a redaction in the *Gospel of Thomas*. He points out that verse 3 ("She didn't know it; she hadn't noticed a problem.") introduces a negative view of the woman and suggests that this sentence may have been a later addition. With its inclusion, the parable can be considered as a warning "against losing the kingdom by not noticing the problem."[44] This parable thus becomes a cautionary tale as a contrast rather than a parallel to Logion 96.

As Pokorný implies, we could allow these parables, especially Logion 97, to challenge the audience's assumption that wisdom is inherently linked, even metaphorically, to wealth, or that wisdom must necessarily fit into our preconceived notions. Perhaps the parable is a pointed challenge to the positive valuation of wealth in the present world system.

Richard Valantasis develops this interpretation using the theme of a critique of "worldliness" in the *Gospel of Thomas*. With more empathy for the woman in the narrative, he acknowledges that the narrative does not describe her "interior state" or evaluate her action:

> This woman's plight describes the life of people who live their lives in the world: they carry jars they think are full, but discover, even after much activity, that they are empty. Unrecognized emptiness characterizes the life lived in the world whose resources (thought to be carefully stored) leak away fruitlessly.[45]

He also proposes intertextual interpretations, connecting the parable to the narrative of the man who amassed grain in storage bins to prepare for the future only to die in the night (Logion 63). This would suggest an emphasis on the futility of attempting to fill a container for provision for the future: "Those who do not make

---

44. Pokorný, *Gospel of Thomas*, 139.
45. Valantasis, *Gospel of Thomas*, 178.

provision for what they will eat do not need to carry jars full of meal."[46] While Valantasis reads the parable as a cautionary tale, he perceives a challenge to "worldliness" that will prove helpful for reading the parable using a hermeneutic of hunger.

A Parable of the Kingdom

Several interpreters assume that the parable carries a positive meaning about the "kingdom of God." A. J. B. Higgins describes its meaning as either "the imperceptible loss of the kingdom, or its coming unnoticed like the meal unknowingly lost by the woman."[47] Similarly, Petr Pokorný likens Logion 97 to the parable of the woman with the yeast in the dough that precedes it. In keeping with themes of the gospel, Logion 97 emphasizes "the imperceptible influence of the kingdom of God on earth" and "may have proclaimed the kingdom that is 'inside of you and outside of you' (log. 3:3)—on the path."[48] This is the interpretation he designates as most likely.

Bernard Brandon Scott suggests that the parable identifies the "kingdom" "with loss, with accident, with emptiness, with barrenness," and as a parable that identifies the "kingdom" with the home, he says it "highlights the female aspects of the home, the system of shame as opposed to male honor."[49] He also sees the parable as a reversal of the story of Elijah's visit to the widow of Zarephath (1 Kgs. 17:8-16) where the widow's jar of meal is not spent.[50] While he does not attempt a happy ending, and acknowledges that "the kingdom is identified not with divine intervention but with divine emptiness," his only further interpretation resorts to invoking the

46. Ibid., 178.
47. Higgins, *Historicity*, 304.
48. Pokorný, *Gospel of Thomas*, 139
49. Bernard Brandon Scott, *Hear Then the Parable: A Commentary on the Parables of Jesus* (Minneapolis: Augsburg Fortress, 1989), 307.
50. Ibid., 307–8.

centurion's insight in Mark 15:39 that the man on the cross is the Son of God.[51] Scott points toward the emptiness of the jar but does not fully look into it or explain the implications of divine emptiness.

April DeConick's apocalyptic interpretation reduces the meaning of the parable to an example of the element of the "surprise" of the coming of the kingdom.[52] DeConick provides no interpretation of Logion 97 in connection with this "reversal of normalcy" that proclaims the blessedness of the poor and the cluelessness of the rich. Yet the "reversal of normalcy" that DeConick associates with the apocalyptic perspective of the earliest part of the *Gospel of Thomas* can be applied here.[53] The interpreters' difficulty with this passage may be precisely that it reverses normalcy so effectively. It requires us to look with the eyes of a food-insecure woman into an empty jar in order to see the kingdom of God.

Kamila Blessing provides a rich layering of interpretation that emphasizes a positive interpretation of the woman and this parable as a parable of the "kingdom."[54] Blessing begins her exploration with the experience of the woman as "the locus of the kingdom."[55] This poses a problem since the woman's unawareness leads to negative consequences, "unrecoverable loss,"[56] but Blessing does not interpret the parable as a cautionary tale. She looks instead to find "a mysterious power at work in this parable, a power that is intended to involve the reader in the Kingdom community."[57] The difficulty in the parable becomes for Blessing a hallmark of a parable as a "therapeutic story"

51. Ibid., 308.
52. DeConick, *Recovering*, 121, 131.
53. Ibid., 140.
54. Kamila Blessing, "The 'Confusion Technique' of Milton Erickson as Hermeneutic for Biblical Parallels," *Journal of Psychology and Christianity* 21 (2002): 161–68.
55. Blessing, "Confusion Technique," 160. She bases her characterization of the "kingdom" as experience in the *Gospel of Thomas* on Miller, "Theme of 'Kingdom,'" 52, quoted above.
56. Blessing, "Confusion Technique," 163.
57. Ibid., 161.

in which the abrupt and unexpected ending opens the hearer's way to a new response.[58] The very difficulty opens multiple possibilities.

Seeking intertextual references to loss, Blessing connects this passage to the parable of "hidden treasure" in Matt. 13:44 and the *Gospel of Thomas*, Logion 109. Blessing's reading of the parable of the Empty Jar brings out the theme of something hidden now revealed.[59] The woman did not know that the meal was escaping, but the fact is revealed when she sees that the jar is empty. The emphasis is on the revelation. Here Blessing makes an interpretive move that influences her other layers of interpretation, saying that the "loss of the physical meal, while unfortunate, is not the point," but the point is the "revelation of previously hidden knowledge."[60] This move away from the physical loss will be an important issue to keep in mind.

Blessing associates the parable's image of the meal "poured out" with the prevalent biblical use of this language for offering and sacrifice.[61] She points in particular to Paul's language in Phil. 2:17, speaking of himself as a "being poured out as a libation" to describe the offering of his life for the gospel.[62] In the meal, as the stuff of life is pouring out from the leaking jar, the sacrifice is transformative: "Upon the completion of the 'sacrifice' . . . the hidden is revealed to her, as if by divine plan."[63] The sacrificial image is combined with the image of the woman's journey as walking in the way of Jesus' life and

---

58. Ibid., 162: "Literature on parables and that on the therapeutic story both show that, faced with such a story, the reader/hearer is emotionally propelled to provide that resolution for herself. " She also suggests that a supposed negative view of women in the *Gospel of Thomas* actually stems from its vision of a return to a primordial androgynous state. This has little effect on her reading of the parable (162–63).

59. Ibid., 167.

60. Ibid.

61. Ibid. She notes exceptions: references to the pouring out of wrath in Jeremiah and love in Rom. 5:5.

62. Ibid., 168.

63. Ibid.

death. The image of the meal spilling out is the imperceptible coming of the "kingdom." The parable shows the process of entry into the "kingdom" in the moment of recognition of the sacrifice.[64] Blessing does not complete a discussion of the implications of this image, but this will be a starting point for an interpretation using a hermeneutic of hunger.

Blessing associates this parable with planting and growing, by association with the parable of the yeast in the dough that precedes it in Logion 96 and the similarity to the image of the sower who also scatters "the kingdom" unknowingly.[65] While Blessing offers a rich variety of avenues for interpretation, her approach relies on reading the "loss of the physical meal," the emptiness of the jar, symbolically and not as "the critical element."[66] With a hermeneutic of hunger, the critical element is the bare fact of the story: the jar is empty and the food the woman would depend on is gone.

Logion 97: A Hermeneutic of Hunger

To read the parable using a hermeneutic of hunger is to accept the real hunger in the text and to allow it to continue as a problem-posing text. This means that the readings may not be the "original meaning" intended by Jesus or the author or community of the *Gospel of Thomas*.

If we return to Karen King's earlier guide to the interpretation of parables framed with the "kingdom is like" in the *Gospel of Thomas*, we would start by reading Logion 97: "To belong to the Thomas community means to be like a woman who set out on a long road carrying a jar of meal. She did not notice that the meal was spilling

64. Ibid., 168–89.
65. Ibid., 170–71.
66. Ibid., 167, 171.

out through the broken handle on the jar as she walked. When she arrived at her home, she set the jar down and saw that it was empty."

What if this woman is, indeed, an example of a wise community member? This woman whose jar has emptied without her realizing it comes to the community with the wisdom attainable only by staring deeply into the prospect of death by starvation, wisdom attainable only by recognizing and living with the consequences of one's own inattention.

If we read it with a hermeneutic of hunger, the wisdom in the parable emerges and opens in several directions as a problem-posing narrative that challenges the "cluelessness of privilege."

A Woman's Life Unconsciously Sacrificed

In reviewing Kamila Blessing's reading of sacrificial imagery in the parable above, I indicated that this image would be a starting point for one layer of interpretation using a hermeneutic of hunger. Given her interpretation, we see the "kingdom" as a woman who is not aware that she is pouring out her life in sacrifice until she discovers her emptiness at the end of the journey. Blessing views sacrifice in positive terms as an imitation of Jesus' life and death and as a ritual action evoking the action of priests. She thus portrays the woman as a positive example of women's inclusion in this priestly action of sacrifice, a sacrifice revealed in the moment of setting the jar down. The sacrifice remains an involuntary action, however, not a product of the woman's decision or agency: she is being poured out.

While Blessing views this sacrifice positively, it can also be taken as emblematic of many women's lives. A key moment for many women in the era of women's consciousness-raising groups in the United States in the 1970s was the awareness of the involuntary sacrifice and loss of self in assumed roles for women. To paraphrase a repeated realization, "I got married because that was what you did, and we had kids and I did what needed to be done for my husband and for them—but what happened to me? I got lost somewhere." She set the jar down and discovered it was empty. Her identity and life had trickled away along the road. This is a sacrifice without agency. She did not make the decision to sacrifice. This is not the same as a voluntary choice to set aside other options to embrace a life of mothering children and maintaining a home and family life with the many sacrifices it requires. That is sacrifice with agency, as a real choice. The woman with the empty jar had no agency in the loss of the meal; it simply trickled away.

Read as an emblem of the sacrifice of women's lives taken for granted in a social system that discourages women's choices about their own lives, the parable becomes, once again, a cautionary tale. It is not so much a warning to keep the meal, the life, from draining away, as it is a caution to become aware of what has been lost. The woman is not blameworthy but simply unconscious, in the sense of the "conscious-raising" movement. The parable cautions not only mindfulness but also the need for the woman to claim herself. In the empty jar we can see the hunger for what is gone, for the life that cannot be retrieved.

The revelation of what is lost can be transformative, however, if we see the woman picking up the empty jar, as the "consciousness-raising" movement did, to say, "Look. See this. This jar is empty. The jar was full and it has been emptied. Something real has been lost." This can be the beginning of the woman claiming herself.

This is a foundational individual action. Each woman must claim herself. Each man must claim himself. This is a claim made, however, in a social context, and the claim holds up the empty jar as a reflection of the emptiness of the "world," the spiritual desolation of "the way things are" in systems that use up the lives of the many and the resources of the earth for the temporary benefit of the few. To hold up the jar to acknowledge individual lives emptied into these systems indicts the emptiness of the system as well.

This is the beginning of the hermeneutics of spiritual hunger that Dorothee Sölle described.

Logion 97—Hermeneutics of Spiritual Hunger
(Individual & Corporate)

Individually discovering, knowing, acknowledging and proclaiming this emptiness, however, is only the beginning. The parable is about what the "kingdom of God" is like. It leads not only toward individual discovery but also toward a world different from "the way things are." A hermeneutic of hunger takes its stance in this other world as a "zone of freedom" that is a mystical grounding for interpretation. The spiritual hunger expressed in this "zone of freedom" is a hunger not only for a different individual life but also for a different world, a world made by unified actions of those who have set the jar down and discovered it empty.

The awareness is thus individual and corporate. The awareness of the empty jar includes the physical hunger of the many. A personal story may help our understanding of this.

Seeing Physical Hunger: Children in Zacatecas

In the early 1980s, I rode into Mexico to a volunteer teaching position arranged through the Arizona Farmworkers' Union. Rogelio, a returning worker, gave me a ride in his van, and on the way we dropped another worker, José, off at his home place in Zacatecas. To get to his home, we meandered off the highway for a couple of hours on dirt tracks, and after a few wrong turns, we came to the top of a wind-swept rocky and barren hill to find José's home. Rogelio stopped the van in the middle of a dusty expanse between two small stone buildings and fences of piled rock. In a patch of shade to our left, we could see a barefoot young girl, maybe twelve years old, in a loose tattered dress. She had a baby on her hip, and a few other children gathered around her. José yelled to the girl, "Come." They met in the desolate yard, and José returned to explain the situation. His sister explained that their parents were off to seek work. She did not know when they would return.

José showed us into one of the buildings and we waited, then walked around a bit, chatted a little with the children, and waited. Late in the afternoon, José came for Rogelio and me, and showed us into the small building that served as a kitchen. There, under a low ceiling, was a table with three chairs. José seated himself at the head of the table to the right and indicated that Rogelio and I should sit on the chairs facing one another in the middle. To the left, his sisters and brothers gathered. Their green eyes were wide. On the table were three flat bowls of thin potato soup. The eyes of the children looked to the bowls and then to us. José sat and began to eat with apparent gusto. Rogelio and I looked at each other. I followed Rogelio's lead. In unison, we took our spoons and found a spoonful of broth with no actual potato chunks in it. We each slurped our spoonful and set our spoon down. Rogelio turned to the twelve-year-old cook to express our thanks. I nodded the same, and we stood. As we found our way out through the low doorway, the children were descending on the two meager bowls of soup.

To interpret Logion 97, we must see the empty jar through the green eyes of these hungry children and all the others like them. Suppose it is their mother who has returned with the jar of meal to feed them, but the jar is empty. How would she see the empty jar? It is a struggle to look into the jar with her, to see starvation and death, to feel her fear and despair. To see into the empty jar is to become as hungry for a different world as the woman in the parable or the green-eyed children in Zacatecas. This is the entry to the "kingdom."

Options for Interpretation: Physical Hunger

This parable can serve as a cautionary tale to those who seek wisdom without hunger. For those who associate wisdom and wealth, the parable cautions the reader who seeks wisdom as an individualistic enterprise to be mindful and attentive, not to let the meal or life slip away unnoticed. From the perspective that associates wealth with foolishness, the parable cautions the same reader that wisdom starts from the perspective of the hungry woman staring into the empty jar, from the very opposite of wealth. To enter the "kingdom" is to follow this disciple, to live a life in solidarity with those green-eyed children in Zacatecas.

Experiencing the Parable with the Woman (Corporate & Individual Participation)

Interpretation of the parable must begin, then, with the experience of the woman in order to join her in entering the "kingdom" of God. We begin by walking with her, feeling the heft of a full jar, the burden that women in the unseen margins of society have carried for millennia and carry today. We walk with her, though, not with a theoretical awareness of the millions and billions in a video-like image that dulls our consciousness, but with a personal awareness of one woman with a full jar. We walk not in paralyzing despair for the many so much as empathy and compassion for the one, a woman whose story is not told in the parable but who has a real life and a real story.

She walks, as the many impoverished women before her and the many after her walk, on a distant road. The bare necessity of the food that she needs is far away, and she must travel to obtain it. On this long walk, we begin to enter the "kingdom of God."

She walks alone. Her jar is damaged. She carries the meal in a low-quality or cast-off jar, equipped in the manner of the impoverished in every generation. The handle of the jar breaks. Gradually the meal leaks out, but she does not notice. Perhaps hunger has dulled her awareness. Perhaps worries rattling in her head make her oblivious. Perhaps her focus on the path and avoiding its dangers distracts her from the meal dripping out behind her. To enter the "kingdom of God," we walk with her and know her hunger and her worries and her focus on avoiding the hazards of the path. We put one foot in front of the other with her.

We arrive with the woman at her home, and as she sets the jar down, we see that there is nothing left in it. The jar is empty. As we look up, we may see an empty house where she lives alone, or we may see the wide eyes of her hungry children, like the green-eyed children in the casita in Zacatecas. But we must look.

To see the empty jar is to look squarely into starvation and death. We must look, each of us, feeling the hunger of the woman and knowing the daily death of the impoverished for lack of food. We must look squarely, each of us, at our own inevitable death, and know ourselves as no different from the woman with the empty jar. We must arrive into a state of solidarity with all who face the empty jar, all humanity. In this way we can see with the eyes of God.

What mystics call "becoming at one" is never a possession that cannot be lost. What really happens in mystical union is not a new vision of God but a different relationship to the world—one that has borrowed the eyes of God. God is no private affair for a few who are naive enough or who are blessed with a fortunate disposition.[67]

---

67. Dorothee Sölle, *The Silent Cry*, 293.

To stare with the woman of the parable into the empty jar is to see with the eyes of God, to learn to interpret not just the text but the world with the "hermeneutic of hunger" of the mysticism Dorothee Sölle describes, and to know the power that lies in the emptiness of the jar.

The Empty Jar, the "Silent Cry" and the "Zone of Freedom"

Attawapiskat Chief Theresa Spence held a long hunger strike that shows how the "kingdom" is like the woman with the empty jar. Her action exemplifies the "performative theology" that Valantasis finds in the *Gospel of Thomas*. She is sacrificing as a voluntary action that takes up the power of hunger on behalf of her people and the earth. Her demand was that the prime minister of Canada and other key governmental officials meet with her and with other First Nations leaders of Canada about recent changes in Canadian law that will have major implications for First Nations rights there, including their ability to protect their lands from environmental devastation.[68] Her action takes up the power of the empty jar in the power to fast.

Her fast is creating a new "zone of freedom" in "Idle No More," a now international movement of indigenous peoples started by four young indigenous women in Canada. This "zone" is becoming manifest in flash mob round dances in major shopping malls and other public places across Canada and now the United States. In the challenge of the empty jar, the flash mobs use drumming and singing and the simple circle and steps of the round dances to create a zone of freedom in the spaces most emblematic of the consuming culture of the "way things are."

This ability to create the zone of freedom is based fundamentally in the ability not to consume, to know one's own hunger as a witness

68. At this writing, Prime Minister Harper has agreed to a form of meeting.

to the "silent cry" of the hunger of the many, to face death squarely and to seize the power of no longer fearing it, to reveal their power to those who believe themselves to be powerless, and to know oneself as part of a reality larger than one's own small life in the world as it was meant to be (the "kingdom.")

Conclusion

In this journey with the parable of the Woman with the Empty Jar, we have seen many possible interpretations and many meanings. Other interpretations, other meanings, are surely possible. We began with the challenge to look into the jar. Many interpretations read the woman's experience as a negative example; others, by acknowledging the parable's reversal of the expectation of divine abundance; still others by seeking various forms of "happy endings." This article has attempted to peer into the empty jar using a hermeneutic of hunger. Perhaps by finding in it a "zone of freedom" we have arrived at just one more invention of a happy ending. Perhaps it is best to let the woman remain in our vision, looking into the empty jar, the jar still empty and the woman still hungry, and to let her gaze and the emptiness of the jar challenge our assumptions about whatever we believe can be contained. Perhaps we need, simply, each one of us, to sit with a life that trickles away along the path, and with the fact that each of us will arrive at the end and that life will be gone. The parable then poses for each of us the problem of finding meaning in our hunger.

9

Including the Hungry *Adelphoi*: Exploring Pauline Points of View in 1 Corinthians 11:17–34

Ma. Marilou S. Ibita

The first Millennium Development Goal is to eradicate extreme poverty and hunger by 2015.[1] In 2006, the former head of the United Nation's Food and Agriculture Organization (FAO), Jacques Diouf, said, "We are confident that the race against hunger can still be won, but only if the necessary resources, political will and correct policies are forthcoming."[2] I agree with his optimism, but as a lay teacher

---

1. "End Proverty 2015 Millenium Campaign," at http://www.endpoverty2015.org/.
2. "World Hunger 'Intolerable,' with Scant Progress in Decade: UN," CBC News, at http://www.cbc.ca/news/world/story/2006/10/30/food-report.html#skip300x250 last modified Oct. 30, 2006.

of the Bible from the Philippines, where hunger is a crucial issue,[3] it is challenging that he did not mention the potential contribution of faith communities as a resource to help combat hunger. Recently, Bread for the World articulated the need to include a more diverse and participative approach to solve the issue by including, among others, the voice of faith groups and the poor themselves.[4] This study explores 1 Cor. 11:17-34 as one of the faith resources that can inspire Christians to contribute to a hunger-free world.

This pericope is a "hidden treasure." It can be used as a reflection of the Christian commitment to address hunger.[5] Liturgically, Catholics only read parts of it on Holy Thursday (vv. 23-26) and on Monday of the Twenty-Fourth week in Ordinary Time (vv. 26, 33).[6] The rest, particularly v. 34, is not heard. Paul's exhortation to correct the Corinthian noncommendable practice does not confront eucharistic practice in the present, whether it is akin to the Corinthians' own dinner (ἴδιον δεῖπνον) or to the Lord's Supper (κυριακὸν δεῖπνον) where the siblings (ἀδελφοί) partake of it together and are satisfied.

One of the interpretations of 1 Cor. 11:34 is to consider it a compromise[7] that reflects love-patriarchalism[8] in the Corinthian

---

3. Philippine data estimates that 4.3 million families experience involuntary hunger in the third quarter of 2012. See "Hunger up 21% in Latest Self-Rated SWS Poverty Survey," in *Philippine Daily Inquirer*, at http://newsinfo.inquirer.net/279278/hunger-up-21-in-latest-self-rated-sws-poverty-survey#sthash.Th8ZJtAb.dpuf, last modified Sept. 29, 2012.

4. See the link to the "2014 Huger Report" provided by Bread for the World Institute website. http://notes.bread.org/religion/.

5. 1 Cor. 11:17-26 was used in Leonardo Z. Legaspi, "To Live in Memory of Him: One Body, One People—A Pastoral Letter on the Eucharist" by the Catholic Bishops' Conference of the Philippines, 21 March 1988.

6. See James Socias, ed., *Daily Roman Missal*, 6th ed. (Chicago: Midwest Theological Forum/ Schiller Park, IL: World Library Publications, 2004), 407 and 1467.

7. Gerd Theissen, "Social Integration and Sacramental Activity: An Analysis of 1 Cor. 11:17-34," in *The Social Setting of Pauline Christianity: Essays on Corinth*, ed. and trans. with an introduction by John H. Schütz (Edinburgh: T & T Clark, 1982), 164.

8. Gerd Theissen, "The Strong and the Weak in Corinth: A Sociological Analysis of a Theological Quarrel," in *Social Setting*, 139–40; See also David G. Horrell, *The Social Ethos of the Corinthian Correspondence: Interest and Ideology from 1 Corinthians to 1 Clement*, Studies of the New Testament and Its World (Edinburgh: T & T Clark, 1996), 126–30.

church (ἐκκλησία). As Gerd Theissen explains, "Wealthy Christians can eat their 'own' meal privately to their hearts content (11:33-34), but in the congregation they are to be satisfied with the Lord's Supper, with the bread and wine of the fellowship."[9] However, from a narrative-critical perspective, this interpretation seems incoherent with Paul's strong criticism of the 'abuses' at the common meal (vv. 17-22). Exploring Paul's points of view in connection with the symbolic universe depicted in 1 Cor. 11:17-34, I propose that Paul takes the side of have-nots (οἱ μὴ ἔχοντες), the hungry siblings (ἀδελφοί, vv. 22, 33-34), in order to uphold the assembly's unity and for everyone to truly partake of the Lord's Supper (κυριακὸν δεῖπνον) at the same time and place.

I. A Narrative Reading of 1 Corinthians 11:17-34

The narrative interpretation of Pauline texts is traceable to two influential works. Richard Hays delved into the narrative substructure of Galatians.[10] Norman R. Petersen analysed the chronological and narrative sequences of the story in the letter to Philemon and characterized the actors' interrelationship in their symbolic universe.[11] Petersen's method, along with more recent narrative approaches to the Pauline letters, tends to be more helpful in analysing the characters, setting, plot, and points of view of a Pauline letter.

The story of Paul's response to the problems in the nascent assembly of the Corinthian Christ followers is found in 1 Corinthians. One subplot is the story of the Lord's Supper (11:17-34),

---

9. Theissen, "The Strong and the Weak," 121–43, 139.
10. See Richard B. Hays, *The Faith of Jesus Christ: An Investigation of the Narrative Substructure of Galatians 3:1—4:11*, SBLDS 56 (Chico: Scholars Press, 1983). For a critical review and application of a narrative approach to Paul, see Bruce W. Longenecker, ed., *Narrative Dynamics in Paul: A Critical Assessment* (Louisville: Westminster John Knox, 2002).
11. See Norman R. Petersen, *Rediscovering Paul: Philemon and the Sociology of Paul's Narrative World* (Philadelphia: Fortress, 1985).

which has the narrative features of "characters, setting and a trajectory."[12] The sequential and consequential connections point to Paul retelling the Corinthians about their divisions at the Lord's Supper, which merit withdrawal of his praise (vv. 17-22) and his attempt to correct them (vv. 23-34). First, he retells the foundational story of the Lord's Supper (vv. 23-25) as a narrative solution.[13] He contrasts it with the Corinthians' practice and he solicits their character identification with the Lord at table. Next, Paul theologizes about the implications of the foundational story for a commendable partaking of the meal (vv. 26-32). Third, addressing the problems in vv. 17-32, he commands them to reform their meal conduct (vv. 33-34).

There are many characters in Paul's narrative. The Corinthian addressees (1:1), the church of God (ἐκκλησία τοῦ θεοῦ, 11:22; 1:2), include have-nots (οἱ μὴ ἔχοντες) and, implicitly, haves (οἱ ἔχοντες, v. 22). Many scholars tend to identify the hungry ones (ὃς πεινᾷ) with the have-nots and those drunk (ὃς μεθύει) with the implied 'haves' (v. 21).[14] From an economic perspective, the have-nots most likely lived at subsistence or below subsistence level, making them more vulnerable to suffer the effects of prolonged hunger such as chronic malnutrition and disease,[15] as v. 30 describes. Second, Paul is the letter's author and narrator of the story of the Corinthians' unpraiseworthy practices at the Lord's Supper (vv. 17-22). Paul retells the Lord's Supper tradition to correct the problems at their common

---

12. See Edward Adams, "Paul's Story of God and Creation: The Story of How God Fulfils His Purposes in Creation," in Longenecker, *Narrative Dynamics*, 23.

13. See Suzanne Watts Henderson, "'If Anyone Hungers . . .': An Integrated Reading of 1 Cor. 11:17-34," *NTS* 48 (2002): 195–208.

14. Nearly all scholars agree, except Joseph A. Fitzmyer who considers that ὃς πεινᾷ refers to οἱ ἔχοντες (*First Corinthians: A New Translation with Introduction and Commentary*, Anchor Yale Bible [New Haven: Yale University Press, 2008], 434).

15. See Steven J. Friesen, "Poverty in Pauline Studies: Beyond the So-Called New Consensus," *JSNT* 26 (2004): 323–61, at 343.

meal. Third, the Lord Jesus (ὁ κύριος 'Ιησοῦς) is a very significant character; he is the protagonist in the foundational narrative (vv. 23-25) to whom the Corinthians are made accountable (vv. 26-27) as the one who will judge them (v. 31-32, 34). Character identification with him will most likely correct the wrongdoings in the Corinthian practice.

Paul takes issue with the story's setting, [16] the dinner (δεῖπνον), in 1 Cor. 11:17-34. Paul contrasts the Corinthians' practice of eating their own dinner (ἴδιον δεῖπνον) with the Lord's Supper, shown through the repeated use of the word *congregate* (συνέρχομαι, vv. 17, 18, 20, 33, 34). The trajectory of Paul's story unfolds in 1 Cor. 11:17-34. The state of equilibrium is described in the Corinthians' coming together for the Lord's Supper. However, as Paul heard, this equilibrium is disturbed by schisms (σχίσματα, v. 18) and heresies (αἱρέσεις, v. 19a) that culminate in the observable effects of hunger and drunkenness in vv. 21-22. Verses 17-34 indicate Paul's attempt to restore this equilibrium. The trajectory in this pericope reflects a problem (vv. 17-22, 30), solution (vv. 23-29, 31-34), and structure.[17]

Apart from these narrative features, Petersen notes that the events in the text construct the narrative elements of point of view, plot, and closure.[18] This contribution analyses Paul's various points of view on the story that indicate including the hungry siblings at the Lord's Supper, with implications for its application to our current situation of some going hungry while others have excess. To clarify Paul's points of view, we will first consider the symbolic universe depicted in the narrative of 1 Cor. 11:17-34.[19]

16. See Seymour Chatman, *Story and Discourse: Narrative Structure in Fiction and Film* (Ithaca: Cornell University Press, 1978), 138–45; Mark Allan Powell, *What is Narrative Criticism?* GBS: NT Series (Minneapolis: Fortress, 1990), 69–75.

17. See Douglas A. Campbell, "The Story of Jesus in Romans and Galatians," in Longenecker, *Narrative Dynamics*, 97–124, at 99.

18. See Petersen, *Rediscovering Paul*, 2–14.

19. Ibid., 14–30.

II. The Symbolic Universe According to the Lord's Supper Story

Petersen says that the symbolic universe includes traditional knowledge known through language and symbols that legitimates the social relations and actions of actors and institutions in the text.[20] It defines and creates a "world."[21] The actions of the actors in the Lord's Supper story help to reconstruct the symbolic universe that legitimates their actions in connection with the conflict and the expected narrative closure. The Corinthian church (ἐκκλησία) and Paul constitute an assembly of people who have different symbolic universes according to their Jewish and non-Jewish backgrounds, living in Roman Corinth in the first century CE.[22] As an assembly of Christ followers, they are in the process of being socialized in their new symbolic world that they all build together. Yet Paul has much say in its architecture as their founding apostle (see 4:15; 9:2; 11:23; 15:1-3).

There are some clues concerning Paul's idea of their recently shared symbolic universe in 1 Cor. 11:17-34. The Corinthian believers gather (συνέρχομαι) in a particular manner, in church (ἐν ἐκκλησίᾳ), to partake of the Lord's Supper (vv. 17-18, 20, 33-34). The meal mirrors the Greco-Roman banquet with the sequence of bread-meal-cup[23] and the problems that beset it. From Paul's

---

20. See ibid., 57. Petersen follows Peter Berger and Thomas Luckmann, *The Social Construction of Reality: A Treatise in the Sociology of Knowledge* (Garden City: Doubleday, 1967), 92–128.

21. See Petersen, *Rediscovering Paul*, 57.

22. See Theissen, "Social Stratification in the Corinthian Community: A Contribution to the Sociology of Early Hellenistic Christianity," in *Social Setting*, 69–119; Wayne Meeks, *The First Urban Christians: The Social World of the Apostle Paul* (New Haven: Yale University Press, 1983), 55–63; Anthony C. Thiselton, *The First Epistle to the Corinthians: A Commentary on the Greek Text*, NIGTC (Grand Rapids: Eerdmans, 2000), 23–29; Richard B. Hays, *First Corinthians*, IBC (Louisville: John Knox, 1997), 6–7. Bruce J. Malina and John J. Pilch, *Social-Science Commentary on the Letters of Paul* (Minneapolis: Fortress, 2006), 14–25, argue for Paul's audience as "Israelites living among non-Israelite peoples outside Judea" (25). See also Nancy Bookidis, "Religion in Corinth: 146 BCE to 100 CE," in *Urban Religion in Corinth: Interdisciplinary Approaches*, ed. Daniel N. Schowalter and Steven J. Friesen, HTS 53 (Cambridge: Harvard University, 2005), 141–64.

description, this meal both demonstrates and creates their symbolic universe, which is why he considers the Corinthians' practice as falling short of the ideal presented in the foundational narrative (vv. 23-25). Paul implies that their table fellowship should reflect the Lord Jesus' conduct at table on the night he was handed over (vv. 23-25) since they partake of it to proclaim the Lord's death until he comes (v. 26). At table, their common identity as church of God (ἐκκλησία τοῦ θεοῦ) that regards Jesus as Lord (vv. 23, 26, 27, 32) and each other as siblings (v. 34) should continue to be affirmed. Unlike the Corinthians' meal where there is disunity, their table fellowship should reaffirm their group identity and their social bonding (vv. 18-19).[24] While table fellowship is an occasion for bestowing honor,[25] for Paul the Lord's Supper should not be an opportunity for some to gain honor as cadets (δόκιμοι) at table (v. 19) while the church of God is despised and the have-nots are shamed (v. 22). Rather, he expects it as an occasion to express mutual responsibility to one another as church of God (v. 22) and as a

23. For scholars who follow the bread-meal-cup sequence, see, for example, C. K. Barrett, *A Commentary on the First Epistle to the Corinthians*, BNTC (Peabody: Hendrickson, 1968), 268; Bruce W. Winter, *After Paul Left Corinth: The Influence of Secular Ethics and Change* (Grand Rapids: Eerdmans, 2001), 150; Peter Lampe, "The Corinthian Dinner Party: Exegesis of a Cultural Context," *Affirmation* 4 (1991): 1–15, and Lampe, "The Eucharist: Identifying with Christ on the Cross," *Int* 48 (1994): 36–49; Bradley B. Blue, "The House Church at Corinth and the Lord's Supper: Famine, Food Supply and the Present Distress," *Criswell Theological Review* 5 (1991): 221–39; Otfried Hofius, "The Lord's Supper and the Lord's Supper Tradition: Reflections on 1 Corinthians 11:23b-25," in *One Loaf, One Cup: Ecumenical Studies of 1 Cor 11 and Other Eucharistic Texts; The Cambridge Conference on the Eucharist August 1988*, NGS 6, ed. Ben F. Meyer (Macon: Mercer University Press, 1993), 75–115, at 80–96; Matthias Klinghardt, *Gemeinschaftsmahl und Mahlgemeinschaft: Soziologie und Liturgie frühchristlicher Mahlfeiern*, Texte und Arbeiten zum neutestamentlichen Zeitalter 13 (Basel: Francke, 1996), 283; James D. G. Dunn, *The Theology of Paul the Apostle* (Edinburgh: T & T Clark, 1998), 610–11, at 618; Dennis E. Smith, *From Symposium to Eucharist: The Banquet in the Early Christian World* (Minneapolis: Fortress Press, 2003), 188.

24. See Smith, *From Symposium*, 9.

25. See, for example, Malina and Plich, *Social-Science Commentary*, 109–10; Smith, *From Symposium*, 10, 196–98. More recently, see the discussion of Rachel M. McRae, "Eating with Honor: The Corinthian Lord's Supper in Light of Voluntary Association Meal Practices," *JBL* 130 (2011): 165–81.

body (v. 29; 10:17, 12:12), especially for the vulnerable have-nots, whose habitual hunger is inadequately addressed at the common meal and who suffer physiologically (vv. 21-22, 30). The socioeconomic stratification[26] dividing the assembly between have-nots (v. 22), who live at or below subsistence level,[27] and those who have plenty (οἱ ἔχοντες) should not eclipse their common identity as Christ followers, as church of God and as siblings to one another. While the social stratification[28] is emphasized by the difference in food and drink distribution,[29] a (mal)practice typical in Greco-Roman meals, Paul greatly censures it (vv. 17-22). All of these show that the Corinthians' meal described in vv. 17-22 and 30 do not properly reflect the world they are attempting to symbolize. Paul judges it: οὐκ ἔστιν κυριακὸν δεῖπνον φαγεῖν. Rather, he calls it ἴδιον δεῖπνον. Thus, in line with the shared symbolic universe he is attempting to articulate for the Corinthians, Paul endeavours to correct their actions. They can more accurately embody the symbolism of the Lord's Supper by including the hungry have-nots so that they partake

26. See Friesen, "Poverty," 323–61; Friesen, "Prospects for a Demography of the Pauline Mission: Corinth among the Churches," in Schowalter and Friesen, *Urban Religion in Corinth*, 351–70. For a critical evaluation, see Peter Oakes, "Constructing Poverty Scales for Graeco-Roman Society: A Response to Steven Friesen's 'Poverty in Pauline Studies,'" *JSNT* 26 (2004): 367–71. Even if Oakes criticizes Friesen's calorific indicator of poverty, his suggested "ordered poverty scale" also has food deprivation as a top indicator. Oakes ("Constructing Poverty Scales," 370) explains "da = adequate diet for survival" and "db = adequate diet for good health." For a critical modification of Friesen's proposal, see Bruce W. Longenecker, "Socio-Economic Profiling of the First Urban Christians," in *After the First Urban Christians: The Social Scientific Study of Pauline Christianity Twenty-Five Years Later*, ed. Todd D. Still and David G. Horrell (New York: T & T Clark, 2009), 36–59; Bruce W. Longenecker, *Remember the Poor: Paul, Poverty and the Greco-Roman World* (Grand Rapids: Eerdmans, 2010). Longenecker discusses the economy scale on 44–59 and discusses it in relation to 1 Cor. 11:17-34 on 11, 144, 153–54, 188, 232, 256, 275, and 289.
27. See Friesen, "Prospects," 368; Longenecker, "Socio-Economic," 54.
28. See Smith, *From Symposium*, 10: "The banquet provided a significant means for one's status in society to be formally recognized and acknowledged" through "reclining" and "ranking" at table. Patron-client is one of the manifestations. The banquet is an occasion for honor. In ancient clubs and associations, those who are low status in society could have a high status in the club.
29. See Pliny, *Ep.* 2.6, Martial, *Epig.* 1.20; 3.60. See also Smith, *From Symposium*, 193.

of the supper with the whole church at the same time, at the same place, and in a way that leaves them satisfied just like the rest, since they are all siblings.

III. Paul's Points of View: Taking the Side of the Hungry Siblings?

Point of view[30] is "the position of a narrator . . . in relation to the actors whose actions are being described."[31] Considering the textual clues from the narrator and the characters in the story, the illusion of point of view "may well be the single most important fiction of narrative."[32] Petersen explains the significance for Paul's letters:

> Each story is governed by Paul's point of view, because all we know of each is learned from him, even the points of view of the characters in his stories, who are sometimes allowed by him as narrator to voice their own points of view, but more often have points of view attributed to them by him.[33]

Since Paul is the author of 1 Corinthians, the narrator[34] of the story of the Corinthians' unpraiseworthy meal, and a character who initiates reforms, we have good reasons to analyse his various points of view

---

30. The point of view is "the position established by the teller of a story vis-à-vis the elements of the story itself." Gary Yamasaki, "Point of View in a Gospel Story: What Difference Does it Make? Luke 19:1-10 as a Test Case," *JBL* 125 (2006): 89–105, at 90. Having studied the different scholars' use of point of view analysis in biblical narratives, including stories in a letter, Gary Yamasaki proposes a comprehensive methodology for studying the spatial, temporal, psychological, phraseological, and ideological points of view. See Gary Yamasaki, *Watching a Biblical Narrative: Point of View in Biblical Exegesis* (New York: T & T Clark, 2008), 152–205; Gary Yamasaki, *Perspective Criticism: Point of View and Evaluative Guidance in Biblical Narrative* (Eugene: Cascade Books, 2012), 18–105; Boris Uspensky, *Poetics of Composition: The Structure of the Artistic and Typology of a Compositional Form*, trans. Valentina Zavarin and Susan Wittig (Berkeley: University of California Press, 1973), 8–119; Yamasaki, "Point of View," 91–93.
31. Petersen, *Rediscovering Paul*, 11.
32. Petersen, *Rediscovering Paul*, 11.
33. Ibid., 15.
34. For the relationship between the authors and narrators of stories, see Wayne Booth, *The Rhetoric of Fiction*, 2nd ed. (Chicago: Chicago University Press, 1983); Seymour Chatman, *Story and Discourse: Narrative Structure in Fiction and Film* (Ithaca: Cornell University Press, 1978), 147–58.

in order to test the suggestion that he wants the Corinthian Christ followers to be inclusive of their hungry siblings when they partake of the Lord's Supper.

As discussed above, Theissen understands Paul's words in 1 Cor. 11:34 (εἴ τις πεινᾷ, ἐν οἴκῳ ἐσθιέτω, ἵνα μὴ εἰς κρίμα συνέρχησθε) as a Pauline compromise, an example of the love-patriarchalism of the Pauline letters. This love-patriarchalism allows social inequities to continue but transfuses them with a spirit of concern, respect and personal solicitude.[35] While other scholars have built on Theissen's insight,[36] some have reservations. Conzelmann says that interpreting v. 34 as eating a separate meal at the private homes of the haves (οἱ ἔχοντες), risks endorsing more divisions.[37] Horrell opines that "the ethos of Paul's instruction . . . is not adequately encapsulated in the term 'love-patriarchalism,' but neither is it a radical ethic of egalitarian redistribution."[38] Moreover, as Suzanne Watts-Henderson observes, "Commentators considering both 11.22 and 11.34 have maintained, often with a touch of embarrassment, that these verses constitute the necessary escape clause of an at-home eating option for the hungering 'haves.'"[39] For his part, Yung Suk Kim argues, "It is not Paul but the rich who seek to practice this 'love patriarchalism': Paul's own view could be described as non-conformist compared to that of the rich."[40]

In exploring Paul's points of view, I will reexamine 1 Cor. 11:17-34 and propose that what Paul puts forward here is a partaking

---

35. Theissen, "The Strong and the Weak," 139.
36. For a brief summary of those who follow Theissen, see Horrell, *Social Ethos*, 126–31. See also Fitzmyer, *First Corinthians*, 448; Raymond F. Collins, *First Corinthians*, SP 7 (Collegeville: Liturgical Press, 1999), 440.
37. See Hans Conzelmann, *1 Corinthians: A Commentary on the First Epistle to the Corinthians*, trans. James W. Leitch, Hermeneia (Philadelphia: Fortress Press, 1975), 203.
38. Horrell, *Social Ethos*, 155.
39. See Watts Henderson, "'If Anyone Hungers . . . '", 196.
40. Yung Suk Kim, *Christ's Body in Corinth: The Politics of a Metaphor*, Paul in Critical Contexts (Minneapolis: Fortress Press, 2008), 62.

of the Lord's Supper (κυριακὸν δεῖπνον, consisting of bread-meal-cup) that is inclusive of the hungry have-nots.

A. Phraseological Point of View in 1 Corinthians 11:17-34

Phraseology shows stylistic patterns that set apart the one speaking in a particular text and indicates whose point of view the author adopts.[41] Paul's phraseology reveals his position concerning the problems at the Corinthian common meal. In vv. 17 and 22, Paul expresses his judgment concerning the practice at Corinth: οὐκ ἐπαινῶ. This *inclusio* colors his description in vv. 18-22 of the reasons why he does not commend them and implies why he wants correction.

Uspensky notes that variation of points of view may be observed, "even more so" in phraseology, particularly when the author "uses different diction to describe different characteristics or where he makes use of one form or another of reported or substituted speech in his description."[42] A particular point of view can also be detected via phraseology when the speech characteristic of another character is incorporated into that of the narrator.[43] In v. 18, ἀκούω[44] indicates a reported speech and implies Paul's possible oral source(s):[45] Chloe's people (1:10-12);[46] Stephanas, Fortunatus, and Achaicus (16:17);[47] or the Corinthians themselves who are proud of their own achievements (1:4).[48] Some opine that "Paul is here reflecting the view 'from below,'

---

41. See Uspensky, *Poetics*, 15; Yamasaki, *Watching*, 70–71; Yamasaki, *Perspective*, 91–97.
42. Uspensky, *Poetics*, 17.
43. Yamasaki, *Watching*, 172.
44. Yamasaki, *Perspective*, 41–42 also considers it under a psychological plane.
45. See Hans-Josef Klauck, *Das Herrenmahl und hellenistischer Kult: Eine religiongeschichtliche Untersuchung zum ersten Korintherbrief*, NTAbh 15 (Münster: Aschendorff, 1982), 288; Fitzmyer, *First Corinthians*, 432 speaks of some report that Paul received but he does not specifically link it to the oral reports.
46. See Winter, *After Paul*, 159–63. See also Klauck, *Das Herrenmahl*, 288.
47. Barrett, *First Epistle*, 261. See Hays, *First Corinthians*, 193. Contrast Klauck, *Das Herrenmahl*, 288.

whereas the response will be directed towards those 'from above.'"[49] While it is difficult to pinpoint the source of the report(s), it is narratively significant that Paul allows the unnamed reporter(s)' point of view to be known (v. 18a), making it his own, albeit with qualification (v. 18b).

Some scholars claim that v. 19 also reflects a reported speech.[50] Δεῖ is understood to show Paul's acceptance of the αἱρέσεις ἐν ὑμῖν. Nevertheless, analysis of the point of view evidenced by phraseology can prompt one to ask the following: If the factions are necessary, why is Paul at pains to correct this problem? Instead, vv. 18-19 seems to corroborate Paul's negative judgment in v. 17 through his ironic[51] criticism of the necessity of disunity at table based on economic stratification (v. 22).

Paul's sharpest disapproval is expressed in naming[52] the Corinthian meal ἴδιον δεῖπνον, not κυριακὸν δεῖπνον (vv. 20-21). Furthermore, he clearly censures the disunity at table and its negative consequences.

---

48. Barrett, *First Epistle*, 261.

49. Gordon D. Fee, *The First Epistle to the Corinthians*, NICNT (Grand Rapids: Eerdmans, 1987), 537.

50. Some scholars appeal to an alleged noncanonical apocalyptic saying of Jesus (ἔσονται σχίσματα καὶ αἱρέσεις) found in Justin Martyr's *Dialogue with Trypho* 35.3, in *Didascalia* 6.5.2, and in Pseudo-Clementine *Homily* 2.17.4 and 16.21.4. See Joachim Jeremias, *Unbekannte Jesusworte* (Gütersloh: Gütersloher Verlaghaus Gerd Mohn, 1963), 74–75. See also Ben Witherington III, *Conflict and Community in Corinth: A Socio-Rhetorical Commentary on 1 Corinthians* (Grand Rapids: Eerdmans, 1995), 248. However, Otfried Hofius ("Unknown Sayings of Jesus," in *The Gospel and the Gospels*, ed. Peter Stuhlmacher, [Grand Rapids: Eerdmans, 1991], 336–60, esp. 344) argues that the origin of the citation of Justin was 1 Cor. 11:18-19.

51. For Pauline irony in v.19, see Collins, *First Corinthians*, 422; Fee, *First Epistle to the Corinthians*, 538–39; Horsley, *1 Corinthians*, 159; Thiselton, *1 Corinthians*, 859–60; Fitzmyer, *First Corinthians*, 433. Margaret M. Mitchell (*Paul and the Rhetoric of Reconciliation: An Exegetical Investigation of the Language and Composition of 1 Corinthians*, HUT 28 [Tübingen: Mohr, 1991], 263): "Paul begins with great irony in 11:17-18." I consider that the irony extends to v. 19. For more on Pauline irony, see Glenn Holland, "Paul's Use of Irony as a Rhetorical Technique," in *The Rhetorical Analysis of Scripture: Essays from the 1995 London Conference*, ed. Stanley E. Porter and Thomas H. Olbricht JSNTSup 146 (London: Sheffield Academic, 1997), 234–48.

52. Uspensky, *Poetics*, 20–32 regards naming to be part of the phraseological plane of point of view. Yamasaki, *Watching*, 171 considers it under the psychological plane but in *Perspective*, 96, he discusses it under the phraseological plane.

In v. 22, Paul strongly upholds the importance of the unified identity of the church of God and his words imply taking the sides of have-nots.

In vv. 23-34, Paul attempts to correct the Corinthian praxis through identifying with the Lord's character in the foundational narrative (vv. 23-25), theologizing about the implications of this story in Corinth (vv. 26-32), and commanding concretely to change their conduct at the common table (vv. 33-34). The phraseology of the foundational narrative intensifies Paul's arguments to be inclusive. In v. 23, the emphatic position of ἐγώ, the use of the explanatory γάρ to signal the beginning of Paul's reinstruction and its connection with the unpraiseworthy practices in v. 22, the explicit naming of the Lord as the source of the tradition, and Paul's use of a technical language of transmitting tradition (παραλαμβάνω)[53] clearly show his opposition to the Corinthian version. In quoting the tradition of the foundational story and using the words of the Lord Jesus in vv. 24-25 as reported speech, Paul affirms that he wants the Corinthians to partake of the Lord's Supper properly by identifying with the way the Lord did it. The undifferentiated, unqualified ὑπὲρ ὑμῶν (v. 24) addressed to the Lord's unspecified tablemates is now addressed to the Corinthians. It implies an inclusive table fellowship that heeds the commandment τοῦτο ποιεῖτε εἰς τὴν ἐμὴν ἀνάμνησιν (vv. 24, 25). The appeal to the Lord's authority, words, and actions demand character identification with him to correct the faulty practices. Thus, how can Paul compromise his position in v. 34 by separating the sharing of the bread and cup from the full meal, or by telling the haves to privately eat their own satisfying meal according to love-

---

53. See 1 Cor. 15:3-5. See also, for example, Conzelmann, *1 Corinthians*, 196; Barrett, *First Epistle*, 264–65; Anders Eriksson, *Traditions as Rhetorical Proof: Pauline Argumentation in 1 Corinthians*, ConBNT 29 (Stockholm: Almqvist & Wicksell International, 1998), 101–2.

patriarchalism? The foundational story serves as a narrative solution to the Corinthian problems at the common meal.

Paul's phraseology in vv. 26-34 continues his arguments for a Lord's Supper that is discerning of the body and inclusive of the have-nots (v. 29).[54] Finally, Paul specifically commands the Corinthians how to reform their meal by welcoming one another as siblings (v. 33), especially those who hunger (v. 34), when they gather to eat (συνέρχομαι, vv. 17-18, 20, 33-34) the κυριακὸν δεῖπνον. This interpretation contrasts with the claim of love-patriarchalism in v. 34 that Paul wants the hungry οἱ ἔχοντες to eat their more satisfying meal in their private homes apart from the bread and wine at the κυριακὸν δεῖπνον, whether before[55] or after[56] the common meal. By beginning with ἀδελφοί μου, Paul emphatically[57] reminds the Corinthians of their fictive sibling relationship to one another. Paul, the Corinthians, and other Christ believers construct their shared symbolic universe by expressing solidarity with one another[58] as they partake of the Lord's Supper. The divisions and factions dominating the ἴδιον δεῖπνον (δόκιμοι–ἀδόκιμοί, v. 19; οἱ μὴ ἔχοντες–οἱ

---

54. Paul's theologizing about partaking of it together is replete with eschatological (v. 26) and judgment motifs (ἀναξίως, v. 27; ἔνοχος, 27; δοκιμάζω, v. 28; κρίμα, vv. 29, 34; κρίνω and its cognates in vv. 29, 31, 32).

55. See, for example, Jerome Murphy-O'Connor, *1 Corinthians*, NTM 10 (Dublin: Veritas, 1979), 114–15; Barrett, *First Epistle*, 277, 263; Collins, *First Corinthians*, 440; Justin J. Meggitt, *Paul, Poverty and Survival*, Studies of the New Testament and Its World (Edinburgh: T & T Clark, 1998), 190; Lampe, "Corinthian Dinner," 8; Mark P. Surburg ("The Situation at the Corinthian Lord's Supper in Light of 1 Corinthians 11:21: A Reconsideration," *Concordia Journal* (2006): 17–37, at 35–37) understands προλαμβάνω to mean "take before" but the reference point of "before" is not the arrival of οἱ μὴ ἔχοντες (considered as later than others), but when οἱ ἔχοντες begin eating ahead of the rest despite everyone being present together at the meal.

56. For instance, see Joachim Jeremias, *The Eucharistic Words of Jesus*, NTL (London: SCM, 1966), 133; Peter Stuhlmacher, "Das neutestamentliche Zeugnis vom *Herrenmahl*," *ZTK* 84 (1987): 1–35, at 21. Contrast Klinghardt, *Gemeinschaftsmahl*, 279–81.

57. See Reidar Aasgaard, *"My Beloved Brothers and Sisters!": Christian Siblingship in Paul*, JSNTSup 265 (New York: T & T Clark, 2004), 279–80.

58. See Aasgaard, *"My Beloved Brothers and Sisters!"*, 297.

ἔχοντες, v. 21-22) are deemed to be overturned through the vocative ἀδελφοί, which underscores their newly shared common identity.[59]

Analyzing the phraseology indicates that Paul favors correcting the Corinthian's version of the κυριακὸν δεῖπνον for it to be more inclusive of the hungry ἀδελφοί.

B. Psychological Point of View in 1 Corinthians 11:17-34

In 1 Cor. 11:17-34, one can detect Paul's perspective on the psychology of the Corinthians in their current practice, Paul internal psychology as the narrator, and understand how he attempts to use this psychology to convince the Corinthians to reform their practice.[60] Paul describes the psychology of the Corinthians from a point of view. His perspective is that the Corinthians have a problem because disunity prevails at table (vv. 18-19). He also illustrates their diminished sense of social obligation[61] since some ate ahead in the presence of others[62] and were drunk, while others experienced hunger (vv. 21-22). He condemns their psychological state, evident in his negative judgment on the Corinthian meal (v. 20) that pales in comparison with the foundational story (vv. 23-25). It is also underscored in v. 22. These clues contrast with what Paul considers as praiseworthy partaking of the Lord's Supper that is inclusive of everyone at the meal (vv. 26-29, 31-34).

---

59. See Meeks, *First Urban Christians*, 88 on the Pauline employment of affective language to underscore "the break with the past and integration into the new community."

60. Yamasaki explains that the psychological "point of view relates to whether the narrator is establishing a point of view inside or outside a character's mind." Uspensky elaborates that "if the behavior of A is described through the perception of B (A and B being characters in the same narrative), then A is described from an external point of view, while B is described from an internal point of view." Paul's psychological point of view reflects his multiple roles as author, narrator, and actor in the story. Simultaneously playing all these roles, one can detect Paul's external and internal point of view concerning the Corinthians' problems (vv. 17-22) as well as his internal point of view about the solution (vv. 23-34).

61. Smith, *From Symposium*, 10: the "ethical obligation of the diners toward one another."

62. Surburg, "Corinthian Lord's Supper," 35–37.

Paul's psychological analysis of the Corinthians in v. 30 relates the resultant physiological manifestations with the unpraiseworthy meal practices in Corinth: διὰ τοῦτο ἐν ὑμῖν πολλοὶ ἀσθενεῖς καὶ ἄρρωστοι καὶ κοιμῶνται ἱκανοί. It is an "indefinite detail of perception"[63] because Paul does not specify who the referents are, ἐν ὑμῖν πολλοί, even if the physical manifestations among the Corinthians are concrete. Most likely, they are οἱ μὴ ἔχοντες who are more prone to suffer the results of chronic and habitual hunger because of their economic situation. In the midst of vv. 27-34, where the judgment theme is concentrated and introduced by διὰ τοῦτο, v. 30 emphatically articulates the physiological consequences of the malpractices at the common meal.

Paul expresses his internal psychology using *verba sentiendi,* illustrating that he takes the side of the hungry have-nots. *Verba sentiendi* refer to verbs of feeling that describe internal consciousness ("he thought," "he felt," and others).[64] For example, ἐπαινέω means "to speak of the excellence of a person, object, or event."[65] Οὐκ ἐπαινῶ (vv. 17, 22) expresses Paul's internal psychology as a letter-writer, narrator and character. It frames the way he negatively regards the problem in Corinth and influences how his addressees ought to reconsider their practices. Paul's repeated and explicit nonpraise of the noninclusive Corinthian meal implicitly defends the hungry οἱ μὴ ἔχοντες. Paul's internal psychology is also found in πιστεύω (v. 18, "to believe something to be true, and hence, worthy of being trusted")[66] qualified with μέρος, an indefinite detail of perception.[67] Moreover, Paul's ironic remark in v. 19, along with v. 22, points out

63. See Yamasaki, *Watching*, 171.
64. See Uspensky, *Poetics*, 85–87; Yamasaki, *Watching*, 169.
65. Johannes P. Luow and Eugene A. Nida, *Greek-English Lexicon of the New Testament Based on Semantic Domains*, 2 vols., 2nd ed. (New York: United Bible Societies, 1989), 1:429, no. 33.354.
66. Ibid., 1:370, no. 31.35.
67. Yamasaki, *Watching*, 171.

that the divisions at table are a consequence of their socioeconomic stratification and not a divinely sanctioned disunity. All of these reflect Paul's psychology that further influences the reasons for his criticisms in vv. 20-22 and the repeated non-commendation in v. 22.

Paul's psychology is also expressed in his naming practices:[68] pointing out the σχίσματα and αἱρέσεις, calling the Corinthian meal ἴδιον δεῖπνον (v. 21) and not κυριακὸν δεῖπνον (v. 20), mentioning those who suffer the consequence of the problems, namely the despised ἐκκλησία τοῦ θεοῦ and the shamed οἱ μὴ ἔχοντες (v. 22). The naming practice also helps in giving clues for the solution to the problems: naming the Lord as the source of the practice, explicitly describing it (vv. 23-25), and calling the Corinthians ἀδελφοί μου (v. 33). Verse 22 also hints at Paul's internal negative mindset towards the conduct of οἱ ἔχοντες. Louw and Nida explain that καταφρονέω denotes "to feel contempt for someone or something because it is thought to be bad or without value,"[69] while καταισχύνω means "to cause someone to be much ashamed—'to humiliate, to disgrace or put to shame.'"[70] As a result, Paul's internal psychology intensifies his external description of the unpraiseworthy conduct of οἱ ἔχοντες at their table fellowship. It implicitly highlights that he takes the side of οἱ μὴ ἔχοντες and decries the despising of the ἐκκλησία.

Analysing Paul's psychological point of view helps to understand vv. 33- 34. His internal view of himself as the faithful transmitter of the tradition of the foundational story (vv. 23-25) impels him to correct the Corinthians. From his external point of view, the example of the Lord is the correct way. The Corinthians' need is to conform to the Lord's example, since the meal is in his memory. The psychological appeal of ἀδελφοί μου (v. 33) aims to influence

68. Ibid., 171–72.
69. Louw, and Nida, *Greek-English Lexicon*, 1:763, no. 88.192.
70. Ibid., 1:310, no. 25.194.

the change in their conduct in vv. 33-34, reminding them of their kinship relationship in their symbolic relationship when they welcome each other at their common meal in the ἐκκλησία space.[71] Paul recognizes that the psychological problem of hunger at the κυριακὸν δεῖπνον can be resolved by the Corinthian ἐκκλησία τοῦ θεοῦ itself (εἴ τις πεινᾷ, ἐν οἴκῳ ἐσθιέτω, v. 34) so that their gathering will be for their good (cf. v. 17) and not for their condemnation (v. 34). These clues support the proposal that Paul wants the Corinthians to be united and inclusive of those who hunger in partaking of the κυριακὸν δεῖπνον.

C. Ideological Plane of Point of View in 1 Corinthians 11:17-34

"Whose point of view does the author assume when he evaluates and perceives ideologically the world he describes?"[72] The author's ideology impacts the audience's evaluation of everything in the story.[73] Paul's ideology is explicit in the whole pericope. The οὐκ ἐπαινῶ *inclusio* (vv. 17, 22) illustrates his stern disapproval of the current Corinthian meal practice.[74] Verses 23-34 contrast with the noncommendable practices in vv. 17-22 and affirm Paul's disapproval. The foundational narrative (v. 23-25) expresses Paul's ideological alignment with the Lord, whose dinner is offered to his tablemates in an inclusive manner. Likewise, Paul unmistakably explains the meaning of the meal for the community (v. 26), what it would take to celebrate it rightly (vv. 27-32), and the concrete efforts to correct the abuses (vv. 33-34). All of these reflect what Smith calls

---

71. See Jorunn Økland, *Women in Their Place: Paul and the Corinthian Discourse of Gender and Sanctuary Space*, JSNTSup 269 (New York: T & T Clark, 2004), 137, 143–49. While I agree with her notion of ἐκκλησία space as ritually constructed, from the analysis of Paul's point of view it seems difficult to maintain that Paul wants the separation of the satisfying meal from the bread and wine.

72. Uspensky, *Poetics*, 8.

73. Yamasaki, *Watching*, 174. See also Petersen, *Rediscovering Paul*, 15.

74. See Eriksson, *Traditions*, 177, 182.

the banquet ideology: social boundary and social bonding as a united ἐκκλησία τοῦ θεοῦ, social stratification and social equality as table fellows, as well as a sense of social obligation for one another.[75] These values are important especially in relation to how the members relate to the vulnerable οἱ μὴ ἔχοντες, who continue to hunger even when they gather together to eat the κυριακὸν δεῖπνον in the present situation. Paul aims to affirm the diners' unity at table as one body.[76]

Second, we find examples of "epistemic modality" or "the degree of confidence a speaker has with regard to the truth of a proposition."[77] Paul employs μέρος (v. 18) to qualify his reception of the oral report. Yet his partial believing is confirmed by his ironic remark in v. 19, introduced by δεῖ γάρ. Paul's use of the foundational story in vv. 23-25 to solicit and even implicitly command character identification with the Lord shows his ideological identification with this story.

Third, an exemplary character can provide a "reliable source of the narrator's own ideological point of view."[78] In vv. 23-25, Paul appeals to his audience using an exemplary character to solve the problem of the ἴδιον δεῖπνον—the Lord Jesus. Just as the Lord Jesus shared his farewell meal with his disciples without discrimination through the unqualified ὑπὲρ ὑμῶν (v. 24), so the Corinthians must faithfully follow the Lord's command (vv. 24-25) and address the discrimination and disunity among them (vv. 27-34). Likewise, Paul is a reliable character. He faithfully transmitted the tradition to them (v. 23) and he corrects the Corinthian unpraiseworthy practices by teaching them about the implications of the foundational story and commanding them to eat together (v. 23-34), since he is also their ἀδελφός (v. 33).

---

75. See Smith, *From Symposium*, 9–11.
76. See also 1 Cor. 10:17.
77. Yamasaki, *Watching*, 174.
78. Ibid., 175.

Fourth, what is Paul's ideological point of view about hunger (πεινάω, vv. 21, 34)? It is clear that Paul is not on the side of those who perpetrate the abuses at the meal. Paul takes the side of the hungry have-nots (v. 21) and does not want them shamed (v. 22). He also takes sides with the ἐκκλησία τοῦ θεοῦ that is despised by the abuses (v. 22). From Paul's ideological point of view, his withdrawal of praise (vv. 17, 22) and his attempts to correct the problems (vv. 23-32) back up his commands in vv. 33-34: he wants the members of the ἐκκλησία τοῦ θεοῦ to treat each other as ἀδελφοί when they come to eat the κυριακὸν δεῖπνον.

D. Temporal Point of View in 1 Corinthians 11:17-34

What is the narrator's time period? When does the narrated story take place?[79] There are several clues to Paul's temporal point of view in 1 Cor. 11:17-34. First, while Paul's use of the tenses of the verb keeps on changing,[80] his predominant use of the present tense indicates a sense of immediacy.[81] It puts Paul in a situation synchronous with the Corinthians (vv. 17-22).[82] This is especially significant if Paul knows that his letter is read when the assembly gathers for the κυριακὸν δεῖπνον.[83]

Second, the temporal point of view in vv. 17-34 is governed by Paul's concern for the Corinthians' inclusive eating of the κυριακὸν δεῖπνον. The exact time of the Corinthian κυριακὸν δεῖπνον cannot be pinpointed. However, a δεῖπνον generally denotes the main meal of the day, held usually in the evening.[84] The temporal clues that

---

79. Uspensky, *Poetics*, 57.
80. Tenses: present (vv. 17-22), past (vv. 23-25), future (vv. 26, 27), present (vv. 26a, 27-30, 32-34), past (v. 31) and future (v. 34).
81. For more on verb tenses and point of view, see Yamasaki, *Watching*, 167; Yamasaki, "Point of View," 93.
82. See Yamasaki, *Watching*, 167.
83. See Smith, *From Symposium*,180; Hal Taussig, *In the Beginning Was the Meal: Social Experimentation and Early Christianity* (Minneapolis: Fortress Press, 2009), 36.

the abuses happen *during* the κυριακὸν δεῖπνον are indicated by the repeated use of συνέρχομαι (vv. 17, 18, 20, 33, and 34), particularly the genitive absolute in vv. 18 and 20. Verse 19 underlines ironically that the factions and divisions are evident during the table fellowship that is supposed to underscore their unity. The clearest temporal expression, however, is found in v. 21, which underscores the problem, and vv. 33-34, which highlight Paul's solution.[85]

Temporally, vv. 23-25 go back to the past, as they recall the supper of the Lord. But their appeal is seen in light of the reforms that must be done presently. The temporal perspective in vv. 26-34 is dominated by the concern to reform their practice immediately. In v. 33, συνερχόμενοι εἰς τὸ φαγεῖν ἀλλήλους ἐκδέχεσθε, welcoming one another ought to happen during their communal gathering to eat the κυριακὸν δεῖπνον. Paul does not seem to have a problem with their private meal in their private homes. What he considers unpraiseworthy is the individual supper (ἴδιον δεῖπνον) eaten during the ἐκκλησία's κυριακὸν δεῖπνον. Thus, instead of contrasting v. 34 with v. 33, v. 34 is Paul's more specific response to the abuses *during* the Corinthians' common meal. The problem of hunger of the have-nots during the κυριακὸν δεῖπνον (v. 21-22) is addressed in Paul's command: εἴ τις πεινᾷ, ἐν οἴκῳ ἐσθιέτω (v. 34). The solution is given with a combined spatio-temporal specification: they must eat at the same time and place where the assembly partake of the κυριακὸν δεῖπνον. This point is further underscored by the

---

84. Louw and Nida, *Greek-English Lexicon*, 1:252, no. 23.25. See also Carolyn Osiek and David L. Balch, *Families in the New Testament World: Household and House Churches*, The Family Religion and Culture (Louisville: Westminster John Knox, 1997), 199; Lampe, "The Eucharist,"41.

85. If one translates προλαμβάνω as "to take before" and not "devour" in v. 21, and ἐνδέχομαι as "wait" and not "receive" in v. 33, the temporal plane of point of view is underscored. Contrast Winter, *After Paul*, 159-63, 144-48. Fee (*First Epistle*, 542) favors the translation of προλαμβάνω as "consume" or "devour," but he notes that "one cannot totally rule out a temporal sense." See also Stephen C. Barton, "Paul's Sense of Place: An Anthropological Approach to Community Formation," *NTS* 32 (1986): 225-46, esp. 241.

purpose clause, ἵνα μὴ εἰς κρίμα συνέρχησθε (v. 34). It connects with the temporal meaning of the repeatedly used συνέρχομαι and the judgment theme strongly present in vv. 27-32. Since v. 34 is the last part of Paul's concrete response to the Corinthian problem, his implicit evaluation of the effects of his instructions is expressed temporally in τὰ δὲ λοιπὰ ὡς ἂν ἔλθω διατάξομαι (v. 34). In sum, the evidence from Paul's temporal point of view substantiates the interpretation that Paul wants to ensure that the disunity in the ἐκκλησία, which marginalizes the hungry οἱ μὴ ἔχοντες during the κυριακὸν δεῖπνον, is resolved.

E. Spatial Point of View in 1 Corinthians 11:17-34

Where does the narrated story take place, and what is the position of the narrator and characters in that space? The κυριακὸν δεῖπνον and the ἴδιον δεῖπνον happen in a particular space. Spatial textual clues are found in Paul's reference to ἐπὶ τὸ αὐτὸ (v. 20), [86] οἰκίας (v. 22), and ἐν οἴκῳ (v. 34). Some scholars allege that there is a contrast between ἐν ἐκκλησίᾳ on the one hand and οἰκίαι (v. 22) and οἶκος (v. 34) on the other.[87] Yet, is there indeed a contrast? Scholars agree that οἰκία and οἶκος can be translated interchangeably as "house" or "home."[88] However, when Paul uses οἰκία in v. 22 and οἶκος in v. 34, there seems to be no indication that he is speaking of different venues for the eating of the bread and drinking of the cup of the κυριακὸν δεῖπνον on the one hand, and for the eating of the satisfying meal on the other hand. Instead, what seems recognizable is the parallelism between Paul's acknowledgment of the spatial function of the οἰκία

---

86. See Barton, "Paul's Sense of Place," 240: "The church meal is sacred by virtue of its spatio-temporal location, indicated by συνέρχομαι ('to gather together') (11.17, 18, 20, 33, 34; cf. 14.23, 26), sometimes accompanied by specific locative phrase (e.g. ἐν ἐκκλησίᾳ in 11.18; cf. 14.23; ἐπὶ τὸ αὐτὸ in 11.20; cf 14.23)."
87. Økland, *Women in their Place*, 137; Blue, "House Church," 226–27.
88. Otto Michel, "οἶκος, οἰκία κτλ.," *TWNT*, 5:122–61.

that is εἰς τὸ ἐσθίειν καὶ πίνειν (v. 22), and the οἶκος that is ἐσθίειν
(v. 34) in relation to the communal gathering to eat the κυριακὸν
δεῖπνον. These spatial words indicate the venue when the ἐκκλησία
gathers for a purpose: κυριακὸν δεῖπνον φαγεῖν (v. 20) and εἰς τὸ
φαγεῖν (v. 33).[89]

While ἐν οἴκῳ (v. 34) is generally translated as "at home," from a
spatial point of view, I propose that it is better to translate it as "in
the house," in other words, the houses where they interchangeably
gather together for the κυριακὸν δεῖπνον. Other NT uses of ἐν
οἴκῳ (Mark 2:1; Luke 1:69; 1 Cor. 14:35; 1 Tim. 3:15) are translated
either "at home" or "in the house," depending on the scholars. Apart
from 1 Cor. 11:34 and 14:35, ἐν οἴκῳ without any qualifier is also
employed in Mark 2:1[90] and is rendered either as "at home" or "in
the house," because neither the text nor the context specifies whose
house it is.[91] In 1 Cor. 14:35, *if* it is authentically Pauline, ἐν οἴκῳ
denotes a symbolic space shared by husband and wife, a learning
environment that is clearly differentiated from the ritual space of the
gathered ἐκκλησία.[92] Yet even if Paul wrote 14:35 and ἐν οἴκῳ is
translated as "at home" here, this does not in and of itself mean that ἐν
οἴκῳ has to have the same meaning as in 11:34.

Several narrative clues indicate that ἐν οἴκῳ is better understood
and translated as "in the house" in v. 34. First, if those who hunger
(vv. 21, 34) denote those who live at and below subsistence level, it
is possible that these characters do not necessarily have (enough) food
to eat in their dwelling places. They might not even have a house, or
they might not be beneficiaries of a household.[93] It is significant that

89. See Watts Henderson, "'If Anyone Hungers . . . ,'" 205–6, where she interprets v. 34 as "Let the
hungry in your midst eat!" (206).
90. According to BDAG, "οἶκος," 698, meaning no.1.a.a., the expression ἐν οἴκῳ means "at home"
in a series of extrabiblical texts, as well as in Mark 2:1, 1 Cor. 11:34 and 14:35.
91. For translations of ἐν οἴκῳ as "at home," see RSV, NRSV, NIV, and NAB; translations that
render it as "in the house" include KJV, NKJV, and NJB.
92. See also Økland, *Women in their Place*, 142.

they have the chance to partake of the supper at the common meal as an expression of the group's fulfilment of their social obligation to one another, social bonding, and social boundary.[94].

Second, ἐν οἴκῳ refers to a definite house that they use as ἐκκλησία space for the κυριακὸν δεῖπνον. It rhetorically recalls the houses in v. 22. It is not necessary in Greek to use the definite article in expressions, particularly in prepositional phrases, to express definite or anaphoric content. While ἐν οἴκῳ in v. 34 is singular, it is an expression that can point to plurality of houses (see v. 22).[95] Furthermore, ἐν οἴκοις never appears in the NT or LXX. Thus, v. 34 spatially responds to the problem of hunger at the κυριακὸν δεῖπνον in the same house(s) where the community eats and drinks (v. 21-22) by having the hungry ones eat in the same place.

Third, ἐσθιέτω is a command to those who hunger at the Lord's Supper (vv. 33-34 recall v. 21). The third person command ἐσθιέτω is challenging to translate. The English circumlocution "let" can be misunderstood, as if the one who hungers needs to be permitted to eat in the house by οἱ ἔχοντες. Nevertheless, following Paul's previously established points of view, is it not rather that Paul accentuates that eating together that includes the hungry ones sharing the satisfying meal is not optional? The κυριακὸν δεῖπνον encapsulates the believers' symbolic universe that demands that the hungry ones partake of the κυριακὸν δεῖπνον with the ἐκκλησία τοῦ θεοῦ at the same time and place, in a way that leaves them satisfied just like the rest, since they are all ἀδελφοί.

Fourth, vv. 33-34 reiterates the quality of the partakers' relationship when they partake of the κυριακὸν δεῖπνον in the same place,

---

93. See Longenecker, *Remember the Poor*, 261.

94. Longenecker (*Remember the Poor*, 261) relates the care for the poor and common meal of Jesus groups as one of the "powerful means of attraction, alongside any other 'non-economic' factors" that can persuade those in ES6-7 to join them.

95. 1 Cor. 14:35 uses ἐν οἴκῳ despite the plural τοὺς ἰδίους ἄνδρας.

influenced by their character identification with the Lord Jesus (vv. 23-25). Yamasaki speaks of a spatial clue that considers the function of possessive noun phrases to underscore the relationship of two characters.[96] As members of the ἐκκλησία τοῦ θεοῦ who partake of κυριακὸν δεῖπνον, Paul underscores their relationship in the symbolic universe: interconnected with each other as ἀδελφοί μου and intimately linked to one another in solidarity.

Fifth, Yamasaki also notes the significance of attention to degree of detail to determine where the narrator is positioned.[97] He contrasts the ἴδιον δεῖπνον (vv. 17-22) with the κυριακὸν δεῖπνον (vv. 20, 23-25). Paul's words evoke a very close spatial position, since he describes the disunity, drunkenness, and hunger at the Corinthian meal (vv. 17-22), and how they are to be resolved in vv. 33-34.

These reasons make it difficult to argue that Paul suggest a contrast between ἐκκλησία and οἰκία/οἶκος. Moreover, ἐκκλησία refers not to a space but to the gathering of the believers in Corinth (11:18, 22; 1:2) since it is qualified by the genitive τοῦ θεοῦ and is used as genitive object of καταφρονεῖτε (v. 22). In the Lord's Supper story οἰκία and οἶκος indicate the same material space for the daily life of the believers, but when they partake of the κυριακὸν δεῖπνον with the gathered ἐκκλησία, it functions as a ritual space (ἐκκλησία space)where Paul wants them to relate at table in a more inclusive manner. The contrast, then, is between the quality of the *Corinthians'* desired table fellowship at the κυριακὸν δεῖπνον (v. 20b) and the unpraiseworthy conduct at the ἴδιον δεῖπνον (v. 21a) in the *same* ἐκκλησία space. The former describes a meal sharing according to the example of the Lord Jesus. It is the model, according to Paul's various points of view, that the Corinthians ought to identify with as ἐκκλησία members (vv. 23-34). The κρίμα (v. 34) furthers this

---

96. Yamasaki, *Watching*, 160.
97. Ibid., 158.

point, where it is implied that those who come together to eat in the Corinthians' way will be judged.

IV. Conclusion

The exploration of Paul's points of view as author, narrator, and actor in 1 Cor. 11:17-34 guides the meaning of the κυριακὸν δεῖπνον story in Corinth. The results from this analysis provide strong reasons to say that Paul is consistent in the whole pericope of being inclusive of οἱ μὴ ἔχοντες, the hungry ἀδελφοί, so that the ἐκκλησία will be united and partake of the satisfying κυριακὸν δεῖπνον at the same time and place, unlike the interpretation advanced by love-patriarchalism. Paul's criticism of the problems in vv. 17-22, where the hungry members are marginalized in the ἴδιον δεῖπνον, is followed by his attempts in vv. 23-34 to turn it back to a κυριακὸν δεῖπνον that is attentive to οἱ μὴ ἔχοντες, the hungry ἀδελφοί. He demands reform for a more inclusive gathering where the ἐκκλησία τοῦ θεοῦ partakes of the κυριακὸν δεῖπνον in a way that is inclusive of the hungry οἱ μὴ ἔχοντες.

While the problem of hunger is even more complex today, I hope that this contribution adds 1 Cor. 11:17-34 to the challenging texts that allow us to rethink our understanding of Christian commitment to address hunger. I also hope that this challenges the way we currently interpret the text, particularly its seeming justification of the separation of liturgical eucharistic concerns and the Christian commitment to justice in addressing hunger. It also tests the inclusiveness of our communal meal in remembrance of the Lord and our attentiveness to hungry people. This pericope invites us to creatively find ways to contribute to a hunger-free world.

10

2 Thessalonians vs. the *Ataktoi*: A Pauline Critique of "White–Collar Welfare"

Sheila E. McGinn and Megan T. Wilson-Reitz

Now we command you, beloved, in the name of our Lord Jesus Christ, to keep away from believers who are living in idleness and not according to the tradition that they received from us. For you yourselves know how you ought to imitate us; we were not idle when we were with you, and we did not eat anyone's bread without paying for it; but with toil and labor we worked night and day, so that we might not burden any of you. This was not because we do not have that right, but in order to give you an example to imitate. For even when we were with you, we gave you this command: Anyone unwilling to work should not eat. For we hear that some of you are living in idleness, mere busybodies, not doing any work. Now such persons we command and exhort in the Lord Jesus Christ to do their work quietly and to earn their own living. Brothers and sisters, do not be weary in doing what is right. Take note of those who do not obey what we say in this letter; have nothing to do with them, so that they may be ashamed. Do not regard them as enemies, but warn them as believers. (2 Thess. 3:6-15; NRSV)

The remarks in Second Thessalonians about the *ataktoi*, in particular 2 Thess. 3:10 ("anyone unwilling to work should not eat"), have received great attention from those who use the Bible to promote particular political and economic perspectives. In the United States, verse 10 has been quoted in support of a surprisingly diverse array of political and economic viewpoints, including the Populist platform of 1892, socialist John Spargo, and laissez-faire capitalist William Graham Sumner.[1] Max Weber argued that this passage is at the heart of the Protestant work ethic, which he saw as a necessary condition for the rise of American capitalism.[2] On the other end of the spectrum, Vladimir Lenin claimed the injunction as an essential socialist principle[3]—so that no one would live off the labor of others. The Soviet Constitutions of 1918 and 1936 both employ the phrase.[4]

In recent US political debates, 2 Thess. 3:10 has been utilized in service of a political-economic agenda that undercuts social services, especially unemployment compensation, food stamps, and other supports for persons who have "fallen through the cracks" of our current market economy.[5] These ideologues typically assume that

1. Daniel T. Rodgers, *The Work Ethic in Industrial America, 1850–1920* (Chicago: University of Chicago Press, 1979), 211.
2. "As ordained by God, the purpose of life itself involves work. Paul's maxim applies to everyone without qualification: 'if anyone will not work, let him not eat.' An unwillingness to work is a sign that one is not among the saved." Weber argues that this theology of work, in turn, influenced the rise of capitalism in the modern age. Max Weber, *The Protestant Ethic and the Spirit of Capitalism*, trans. Stephen Kalberg (Chicago: Fitzroy Dearborn, 2001), 106.
3. Vladimir Ilyich Lenin, *The State and Revolution* (New York: International Publishers, 1943). Of course, Lenin used it to argue in favor of requiring the bourgeoisie to work, so that no one would live off the labor of others.
4. The 1918 constitution, for example, gives as the state motto the phrase "he shall not eat who does not work." (Article 2.18, *General Provisions of the Constitution of the Russian Socialist Federated Soviet Republic, 1918*; http://www.marxists.org/history/ussr/government/constitution/1918/.)
5. For example, the Reverend Jerry Falwell described it as "one of ten 'Judeo-Christian principles' at the foundation of American Democracy" and used it "to provide ideological justification for

the text reflects "a straightforward problem with a straightforward solution."[6] The problem, they claim, is that certain lazy Thessalonians are exhibiting "escapist, antisocial behavior" by refusing to work, leading to their poverty and subsequent need to depend upon generous, wealthy members of the community for their sustenance.[7] The solution sounds remarkably similar to the Protestant work ethic: "To live faithfully and productively *in the present moment* and to put everyday energies into *the daily labor that puts bread on the table*."[8] An individual's hard work to earn a living becomes the definition of the Christian life.[9]

This common interpretation relies upon three key assumptions:

1. Since they prefer to depend upon others for support rather than working for a living, the "idlers" *(ataktoi)* must be poor.

2. The letter's original author and audience took for granted that manual labor is a positive cultural force and shared an appreciation of its value.

3. The people reproached here are behaving in a culturally proscribed manner. In other words, "hard work" is the general cultural expectation and "laziness" is antisocial.

---

gutting federal welfare programs" (Neil Elliott, *Liberating Paul: The Justice of God and the Politics of the Apostle* [Maryknoll, NY: Orbis, 1994], 13).

6. Dorothy Jean Weaver, "2 Thessalonians 3:6-15," *Interpretation* 61, no. 4 (October 2007): 426.

7. Robert K. Jewett, "1 and 2 Thessalonians," in *Eerdmans Commentary on the Bible*, ed. James D. G. Dunn and John William Rogerson (Grand Rapids: Eerdmans, 2003), 1413–27, at 1417. Like other commentators, Jewett sees a realized eschatology (e.g., 2 Thess. 2:2) as underlying the problem of the Thessalonian *ataktoi*. While such a relationship is possible, it is equally possible that the two concerns reflect the beliefs and behaviors of different groups (as is the case, e.g., in the Corinthian correspondence). 2 Thessalonians itself makes no direct connection between the assertion "that the day of the Lord is already here" and the behavior of the *ataktoi* described several lines later in 3:6-13.

8. Weaver, "2 Thessalonians 3:6-15," 427.

9. Jewett, "1 and 2 Thessalonians," 1417.

All three of these premises are incorrect when examined within the social context of first-century Thessalonica and in light of internal linguistic evidence and intertextual evidence elsewhere in the New Testament. Instead, these three contexts (sociocultural, linguistic, and intertextual) suggest the following:

1. The *ataktoi* are upwardly mobile social climbers rather than the jobless poor.
2. The value of manual labor is by no means a shared assumption between the author and audience.
3. The author reproaches the *ataktoi* for their *obedience* to the cultural norms of their city and the Empire, rather than their *disobedience* to those cultural norms.

The key to this interpretation is patronage (*clientela*), the basic building block of first-century Roman social, economic, and civic relationships. Every attempt to advance in social standing, gain political office, engage in advantageous business or marital arrangements, or otherwise participate in the Roman economy required a patron who could introduce you to the "right" people and use his/her prestige and influence to help you negotiate the "right" business deals. Patron-client relationships often spanned generations, and "inheriting" an influential patron was as valuable an asset as a family business. An ambitious person's career could be made—or broken—depending upon the favor (and favors) of a powerful and well-connected *patronus*.

James Hollingshead's *The Household of Caesar and the Body of Christ* identifies numerous passages in Paul's letters that demonstrate Paul's unequivocal rejection of the patronage system. It must be emphasized that such a rejection would have been considered radically countercultural. "It is difficult," writes Hollingshead, "to imagine anything that would have been more shocking, or more incomprehensible, to a first-century Roman citizen than Paul's rejection of the routine practices of patronage."[10]

It is, of course, not only in the case of the patronage system that Paul rejects the status quo of Roman imperial life. Throughout the Pauline correspondence, we find overwhelming evidence that Paul rejected many Roman social values and customs.[11] The burden of proof rests, therefore, with those who would assert that the Thessalonian correspondence runs contrary to that trend, urging the community to conform to Roman social standards rather than resist them.[12]

When read with attention to Paul's own "countercultural" bent, it becomes clear that, far from admonishing the poor for freeloading, 2 Thess. 3:6-15 actually critiques ancient "yuppies" who were grasping at upward mobility. As we will demonstrate below, this passage advocates that all members of the Christian community participate in the economic system at the same (low-status) level, abandoning intraecclesial class divisions created by socioeconomic disparities and maintained by the patron-client system. This critique of the *ataktoi*

---

10. James Hollingshead, *The Household of Caesar and the Body of Christ: A Political Interpretation of the Letters from Paul* (Lanham, Md.: University Press of America, 1998), 136; henceforth, *Household*.

11. E.g., the rejection of common prayer and meal practices in 1 Corinthians 11. For more extensive discussion of the anti-imperial aspects of Paul's writing, see Neil Elliott, *Liberating Paul*, passim; cf. John Dominic Crossan and Jonathan L. Reed, *In Search of Paul: How Jesus' Apostle Opposed Rome's Empire with God's Kingdom* (New York: HarperCollins, 2005).

12. This is admitted by scholars such as Cain Hope Felder ("2 Thessalonians," in *True to Our Native Land: An African American New Testament Commentary*, ed. Brian K. Blount [Minneapolis: Fortress, 2007], 404–8, at 407), who admits that the later authors of the Pauline school were more concerned than Paul himself with the Christian community's respectable "public profile" (e.g., Titus 2:7-8). Cf. Raymond F. Collins, *Letters that Paul Did Not Write: The Epistle to the Hebrews and the Pseudepigrapha* (Wilmington, DE: Michael Glazier, 1988), 235; henceforth, *Letters*. Based on this inconsistency with Paul's thinking, Collins and Felder conclude that 2 Thessalonians is the work of a later writer. However, this does not entirely resolve the problem, since 1 Thessalonians takes essentially the same approach to the *ataktoi*, although without the severe penalty.

does not charge them with antisocial behavior, but rather reproaches them for rejecting Paul's example and teaching in order to engage in socially *desirable* behavior—in other words, their participation in the patronage system.[13]

First-Century Roman Thessalonica

Indispensable as it was to the functioning of the Roman Empire, proper observance of the patronage system may have been an issue of particular sensitivity in Thessalonica.[14] By Paul's time, Thessalonica had already been the capital of the Roman province of Macedonia for nearly two hundred years.[15] An important commercial center with a valuable harbor, situated along two busy trade routes, it boasted a diverse cosmopolitan population.[16] After the fall of the Macedonian kingdom in 168 BCE, Thessalonica's economic development became intertwined with that of Rome, first as a city of the Republic and an important trade hub along the *Via Egnatia*, later also as a key harbor among the Greek cities.

Because of its significance as a center of trade and provincial government, the city's fortunes depended heavily upon the patronage of the wealthy Roman citizens who had come to live in the city.[17]

13. The authenticity of 2 Thessalonians is being assumed here, though it should be noted that there is a lack of scholarly consensus on this point. This paper's interpretation, in fact, reveals a certain continuity of thought between 2 Thessalonians and the other undisputed letters of Paul that may serve to support an argument for the letter's authenticity. Given the consistent dynamics of the Roman patronage system throughout the first century, the issue seems less pressing than in regard to other matters of interpretation.

14. Todd D. Still, *Conflict at Thessalonica: A Pauline Church and Its Neighbours*, Journal for the Study of New Testament Supplement Series 183 (Sheffield: Sheffield Academic, 1999), 66. Still relies heavily on the article by Holland Lee Hendrix, "Archaeology and Eschatology at Thessalonica" in *The Future of Christianity: Essays in Honor of Helmut Koester*, ed. Birger A. Pearson (Minneapolis: Fortress, 1991), 107–18.

15. Wayne A. Meeks, *The First Urban Christians: The Social World of the Apostle Paul* (New Haven: Yale University Press, 1983), 45.

16. Meeks, *First Urban Christians*, 46.

17. Eugenio L. Green, "¡Patrón! La Clientela en Tesalónica Romana," *Kairós* 43 (July–December 2008): 80.

"Patronage," says David Braund, "was a principal channel by means of which foreign relations and provincial administration were conducted" throughout the Empire, and the city of Thessalonica was no exception.[18] Many residents would not have held the status of citizens—a grant of Roman citizenship may have been one of the enticements for the Jewish colonists who arrived in the first century BCE—so non-citizens would need to cultivate positive relationships with the city's Roman citizens if they wished to prosper in trade or have any influence with Roman officials.[19] As Karl Donfried points out, "It was necessary for the Thessalonians to develop ways to honour their Roman benefactors so that their benefaction and favours would continue."[20]

One way that the Thessalonians did this was by establishing a public cult in honor of Dea Roma and of the Emperor. Eugenio Green notes that "Not a few inscriptions from the city make mention of 'the Roman benefactors' . . . on a par with the Dea Roma (the Roman goddess) and indicate that a priesthood functioned in their honor."[21] The cultic and civil honor paid to the Roman citizens mirrors that of the imperial cult, which in Thessalonica dates as far back as 27 BCE. By the time of Augustus there was a temple to Caesar in the city.[22] Green calls the imperial cult "a manifestation

---

18. David Braund, "Function and Dysfunction: Personal Patronage in Roman Imperialism," in *Patronage in Ancient Society*, ed. Andrew Wallace-Hadrill (London: Routledge, 1989), 137–52, at 139.

19. All citizens of colonies also were granted Roman citizenship; free Greek cities annexed to the Empire did not have this privilege. They did, however, have their own constitutions and some autonomy in local governance. Luke is historically accurate in describing Thessalonica's local leaders as *politarchai*, a term used in Acts only in reference to government in Thessalonica. These authorities would be responsible for local governance and maintaining order (hence their swift involvement in the conflict in Acts 17), but they remained economically dependent upon the patronage of Rome. Hollingshead, *Household*, 8; cf. Meeks, *First Urban Christians*, 47.

20. Karl Donfried, "The Theology of 1 Thessalonians," in *The Theology of the Shorter Pauline Letters*, ed. Karl Donfried and I. Howard Marshall (New York: Cambridge University Press, 1993), 1–79, at 17.

21. Green, "¡Patrón!," 80; our translation.

22. Donfried, "Theology of 1 Thessalonians," 18.

of the same phenomenon" as the cultic honor paid to the Roman benefactors, because "the emperor was the benefactor *par excellence* of the city."[23] Preserving the good relationships between the city, its resident Roman benefactors, and the emperor was fundamental for the city's overall well-being. The patronage system, requiring a client's personal fidelity to the patron, operated on a large scale as well; to sustain its well-being, the city needed to demonstrate public fidelity to its Roman benefactors and to the Emperor.

To demonstrate public fidelity to the Roman emperor was a matter both political and religious.[24] Loyalty to the emperor entailed public acknowledgement both of his political position as *imperium maius* ("highest authority")[25] and his religious position as *divi filius* ("son of god").[26] "Thessalonica acknowledged Julius [Caesar] as a god," and the emperor, as son of the divine Julius, had divine status in his own right.[27] The imperial cult had its own temple and priesthood, and the citizens of Thessalonica were expected to participate in this cult—or at least not oppose it.[28]

The gospel message preached by Paul was dangerously political (Acts 17:6),[29] disturbing to imperial "peace and security" (1 Thess.

---

23. Green, "¡Patrón!," 81; our translation.
24. Hollingshead points out, "The separation of religion and politics is a modern phenomenon, and was unknown to the ancient world" (*Household*, 112). As far as the Romans were concerned, the cosmic order and the earthly order reflected one another (46–47).
25. Ibid., 6.
26. Donfried, "Theology of 1 Thessalonians," 18.
27. Ibid.
28. The Jews, as a traditionally monotheistic community, were permitted to avoid participation in emperor worship. However, they were still expected to behave in socially acceptable ways, including refraining from direct opposition to the civic cults.
29. Cf. Acts 17:1-10. Caution is necessary when attributing historical accuracy to the account in Acts; nevertheless, as Still argues, "one should not reject out of hand the possibility that Acts accurately reports Paul's context and conflict with Thessalonian Jews" (Still, *Conflict at Thessalonica*, 66). The references to the Thessalonians' suffering and persecution in both letters [e.g., 1 Thess. 2:14-16 and 2 Thess. 1:4-6] hint at a situation consonant with the Acts account. Even Luke's unusual use of the term *politarchai* to describe the city leaders has been archaeologically verified (Donfried, "Theology of 1 Thessalonians," 15).

5:3).[30] From the Roman vantage point, Paul's message was both seditious and treasonous;[31] by claiming Christ as emperor (*basileus*) they set him up as Caesar's rival.[32]

If, as suggested above, Thessalonica's prosperity depended upon the goodwill of Roman benefactors, then there would be good reason for the leaders of the Jewish community, as well as the city authorities, to be concerned about Paul's preaching. The preaching of Paul and his companions rejected the theological claims of the imperial cult, instead proclaiming "the central role of Jesus in salvation and his divine election as the *Christos*,"[33] which "would easily be feared in such a multi-religious community as a reversal of value-system."[34] By preaching the gospel publicly in Thessalonica, Paul and his companions challenged not only the religious claims of the imperial cult, but also the political claims of the emperor as patron of the people— thereby subverting "the foundational institutions of Greco-Roman society."[35] The apostles' public preaching stood in direct opposition to the public observation of the patron-client relationship between the city and the Empire.[36] To question this relationship would create a social disruption that was potentially dangerous for the city and its citizens if it caused any displeasure to the Romans.

30. Still (*Conflict at Thessalonica*, 260–66) suggests that Paul's use of the phrase "peace and security" in 1 Thess. 5:3 can be understood as a direct criticism of the language used in the political propaganda of the *Pax Romana*.
31. Still, *Conflict at Thessalonica*, 74.
32. They may even have flouted a specific law requiring loyalty to the emperor, which would explain the charge in Acts that "they are all acting contrary to the decrees of Caesar" (17:7). Cf. E. A. Judge, "The Decrees of Caesar at Thessalonica," *Reformed Theological Review* 30 (1971): 2–7.
33. Chris Ukachukwu Manus, "Luke's Account of Paul in Thessalonica (Acts 17:1-9)," in *The Thessalonian Correspondence*, ed. Raymond F. Collins (Leuven: Leuven University Press, 1990), 27–38, at 33; henceforth, "Paul in Thessalonica."
34. Manus, "Paul in Thessalonica," 33.
35. Ibid.
36. Of course, the imperial cult's theological claims were integrally connected with its political claims.

Patrons and Clients in the Roman Empire

David Braund summarizes the significance of the Roman patronage
system. "Since personal patronage was all-pervasive in Roman
society, it is hardly surprising that it played a leading role in what
was perhaps the greatest issue of that society—namely, the creation,
retention, administration and expansion of Rome's empire."[37] To
reject the patronage system was to reject the entire imperial order;
indeed, the system of patrons and clients "bound the Empire
together."[38]

2 Thess. 3:6-15 opposes the patronage system both at the
individual level and at the level of the imperial cult as present in
the city. While modern readers may see them as very different kinds
of relationship, they are in fact only different levels of the same
imperial design, and are therefore intimately connected. "Public and
private are scarcely distinguishable as the complex of patronage is
deepened and extended. . . . Patronage became the very currency of
government."[39]

The Roman Empire was built upon a rigid hierarchy headed by
the emperor as the *pater patriae* ("father of the people").[40] "The empire
became a sort of extended household with provincial governors and
prefects and client kings owing their positions and their allegiance
directly and personally to [the Emperor]. . . . The empire was a single
continuous hierarchy."[41] Each social stratum had a specific place in
this hierarchy, from the governors of provinces to benefactors of
cities (as in Thessalonica) to heads and members of individual
households.

37. Braund, "Function and Dysfunction," 137.
38. Hollingshead, *Household*, 107.
39. Braund, "Function and Dysfunction," 142–43.
40. Hollingshead, *Household*, 108.
41. Ibid., 6, 10.

The fundamental building block of this system, at every level of Roman society, was the patron-client relationship, which had three basic characteristics: based upon an exchange of goods and services, it comprised a personal relationship of indefinite length, and was marked by asymmetry—the patron always boasted a higher status and more power than the client.[42] Due to the personal nature of the patron-client relationship, all transactions were viewed as gift exchanges. "'Gift-exchange' between patrons and clients was the most important means of economic interaction in the empire."[43] This ethic applied to commercial transactions as well; even prostitutes offered their favors as "gifts" (for which a return "gift" was expected), rather than as services rendered for payment.[44]

This gift-exchange understanding of economic activity meant that purely commercial transactions, especially manual labor performed for pay, was considered shameful in Roman society. Plutarch makes it clear that the products of manual labor may be appreciated, but not the laborer:

> When we are pleased with the work, we slight and set little by the workman or artist himself. . . . We are taken with the things themselves well enough, but do not think [their makers] otherwise than low and sordid people. . . . He who busies himself in mean occupations produces, in the very pains he takes about things of little or no use, an evidence against himself of his negligence and indisposition to what is really good. . . . For it does not necessarily follow that, if a piece of work please for its gracefulness, therefore he that wrought it deserves our admiration.[45]

Furthermore, many laborers were slaves, so manual labor was equated with slavery. This point of view is expressed by Cicero, who writes,

---

42. Richard Saller, "Patronage and Friendship in Early Imperial Rome: Drawing the Distinction," in Wallace-Hadrill, *Patronage in Ancient Society*, 63–87, at 63; henceforth, "Patronage."
43. Hollingshead, *Household*, 104.
44. Ibid., 104.
45. *Pericles*, in *Plutarch's Lives*, trans. John Dryden (New York: Random House, n.d.), 182-83.

"Unbecoming to a gentleman, too, and vulgar are the means of livelihood of all hired workmen whom we pay for mere manual labour, not for artistic skill; for in their case the very wages they receive is a pledge of their slavery. . . . All mechanics are engaged in vulgar trades; for no workshop can have anything liberal about it."[46] Since slaves were not legally human persons in the Roman Empire, it stands to reason that a slave's labor would be understood as less than "dignified."

Modern commentators on 2 Thessalonians 3 frequently assume that the letter's audience valued manual labor, especially given the "work ethic" that has made its way into the value systems of the societies most influenced by Christianity. On the contrary, as demonstrated above, Roman society placed little value upon physical labor and did not understand it as a positive cultural force. Recognizing this cultural antipathy toward manual labor is essential to recognizing the countercultural force of the argument in this letter.

The Roman elite's disdain for manual labor must be understood within the context of the patron-client system, which grounded the social fabric of the empire. Those who did not participate in the patron-client system—or who participated on the fringe of this system as slaves or laborers—were seen as belonging to a lower order of humanity.[47] Because, in Roman society, a person who did manual

---

46. Cicero, *De Officiis* 1.42; translated by Walter Miller (New York: Putnam, 1928); electronic book at www.archive.org.
47. Neal Wood, *Cicero's Social and Political Thought* (Berkeley: University of California Press, 1991), 94–100. Note, of course, that this is true only for men. A woman was never considered a full human being in Roman society, regardless of her work or rank. Paul's writing, by embracing the participation and leadership of women, and through his use of the egalitarian baptismal formula quoted in Gal. 3:28, may be considered "subversive" in this regard as well. See Elisabeth Schüssler Fiorenza, *In Memory of Her: A Feminist Theological Reconstruction of Christian Origins* (New York: Crossroad, 1983), chapter 6.

labor to earn a living was not a full human being, the patronage system was the only route to full personhood.

The New Testament Perspective on Patronage

Full personhood and dignity, to Paul, was granted by virtue of baptism (Gal. 3:26-29), rather than by one's social status in the larger culture. These two routes to dignity and personhood were understood by Paul to be diametrically opposed.[48] The *ataktoi* of 2 Thessalonians seem to be attempting to assert their dignity in the Christian community while also maintaining their status and personhood in Roman terms—a bargain that Paul rejects outright.

2 Thessalonians 3:6-15 is by no means unique within the Pauline corpus. Rather, each of Paul's letters attests to his view that the gospel of Jesus Christ demanded the rejection of existing systems of social division and acceptance of the humble "slavery" of the Christian life.[49] In harmony with this countercultural stance toward Roman social structures, we also find many instances where the apostle rejects the patronage system. By way of example, we will look at a few pericopes from 1 Corinthians.

The opening salvo in 1 Corinthians involves Paul's rejection of patron-client relationships with respect to the Corinthian community, and the theme is repeated at several other points in the letter.[50] Paul refuses to acknowledge those who consider themselves his clients, thanking God that "no one can say that you were baptized in my name" (1 Cor. 1:15). He presents an extended defense of his refusal to accept the financial patronage of the Corinthian community (1 Cor. 9:18), and even calls his own economic self-

---

48. E.g., "Has not God made foolish the wisdom of the world" (1 Cor. 1:20)?
49. E.g., 1 Cor. 9:19-22; Gal. 3:28; 5:13-15; Phil. 2:3-8. Some members of the Pauline communities resisted this radical change in social status (see, e.g., 1 Cor. 11:17-22, esp. v. 22.
50. See also 1 Thess. 2:4b-7a. Hollingshead (*Household*, 135–36) argues that 1 Corinthians as a whole "can be read as a critique of patron-client relations."

sufficiency a "ground for boasting" (1 Cor. 9:15). In most of his letters, Paul makes a point of discussing his manual labor (e.g., 1 Thess. 2:9), and goes so far as to describe himself in many places as a "slave," which "would have been demeaning not only to [Paul] himself, but to those who thought themselves either his clients or his patrons, and to the very Roman order itself."[51]

If Cicero and Plutarch are representative of the Roman elite's perspective toward working for a living, then Paul's attitude on the subject must be considered extremely countercultural. He rejects as inimical to the gospel the Corinthians' use of a customary symposium meal for the Lord's Supper (1 Cor. 11:17-34).[52] Participation in such a meal was designed to increase the honor and status of the patron while humiliating the clients—to Paul, an unconscionable practice that flaunted and fostered social status divisions. As Hollingshead remarks, "Roman honor becomes Christian disgrace."[53] In short, Paul seems clearly opposed to the entire patron-client system as contrary to the gospel.[54]

Nor is this perspective unique to 1 Corinthians. In 1 Thessalonians, Paul immediately distances himself from any desire to act as patron or client to the community. He describes his relationship to the community in familial rather than patronage terms (2:7, 11). He insists that all Christians are brothers and sisters, with God as "Father of us [all]" (3:11). Lastly, Paul urges the Thessalonians to demonstrate their love for one another by abandoning participation in the patron-client system: "Aspire to live quietly, to mind your own affairs, and to work with your hands, as we directed you, so that you may behave properly toward outsiders and be dependent on no one" (1

---

51. Hollingshead, *Household*, 129.
52. Ibid., 135. Cf. Gerd Theissen, *The Social Setting of Pauline Christianity: Essays on Corinth*, ed. and trans. John H. Schütz (Philadelphia: Fortress, 1982), 145–74.
53. Hollingshead, *Household*, 135.
54. Ibid., 136. Cf. Winter, "Work," 313–15.

Thess. 4:11-12). Those who fail to do these things, Paul describes as *ataktoi*, "timid" *(oligopsuchoi)*, and "weak" *(asthenoi)*, who must be admonished, encouraged, and helped with patience.

The Patronage System in 2 Thess. 3:6-15

This pericope from 2 Thessalonians takes up the tradition of 1 Thessalonians, outlining a stark contrast between those who are "living in idleness" *(ataktōs peripatountos)* and those who are living "according to the tradition" *(kata tēn paradosin)* established by Paul (3:6). The author defines this "tradition" by Paul's own behavior, reminding his audience that, while in Thessalonica, Paul worked as a laborer to support himself, rather than depending on financial support from the community (3:7-9; cf. 1 Thess. 2:9). By refusing the community's support, Paul placed himself outside of the social conventions of the patron-client institution, implicitly rejecting them. While acknowledging that these social conventions give Paul, as the community's founder and patron, the right to claim ecclesial support, Paul declined this custom and instead engaged in paid labor to support himself (3:9; cf. 1 Thess. 2:5-7). The Thessalonian community should follow this example, imitating Paul in working for pay rather than depending upon others for financial support (3:9, 12).

That this passage refers to the customs of the patronage system may be demonstrated through a careful examination of the language of the text, especially Paul's description of certain members of the community as *ataktoi* and *periergazomenoi* (2 Thess. 3:11).

Ataktoi and *Periergazomenoi*

The term *ataktoi* is unique to the Thessalonian correspondence; three of the four NT uses appear in this passage (1 Thess. 5:14; 2 Thess. 3:6,

7, and 11). This pericope, therefore, has tremendous significance for understanding the biblical usage of the word.[55] Clearly the *ataktoi* in Thessalonica are refusing to work, depending instead upon others for their support. Translations such as "idlers" assume that laziness, rather than ideology, motivates their actions. However, the Greek root *atakt-* can mean any kind of disruptive or antisocial behavior.[56] In other early Christian literature, the word usually means "disorderly" or "insubordinate,"[57] which Ceslas Spicq argues should also be the case here: "The basic meaning of the term is standing against the order of nature or of God. . . . The word was typically used in military contexts to depict someone who would not keep step or follow commands."[58]

Translating *ataktoi* not as "idlers" but "disorderly" or "insubordinate" highlights the group's refusal to work as a flouting of ecclesial or apostolic authority.[59] The decision not to work for a living makes them "insubordinate" to church teachings. Meanwhile, the church is being persecuted by other Thessalonians who oppose those teachings (cf. 2 Thess. 1:4–8). Perhaps the insubordination of the *ataktoi* involves following the ways of the persecutors instead

55. Translators typically render the term as "idlers" (NRSV, NIV) or "loafers," which Jewett suggests are "outmoded translation[s]." The older KJV and Douay-Rheims, by contrast, prefer "disorderly," which may be more correct, as Jewett (*Thessalonian Correspondence*, 105) points out.

56. Collins, *Letters*, 234.

57. William F. Arndt and F. Wilbur Gingrich, *A Greek-English Lexicon of the New Testament and Other Early Christian Literature*, 4th ed. (Chicago: University of Chicago Press, 1957), 119.

58. Ceslas Spicq, "Les Thessaloniciens 'inquiets' étaient-ils des paresseux?" *Studia Theologica* 10 (1956): 1–13. Spicq translates *ataktoi* as *refractaires* (insubordinate); cited in Jewett, *Thessalonian Correspondence*, 104–5.

59. This interpretation is strengthened by the word's context in the Greco-Roman military world to describe one who "steps out of line." See, e.g., Willi Marxsen (*Der erste Brief an die Thessalonicher* [Zurich: Theologischer Verlag, 1979], 62, 72), who argues based upon Paul's appeal in 1 Thess. 5:12 to "respect those who labor among you, and have charge of you in the Lord" that the *ataktoi* are disrespecting the authority of the apostles and of their local leaders; cited in Jewett, *Thessalonian Correspondence*, 105. Cf. Ceslas Spicq, "Les Thessaloniciens 'inquiets' étaient-ils des paresseux?," , cited in Collins, *Letters*, 234.

of the ways of the church, by becoming clients to wealthy patrons. Choosing to participate in the patronage system rather than follow the apostolic example of manual labor for pay may indeed be criticized as "insubordinate" behavior, particularly because this is the second letter to the Thessalonian church that addresses this same issue (cf. 1 Thess. 2:9-12).

Much of the confusion in translating the word *ataktoi* results from Paul's use of the term as an antonym for hard work. However, he also presents the word in parallel with the term *periergazomenoi*. A close examination of this expression can help clear up the confusion surrounding the term *ataktoi*. It also lends support to the claim that the *ataktoi* are participating in the patronage system as clients.

The word *periergazomenoi* is almost universally translated as "busybodies."[60] Where it appears in other Greek texts, the root word *periergos* generally means someone who is meddlesome or curious.[61] It appears to be a clear contrast to Paul's command in 1 Thess. 4:11 to "mind your own affairs, and to work with your hands, as we directed you." A *periergos*, according to 2 Thess. 3:11, is doing neither.

The word *periergazomenoi* is related to the expression *perierchomai*, "to go from place to place" or "wander about."[62] This last expression can cast some light on the social context of the word: to "go from place to place" is a fairly accurate description of what would be expected of a client in the Roman world. If the misconduct of the *ataktoi* comprises their behavior as *periergazomenoi*, then it is quite likely that Paul is referring to participants in the patronage system.

60. Nearly all the English versions translate the word this way. The Douay-Rheims substitutes the expression "curiously meddling." The paraphrased "The Message" Bible eliminates all complexity, and a good deal of accuracy, by condensing the words *ataktoi* and *periergazomenoi* into the expression "a bunch of lazy good-for-nothings."
61. The word appears, for example, to describe the behavior of the young widows in 1 Tim. 5:13.
62. Cf. Job 2:9; Acts 13:6, 19:13; Heb. 11:37.

Patronage and the *Ataktoi*

The *ataktoi* are criticized for violating apostolic instructions by minding other people's affairs; but taking care of someone else's business is precisely what clients in the Roman patronage system are expected to do. Clients had to adjust their lifestyles and daily schedules to those of the patron. "Honoring one's patron was a highly formal and daily routine,"[63] beginning with the *salutatio* first thing in the morning—a practice intended to reinforce the dependency of the client and the power of the patron. "The early morning scramble to the house of the patron was an imposition that put the caller in his place."[64] It was not uncommon for clients to spend a good part of their day in some form of service to the patron. Some might attend meetings of the Senate in their patron's place; others might run errands, conduct business transactions, or simply accompany the patron in daily affairs to ensure a large entourage to promote the patron's prestige. This practice of spending one's day attending to the affairs of the patron was routine for clients; it would leave them little or no time to do any work for themselves.[65] Plutarch advises one young aristocrat against seeking wealth through *clientela* for this reason, because "most public men grow old haunting the doors of other men's houses and leaving their own affairs neglected."[66] Owing to this heavy commitment of time to the patron, clients were unable to work for their own living or to "eat their own bread" (2 Thess.

---

63. Hollingshead, *Household*, 146. Cf. H. H. Scullard, *From the Gracchi to Nero: A History of Rome 133 BC to AD 68* (London: Methuen, 1982), 338.
64. Saller, "Patronage," 57.
65. For example, an artisan who wanted to become someone's client would have to abandon the trade to make enough time in the day to pursue his new "occupation" of waiting on the whims of the patron.
66. Plutarch, *Moralia* 814D; cited in Saller, "Patronage," 58. One occasionally finds women patrons or clients, but this was still unusual in the first century CE. Cf. Hollingshead, *Household*, 146n60.

3:8, 11-12); they were completely dependent upon their patron to provide for their needs.

The patron-client arrangement is often misunderstood by modern commentators as a sort of ancient "welfare system," in which the generous rich provide for the dependent poor.[67] However, this ignores the most central characteristic of the patron-client relationship, its *reciprocity*. Clients became members of their patrons' household and depended upon gifts and favors from their patrons, but patrons also benefited, increasing their prestige and social standing by increasing the number and status of clients in their entourage.[68] Clients had to have sufficient social capital to add to the status of their patrons. The poor and working classes had no social capital to offer potential patrons and thus would be unwelcome as clients.[69]

Since admonitions to earn a living by manual labor would be "unsympathetic and impractical" if no employment could be found,[70] it seems safe to conclude that the *ataktoi* were not suffering from a forced unemployment. "The fundamental problem in the congregation was not that they *could* not work (cf. 1 Thess. 4:11-12), but that certain individuals wished to be clients instead of workers."[71] These higher-status members of the community are *refusing* to compromise their status by engaging in the humbler professions requiring physical labor.

Intertextual evidence supports a claim that the Thessalonian community was marked by such economic diversity. Acts 17

---

67. Bruce Winter, for instance, quotes P. Garnsey (*Food and Famine*) who claims that "without the existence of the institution of patronage, the free poor would not have received their daily bread." (Bruce W. Winter, "'If a Man Does Not Wish to Work . . .': A Cultural and Historical Setting for 2 Thessalonians 3:6-16," *Tyndale Bulletin* 40, No. 2 (1989): 306; cf. 309; henceforth "Work.") Cf. R. Russell, "The Idle in 2 Thess 3:6-12," *New Testament Studies* 34 (1988): 108.
68. Hollingshead, *Household*, 103.
69. See Saller ("Patronage," 52–53) on *clientela* among the leisured classes.
70. Winter, "Work," 304.
71. Green, "¡Patrón!," 85.

mentions upper-class people among the Thessalonian converts: "A great many of the devout Greeks and not a few of the leading women" (17:4), particularly one Jason who hosted the apostles in his home (17:7).[72] When the fledgling church ran afoul of the local authorities, Jason and others are arrested; all pay bail before being released (17:9), which shows their ready access to money. Acts 19:29 and 20:4 also mention a Thessalonian companion of Paul named Aristarchus, and Thessalonian inscriptions attest to a leading citizen by that name during Paul's time.[73] Individuals like Jason, Aristarchus, and the "leading women" were wealthy enough to serve as patrons to members of the community. They also had the kind of social position that would warrant having Roman patrons of their own.

As noted above, a common interpretation of this passage assumes that the *ataktoi* were working-class people who abandoned their gainful labor in favor of idleness, living off the generosity of wealthy church members.[74] A more likely scenario is that the *ataktoi* belonged to a class that simply did not participate in manual labor. The severe limits on social mobility in the Roman Empire made it incredibly difficult for laborers to transcend their social status and become the client of a wealthy patron.[75] Yet the *ataktoi* are numerous enough to be causing a problem in the Thessalonian community. Few (if any) can have been manual laborers who quit work to become clients of the wealthy.

---

72. Acts portrays Jason as the apostles' host; 2 Thess. 3:8 asserts that Paul did not accept anyone's hospitality "without paying for it," which implies that he stayed as a paying boarder rather than a guest. See Green, "¡Patrón!," 94

73. We cannot be sure, of course, that this is the same Aristarchus, but the coincidence is suggestive. See Green, "¡Patrón!," 84.

74. E.g., Jewett, *Thessalonian Correspondence*, 120–21, 104; Beverly Roberts Gaventa, *First and Second Thessalonians*, Interpretation: A Bible Commentary for Teaching & Preaching (Louisville: John Knox Press, 1998), 128.

75. Hollingshead, *Household*, 14.

There is no textual evidence indicating that the *ataktoi* ever engaged in manual labor. Given the limits on social mobility, more likely the *ataktoi* were members of the client class all along, who did not work for a living, rather than workers who were abandoning their labors in favor of becoming clients. Because the author speaks extensively about the value of manual labor, commentators have concluded that the audience must comprise working-class people.[76] As demonstrated above, however, it seems clear that the Thessalonian community included wealthy individuals as well. For them, manual labor would constitute a humiliating reduction in social status. If the author was addressing individuals accustomed to manual labor, why the exhortation to work with their hands? Those who must work for a living are not likely to dispute the regulation that "anyone unwilling to work should not eat" (2 Thess. 3:10). On the other hand, the affluent members of the congregation who participate in the patronage system might well balk at this injunction. To give up their patrons and adopt lives of manual labor would require voluntary acceptance of serious downward mobility on their part—similar to what Paul extolls in the *kenosis* hymn of Phil. 2:6-11. Such a challenging command easily might inspire "insubordination" against the apostle's authority.

The penalty for their disobedience is equally challenging: excommunication. The ruling that "anyone unwilling to work should not eat" (2 Thess. 3:10) should be viewed in the context of the community's *agapē* meal, not one's "daily bread." This excommunication of the *ataktoi* is supported by the injunction to shun them (3:14). Still, they are not to be banished altogether: "Do not regard them as enemies, but warn them as believers" (3:15). These

---

76. E.g., Jewett, *Thessalonian Correspondence*, 120.

disciplinary actions are intended to shame them into correcting their insubordinate behavior (3:14).

Conclusion: Implications for Today's Christians in Empire

Downward mobility is as countercultural in today's world as it was in Paul's. However, traditional interpretations of this passage have watered down its countercultural message, treating it instead as an apostolic ratification of the world's economic and social system. As such, the text has been used to justify profoundly un-Christian behavior and social policies. Commentators writing from the perspective of the cultural elite have made assumptions about the passage that have prevented them recognizing the radically countercultural viewpoint expressed therein.

A thorough examination of the sociohistorical context of this passage reveals a radical, antipatronage viewpoint "corrosive to the existing Roman hierarchy."[77] The author's insistence upon overturning the routine social divisions of the patron–client system effectively challenges the Thessalonian Christians to downward mobility. For a Roman aristocrat, to live as Paul commands would entail a significant loss of power, social status, wealth, and dignity. It would be a humiliating venture. When read through this lens, the challenge to the present-day reader may be much stronger than assumed by prior commentators.

The United States, in its global economic supremacy, political domination, and military hegemony, is the modern world's closest parallel to the ancient Roman Empire. The enormous wealth of the United States (most especially the top 1 percent of its wealth holders) masks an enormous (and growing) global disparity between rich and poor, creating a situation of extreme social divisions much

---

77. Hollingshead, *Household*, 128.

like those Paul consistently rejects in his letters.[78] The upwardly mobile social climbers who utilize a system of social division and disparity to attain personal wealth and status—those whom Paul called *ataktoi*—are still with us today. Members of the upper middle class in this country (including the small percentage of the population holding advanced university degrees) may in fact be uncomfortably similar to the Thessalonian *ataktoi* both in behavior and attitude.

If Paul rejects the fundamental building block of his own society, and asks his readers to do the same, what might be an appropriate analogy for living Paul's commands in today's context? What does "downward mobility" mean to a middle-class Christian living in the United States? To reject the dominant paradigm of our society, as Paul does of his own, may require embracing loss of power, social status, wealth, and dignity. It certainly could mean humiliation.

There is some precedent, however, for the model of "downward mobility." The Christian community always has had a vocal minority who reject the status quo insofar as it creates false divisions between people.[79] Those who understand a rejection of the dominant system to be a fundamental component of Christian discipleship will find much to support their understanding in this discussion of 2 Thess. 3:6-15. In addition, the instructions to the *ataktoi* may serve as guidelines for an alternative way of being church in the midst of a status-hungry society. "To seek to 'negate' the discourses and practices of the dominant culture," writes scholar-activist Ched

---

78. North America, with only 4.5 percent of the global population, currently controls a full 32.8 percent of global household wealth, while 1 percent of the global population controls 46 percent of all wealth worldwide. Approximately 1 percent of the world's resources are divided among the lower half of the global population. Credit Suisse Research Institute, *Global Wealth Report 2013* (Credit Suisse Research Institute, October 2013; https://www.credit-suisse.com/ch/en/news-and-expertise/research/credit-suisse-research-institute/publications.html), 10-11.

79. E.g., mendicant orders, Beguines, and Anabaptists, along with modern lay movements such as the Catholic Worker or New Monastic communities, have chosen countercultural lifestyles in obedience to the gospel.

Myers, "presumes that there is some other discursive and practical place to stand." This "other place," for Myers, is the gospel concept of the kingdom of God, a vision for the church that many consider to be no more than a "dangerous memory."[80]

Second Thessalonians' rejection of the patronage system and censure of the *ataktoi* continues to inspire those who honor the "dangerous memory" of Paul's gospel. Likewise, the call to egalitarian downward mobility poses a stark challenge for those who hope to maintain social power and status while still calling themselves Christian. For those who reject the dominant paradigm, Paul's words encourage their efforts to live as Christians in the hope of a radically subversive kingdom of God.

---

80. Ched Myers, *Who Will Roll Away the Stone? Discipleship Queries for First World Christians* (Maryknoll, NY: Orbis, 1994), 163.

Contributors

Mary Ann Beavis, Ph.D. (Cambridge University), is professor in the Department of Religion and Culture, St. Thomas More College, University of Saskatchewan (Saskatoon, Canada). Her recent book-length publications include a commentary on the Gospel of Mark (Ada, MI: Baker Academic, 2011), *Jesus and Utopia: Looking for the Kingdom of God in the Roman World* (Minneapolis: Fortress Press, 2006), as well as many peer-reviewed articles and two edited works, *Feminist Theology with a Canadian Accent: Canadian Perspectives on Contextual Feminist Theology* (Toronto: Novalis, 2008), and *The Lost Coin: Parables of Women, Word and Wisdom* (Sheffield, UK: Sheffield Academic, 2002). Her most recent book, which she coauthored with HyeRan Kim-Cragg, is the volume on Hebrews for the Wisdom series of feminist biblical commentaries (Collegeville,MN: Liturgical Press, 2015). Professor Beavis is the founding editor of two academic journals, the *Canadian Journal of Urban Research* and *The Journal of Religion and Popular Culture.*

Carol J. Dempsey, OP, Ph.D. (Catholic University of America, 1994), has expertise in the Old and New Testaments and the biblical languages. Among her major publications are *Isaiah: God's Poet of*

Light (Atlanta: Chalice, 2010), *Justice: A Biblical Perspective* (Atlanta: Chalice, 2008), and *Jeremiah: Preacher of Grace, Poet of Truth* (Collegeville, MN: Liturgical, 2007). She recently published a series of eighteen lectures on CDs, *Understanding Old Testament Prophets* (Now You Know Media, 2010). She is the lead editor and a contributor to an exciting new interdisciplinary series for Orbis Books entitled Theology in Dialogue. Dr. Dempsey also serves on the editorial boards for the *Journal of Catholic Higher Education* and *Dominican Studies*. Professor Dempsey has been a Dominican for thirty-five years and has two little parrotlets, Kelli Mae and Kristi Belle, and a zebra finch, Holly.

Susan M. (Elli) Elliott, Ph.D. (Loyola University Chicago), is a writer, workshop leader and environmental activist based in Red Lodge, Montana, who currently is organizing a grassroots think tank in the Big Sky Region. She is the author of *Cutting Too Close for Comfort: Paul's Letter to the Galatians in Its Anatolian Cultic Context*, Library of New Testament Studies 248 (T & T Clark, 2003, 2008). Her current book project, *Family Empires,* investigates family relationships and metaphors in the construction of the Roman Empire, and early Christian experimentation in constructing alternative visions of "Empire" by reconstructing familial relationships. Her articles and reviews have appeared in the *Journal of Biblical Literature, Biblical Research, Semeia, Listening, Catholic Biblical Quarterly, Bryn Mawr Classical Review, The 4th R,* and in dictionaries of the Bible.

Bradley C. Gregory, Ph.D. (University of Notre Dame, 2009), is assistant professor of Scripture at the University of Scranton. He is the author of *Like an Everlasting Signet Ring: Generosity in the Book* *of Sirach* (Berlin/Boston: Walter de Gruyter, 2010) as well as various articles on Sirach and Second Temple Judaism. His research interests include biblical ethics, hermeneutics, and the development of the wisdom tradition. He lives with his wife, Mendy, and two children in Scranton, Pennsylvania.

Ma. Marilou S. Ibita, Ph.D. (Katholieke Universiteit Leuven, 2012), serves as lecturer at the Institute of Formation and Religious Studies in Quezon City, Philippines, and postdoctoral researcher of New Testament exegesis at the Faculty of Theology and Religious Studies, Katholieke Universiteit Leuven. Her doctoral dissertation is entitled "If Anyone Hungers, He/She Must Eat in the House" (1Cor 11:34): A Narrative-Critical, Socio-Historical, and Grammatical-Philological Analysis of the Story of the Lord's Supper in Corinth (1Cor 11:17–34)". Her latest publication is "A Conversation with the Story of the Lord's Supper in Corinth (1Cor 11:17–34): Engaging the Scripture Text and the Filipino Christians' Context" in *1 & 2 Corinthians*, ed. Yung Suk Kim (Texts @ Contexts; Minneapolis: Fortress Press, 2013). Her research interests include the Pauline letters, the Gospel of Luke, meals and famine in antiquity and in the biblical accounts, as well as the relationship of material evidence and the study of the New Testament.

Linda Maloney, Th.D. (Eberhard-Karls-Universität Tübingen), is a priest of the Episcopal Diocese of Vermont. She studied New Testament theology at the University of Tübingen under the supervision of Prof. Dr. Gerhard Lohfink and was the first woman to receive the Th.D. in Scripture Studies (in 1990) from the Catholic faculty at Tübingen.

J. L. Manzo, SSL (Pontifical Gregorian University in Rome), Ph.D. (Catholic University of America), holds a License in Sacred Scripture and the Ph.D. in theology, with a specialty in Hebrew Scripture. Her doctoral dissertation concerns the traditional-historical background of the imagery surrounding the personification of wisdom in Sirach 24. Professor Manzo currently serves as associate professor of Scripture at the University of St. Thomas in Houston, Texas.

Sheila E. McGinn, Ph.D. (Northwestern University, 1989), currently holds the post of professor and chair in the Department of Theology and Religious Studies at John Carroll University, the Jesuit university in Cleveland, Ohio. A frequent lecturer and author of numerous articles and books, her main area of interest concerns the development of the earliest churches (including "dissenting" movements) and of early Christian writings in their social and cultural environments. Her works include commentaries on the Gospel according to Matthew, the Montanist Oracles, and the Acts of Thecla; a comprehensive bibliography on the book of Revelation; studies on several letters in the Pauline corpus, most recently Paul's letter to the Romans; as well as works on engaged methods of pedagogy. Currently writing the *Wisdom Commentary on Romans* (Collegeville, Minn.: Liturgical Press, 2015) and a survey of the first Christian century (Winona, Minn.: Anselm Academic, 2014), she also serves as general editor of *Conversations with the Biblical World: Proceedings of the Eastern Great Lakes Biblical Society and the Midwest Region Society of Biblical Literature.* Professor McGinn lives in Cleveland with her two college-age children.

Lai Ling Elizabeth Ngan, Ph.D. (Golden Gate Baptist Theological Seminary, 1991), holds the post of associate professor of

Christian Scriptures at the George W. Truett Theological Seminary of Baylor University, in Waco, Texas. She is a native of Hong Kong and came to the United States in her late teens. Her research interests and commitment to social justice and racial and gender equality are shaped by her experience as a Chinese-American woman, as well as the experiences of other Asian-American immigrants. A frequent speaker in churches and conferences, Professor Ngan is the author of several commentaries and articles on the prophets and women in the Hebrew Bible.

Kathleen M. O'Connor, Ph.D. (Princeton Theological Seminary, 1984), is the William Marcellus McPheeters Professor of Old Testament at Columbia Theological Seminary in Decatur, Georgia. Author of several books and essays relating to biblical interpretation, her recent volume, *Shaking Heaven and Earth: Essays in Honor of Walter Brueggemann and Charles B. Cousar, Lamentations and the Tears of the World* (Maryknoll, NY: Orbis, 2002) received the first place award for Scripture from the Catholic Press Association in 2003.

Ahida E. Calderón Pilarski, Ph.D. (Lutheran School of Theology at Chicago, 2008), holds the post of associate professor of theology at Saint Anselm College, Manchester, New Hampshire. A native of Perú, she works in the areas of feminist studies and Latin American hermeneutics. Professor Pilarski has several essays on various topics relating to feminist hermeneutics, Latino/a Studies, biblical interpretation, particularly of the Hebrew Bible, as well as two forthcoming books, *Introducción al Pentateuco en Perspectiva Latinoamericana*, coedited with Alejandro F. Botta (Estella [Navarra]: Editorial Verbo Divino, 2014) and the commentary on Jeremiah in the Wisdom Commentary Series (Collegeville, MN: Liturgical, 2016).

Christine Vladimiroff, OSB, Ph.D. (Universidad Internacional, Mexico), Prioress of the Benedictine Sisters of Erie, Pennsylvania, is a past Executive Director of Second Harvest, a nonprofit, anti-hunger advocacy group. In August of 2003, Sr. Christine was elected into the presidency of the Leadership Conference of Women Religious (LCWR) and served in the presidency from August 2003 to August 2006. She has served on the National Board for Bread for the World and chaired the Board for three years (2000–2003), and also, on the National Council of Pax Christi (USA). Sr. Christine was the US delegate and co-chaired the Food Security Committee of the United Nations Food and Agricultural Organization in Rome, Italy (1996–2000).

Lauress L. Wilkins, Ph.D. (Boston University, 2005), serves as associate professor of religious studies and director of the Honors Program at Regis College in Weston, Massachusetts. A 1978 graduate of Smith College majoring in Latin American studies, she earned her M.Div. at Boston University in 1988, followed by the Ph.D. in Hebrew Bible at the same institution. Her commitment to social justice and community service has recently led her on international mission trips to Villa el Salvador, Peru and Port-au-Prince, Haiti. Professor Wilkins's publications include *The Book of Lamentations and the Social World of Judah in the Neo-Babylonian Era* (Piscataway, NJ: Gorgias, 2010).

Megan T. Wilson-Reitz, M.A. (John Carroll University, 2010), is part of the Cleveland Catholic Worker extended community, a mother of two putative Christian radicals, and a lecturer in theology and religious studies at John Carroll University. She presents workshops and retreats on the themes of nonviolence, economic justice, and radical discipleship in Scripture.

Select Bibliography

Aasgaard, Reidar. *"My Beloved Brothers and Sisters!" Christian Siblingship in Paul.* JSNTSup 265. New York: T & T Clark, 2004.

Adams, Edward. "Paul's Story of God and Creation: The Story of How God Fulfills His Purposes in Creation." In *Narrative Dynamics in Paul: A Critical Assessment,* edited by Bruce W. Longenecker, 19–43. Louisville: Westminster John Knox, 2002.

Alter, Robert. *Genesis: Translation and Commentary.* New York: W. W. Norton, 1996.

Anderson, Bernhard W. "The Tower of Babel: Unity and Diversity in God's Creation." In *From Creation to New Creation: Old Testament Perspectives.* OBT. Minneapolis: Fortress Press, 1994.

Arnal, William E. "The Rhetoric of Marginality: Apocalypticism, Gnosticism, and Sayings Gospels." *HTR* 88 (1995): 471–94.

Arndt, William F. and F. Wilbur Gingrich. *A Greek-English Lexicon of the New Testament and Other Early Christian Literature.* 4th ed. Chicago: University of Chicago Press, 1957.

Avorti, Solomon. "Genesis 11:1–9: An African Perspective." In *Return to Babel: Global Perspectives on the Bible,* edited by Priscilla Pope-Levinson and John R. Levinson, 17–26. Louisville: Westminster John Knox, 1999.

Baden, Joel S. "The Tower of Babel: A Case Study in the Competing Methods of Historical and Modern Literary Criticism." *JBL* 128 (2009): 209–24.

Baker, David L. *Tight Fists or Open Hands? Wealth and Poverty in Old Testament Law*. Grand Rapids: Eerdmans, 2009.

Bandstra, Barry. *Genesis 1–11: A Handbook on the Hebrew Text*. Baylor Handbook on the Hebrew Bible. Waco, TX: Baylor University Press, 2008.

Barré, Michael L. "Fasting in Isaiah 58:1-12: A Reexamination." *BTB* 15 (1985): 94–97.

Barrett, C. K. *A Commentary on the First Epistle to the Corinthians*. BNTC. Peabody, MA: Hendrickson, 1968.

Barton, Stephen C. "Paul's Sense of Place: An Anthropological Approach to Community Formation." *NTS* 32 (1986): 225–46.

Beard, Robert. "1936 Constitution of the U.S.S.R." 1996. http://www.departments.bucknell.edu/russian/const/1936toc.html.

Beavis, Mary Ann. *Mark*. Paideia Commentaries on the New Testament. Grand Rapids: Baker Academic, 2011.

Beckman, David. *Exodus from Hunger: We Are Called to Change the Politics of Hunger*. Louisville: Westminster John Knox, 2010.

Ben-Dov, Jonathan. "The Poor's Curse: Exodus XXII 20-26 and Curse Literature in the Ancient World." *VT* 56 (2006): 431–51.

Benedict XVI. *Caritas in Veritate*. http://www.vatican.va/holy_father/benedict_xvi/encyclicals/documents/hf_ben-xvi_enc_20090629_caritas-in-veritate_en.html.

Berger, Peter and Thomas Luckmann. *The Social Construction of Reality: A Treatise in the Sociology of Knowledge*. Garden City: Doubleday, 1967.

Blenkinsopp, Joseph. *Isaiah 56–60: A New Translation with Introduction and Commentary*. AB 19B. New York: Doubleday, 2003.

Blessing, Kamila. "The 'Confusion Technique' of Milton Erickson as Hermeneutic for Biblical Parables." *Journal of Psychology and Christianity* 21 (2002): 161–68.

Blue, Bradley B. "The House Church at Corinth and the Lord's Supper: Famine, Food Supply and the Present Distress." *Criswell Theological Review* 5 (1991): 221–239.

Boadt, Lawrence. Review of *The Old Testament: Canon, Literature and Theology: Collected Essays of John Barton*, by John Barton. *CBQ* 71 (2009): 665–66.

Bookidis, Nancy. "Religion in Corinth: 146 BCE to 100 CE." In *Urban Religion in Corinth: Interdisciplinary Approaches*, edited by Daniel N. Schowalter and Steven J. Friesen, 141–64. HTS 53. Cambridge, MA: Harvard University Press, 2005.

Booth, Wayne. *The Rhetoric of Fiction*. 2nd ed. Chicago: University of Chicago Press, 1983.

Boring, M. Eugene. *Mark: A Commentary*. NTL. Minneapolis: Fortress Press, 2006.

Box, G. H. and W. O. E. Oesterley. "The Book of Sirach." In *The Apocrypha and Pseudepigrapha of the Old Testament in English, with Introductions and Critical and Explanatory Notes to the Several Books*, edited by R. H. Charles, 268–517. 2 vols. Oxford: Clarendon, 1913.

Braund, David. "Function and Dysfunction: Personal Patronage in Roman Imperialism." In *Patronage in Ancient Society*, edited by Andrew Wallace-Hadrill, 137–52. London: Routledge, 1989.

Bread for the World Institute, "2014 Hunger Report." http://notes.bread.org/religion/.

Brueggemann, Walter. *Deuteronomy*. Nashville: Abingdon, 2001.

———. *An Unsettling God: The Heart of the Hebrew Bible*. Minneapolis: Fortress Press, 2009.

Callahan, A. "'No Rhyme or Reason': The Hidden Logia of the *Gospel of Thomas*." *HTR* 90 (1997): 411–26.

Campbell, Douglas A. "The Story of Jesus in Romans and Galatians." In *Narrative Dynamics in Paul: A Critical Assessment*, edited by Bruce W. Longenecker, 97–124. Louisville: Westminster John Knox, 2002.

Carroll, Robert P. *The Book of Jeremiah*. OTL. Philadelphia: Westminster, 1986.

Casey, Damien. "The 'Fractio Panis' and the Eucharist as Eschatological Banquet." *McAuley University Electronic Journal* (18 Aug 2002). http://www.womenpriests.org/theology/casey_02.asp.

CBC News. "World Hunger 'Intolerable,' with Scant Progress in Decade: UN." http://www.cbc.ca/news/world/world-hunger-intolerable-with-scant-progress-in-decade-un-1.611024#skip300x250; modified 30 Oct 2006.

Chatman, Seymour. *Story and Discourse: Narrative Structure in Fiction and Film*. Ithaca, NY: Cornell University Press, 1978.

Churches Together: Supporting Station 20 West. http://ecumenism.net/archive/2010/11/churches_together_supporting_station_20_west.htm.

Cicero. *De Officiis*. Translated by Walter Miller. LCL. New York: G. P. Putnam's Sons, 1928.

Collins, Raymond F. *First Corinthians*. SP 7. Collegeville: Liturgical Press, 1999.

———, ed. *The Thessalonian Correspondence*. Leuven: Leuven University Press, 1990.

Conzelmann, Hans. *1 Corinthians: A Commentary on the First Epistle to the Corinthians*. Translated by James W. Leitch. Hermeneia. Philadelphia: Fortress Press, 1975.

Corley, Jeremy. "Searching for Structure and Redaction in Ben Sira: An Investigation of Beginnings and Endings." In *The Wisdom of Ben Sira: Studies on Tradition, Redaction, and Theology*, edited by Angelo Passaro and Giuseppe Belllia, 21–48. Deuterocanonical and Cognate Literature Studies 1. Berlin: Walter de Gruyter, 2008.

Corley, Kathleen. *Private Women, Public Meals: Social Conflict in the Synoptic Tradition.* Peabody, MA: Hendrickson, 1993.

Crenshaw, James. "The Primacy of Listening in Ben Sira's Pedagogy." In *Wisdom You Are My Sister: Studies in Honor of Roland E. Murphy, O.Carm., on the Occasion of His Eightieth Birthday,* edited by M. L. Barré, 172–87. CBQMS 29. Washington, DC: Catholic Biblical Association of America, 1997.

Croatto, J. Severino. "A Reading of the Story of the Tower of Babel from the Perspective of Non-Identity: Gen 11:1–9 in the Context of Its Production." In *Teaching the Bible: The Discourses and Politics of Biblical Pedagogy,* edited by Fernando F. Segovia and Mary Ann Tolbert, 203–23. Minneapolis: Fortress Press, 2009.

Crossan, John Dominic. *The Historical Jesus: The Life of a Mediterranean Jewish Peasant.* New York: HarperCollins, 1992.

Crossan, John Dominic and Jonathan L. Reed. *In Search of Paul: How Jesus' Apostle Opposed Rome's Empire with God's Kingdom.* New York: Harper Collins, 2005.

Crüsemann, Frank. *The Torah: Theology and Social History of Old Testament Law.* Edinburgh: T & T Clark, 1992.

Davies, James, *et al. The World Distribution of Household Wealth: Discussion Paper No. 2008/03.* Feb. 2008. Http://www.wider.unu.edu/publications/working-papers/discussion-papers/2008/en_GB/dp2008-03/.

Davies, Stevan L. "The Christology and Protology of the Gospel of Thomas." *JBL* 111 (1992): 663–82.

DeConick, April D. *The Original Gospel of Thomas in Translation: With a Commentary and New English Translation of the Complete Gospel.* LNTS 287. New York: T & T Clark, 2007.

DeSilva, David A. "The Wisdom of Ben Sira: Honor, Shame, and the Maintenance of the Values of a Minority Culture." *CBQ* 58 (1996): 433–55.

The Didascalia Apostolorum in English. Translated by Margaret Dunlop Gibson. New York: Cambridge University Press, 2011.

Donahue, John R. and Daniel J. Harrington. *The Gospel of Mark.* SP 2. Collegeville: Liturgical Press, 2002.

Donfried, Karl P. "The Feeding Narratives and the Markan Community: Mark 6,30–45 and 8,1–10." In *Kirche: Festschrift für Günther Bornkamm zum 75. Geburtstag,* edited by D. Lührmann and G. Strecker, 95–103. Tübingen: Mohr Siebeck, 1980.

———. "The Theology of 1 Thessalonians." In *The Theology of the Shorter Pauline Letters,* edited by Karl Donfried and I. Howard Marshall, 1–80. New York: Cambridge University Press, 1993.

Doran, Robert. *Hellenistiches Judentum in römischer Zeit, ausgenommen Philon und Josephus.* ANRW II.20.1. Berlin & New York: Walter de Gruyter, 1987.

———. "Jewish Education in the Seleucid Period." In *Second Temple Studies III: Studies in Politics, Class, and Material Culture,* edited by Philip R. Davis and John M. Halligan, 116–32. JSOTSup 340. London, Sheffield: 2002.

Douglas, J. D., Robert K. Brown, and Philip W. Comfort. *The New Greek-English Interlinear New Testament.* Carol Stream, IL: Tyndale House, 1990.

Dube, Musa W. *Postcolonial Feminist Interpretation of the Bible.* St. Louis: Chalice, 2000.

Dunn, James D. G. *The Theology of Paul the Apostle.* Edinburgh: T & T Clark, 1998.

Dunn, James D. G. and John William Rogerson. *Eerdmans Commentary on the Bible.* Grand Rapids: Eerdmans, 2003.

Eberharter, Andreas. *Das Buch Jesus Sirach oder Ecclesiasticus.* Bonn: Hanstein, 1925.

Elliot, J. K., ed. "The Pseudo-Clementine Literature." In *The Apocryphal New Testament: A Collection of Apocryphal Christian Literature in an English Translation Based on M. R. James*, 431–38. Oxford: Oxford University Press, 2005.

Elliott, Neil. *Liberating Paul: The Justice of God and the Politics of the Apostle*. Maryknoll, NY: Orbis, 1994.

Elliott, Susan M. "Probing and Prompting." The Listening Resource, Oct. 1, 2012. http://www.qualitative-researcher.com/listening/probing-and-prompting/

End Poverty 2015 Millennium Campaign. http://www.endpoverty2015.org/.

Eriksson, Anders. *Traditions as Rhetorical Proof: Pauline Argumentation in 1 Corinthians*. ConBNT 29. Stockholm: Almqvist & Wicksell International, 1998.

Fee, Gordon D. *The First Epistle to the Corinthians*. NICNT. Grand Rapids: Eerdmans, 1987.

Fehribach, Adeline, Gerald Caron and Aldina Da Silva. *The Women in the Life of the Bridegroom: A Feminist Historical-Literary Analysis of the Female Characters in the Fourth Gospel*. Collegeville: Liturgical Press, 1998.

Felder, Cain Hope. "2 Thessalonians." In *True to Our Native Land: An African American New Testament Commentary*, edited by Brian K. Blount, 404–8. Minneapolis: Fortress Press, 2007.

Fitzmyer, Joseph A. *First Corinthians: A New Translation with Introduction and Commentary*. AB 32. New Haven: Yale University Press, 2008.

Fokkelman, J. P. *Narrative Art in Genesis: Specimens of Stylistic and Structural Analysis*. SSN 17. Assen: Van Gorcum, 1975.

Fowler, Robert M. *Loaves and Fishes: The Function of Feeding Stories in the Gospel of Mark*. SBLDS 54. Chico, CA: Scholars Press, 1981.

Fox, Everett. *The Five Books of Moses: Genesis, Exodus, Leviticus, Numbers, Deuteronomy. A New Translation with Introductions, Commentary, and Notes.* Schocken Bible 1. New York: Schocken, 1995.

Fox, Michael V. *Proverbs 1–9: A New Translation with Introduction and Commentary.* AB 18A. New York: Doubleday, 2000.

Freire, Paulo. *Pedagogy of the Oppressed.* Translated by Myra Bergman Ramos. New York: Seabury, 1974.

Fretheim, Terence. *Jeremiah.* Smyth & Helwys Bible Commentary. Macon, GA: Smyth & Helwys, 2002.

Friesen, Steven J. "Poverty in Pauline Studies: Beyond the So-Called New Consensus." *JSNT* 26 (2004): 323–61.

Friesen, Steven J. "Prospects for a Demography of the Pauline Mission: Corinth among the Churches." In *Urban Religion in Corinth: Interdisciplinary Approaches,* edited by Daniel N. Schowalter and Steve J. Friesen, 351–70. HTS 53. Cambridge, MA: Harvard University Press, 2005.

Funk, Robert W. and Roy W. Hoover, eds. *The Five Gospels: The Search for the Authentic Words of Jesus.* New York: MacMillan, 1993.

Garnsey, Peter. *Famine and Food Supply in the Græco-Roman World: Responses to Risk and Crisis.* New York: Cambridge University Press, 1988.

Gaventa, Beverly Roberts. *1 and 2 Thessalonians.* IBC. Louisville: John Knox, 1998.

Gerlak, Andrea K. and Margaret Wilder. "Exploring the Textured Landscape of Water Insecurity and the Human Right to Water." *Environment: Science and Policy for Sustainable Development* (March–April 2012): 4–17.

Gilbert, Maurice. "Prêt, aumône et caution." In *Der Einzelne und seine Gemeinschaft bei Ben Sira,* edited by R. Egger-Wenzel and I. Krammer, 179–89. BZAW 270. Berlin: Walter de Gruyter, 1998.

Goodacre, Mark. *Thomas and the Gospels: The Case for Thomas's Familiarity with the Synoptics.* Grand Rapids: Eerdmans, 2012.

Green, Eugenio L. "¡Patrón! La Clientela en Tesalónica Romana." *Kairós* 43 (2008): 79–86.

Greenfield, Jonas. "Two Proverbs of Ahiqar." In *Lingering over Words: Studies in the Ancient Near Eastern Literature in Honor of William L. Moran*, edited by T. Abusch, J. Huehnergard, and P. Steinkeller, 195–201. HSS 37. Atlanta: Scholars Press, 1990.

Gregory, Bradley C. *Like an Everlasting Signet Ring: Generosity in the Book of Sirach*. Deuterocanonical and Cognate Literature Studies 2. Berlin: Walter de Gruyter, 2010.

Gundry Volf, Judith M. *Paul and Perseverance: Staying In and Falling Away*. WUNT 2/37. Tübingen: Mohr Siebeck, 1990.

Gunkel, Hermann. *Genesis*. Translated by Mark Biddle. Mercer Library of Biblical Studies. 3rd ed. Macon, GA: Mercer University Press, 1910, 1997.

Gutiérrez, Gustavo. *On Job: God Talk and the Suffering of the Innocent*. Translated by Matthew J. O'Connell. Maryknoll, NY: Orbis, 1987.

Harper, Dan. "2009 in Review: Trends and Possibilities I'll Be Watching in 2010." *Yet Another Unitarian Universalist, Vol. 1* (blog), Dec. 28, 2009. http://www.danielharper.org/blog/?p=6133.

Hays, Richard B. *The Faith of Jesus Christ: An Investigation of the Narrative Substructure of Galatians 3:1—4:11*. SBLDS 56. Chico, CA: Scholars Press, 1983.

———. *First Corinthians*. IBC. Louisville: John Knox, 1997.

Henderson, Suzanne Watts. "'If Anyone Hungers . . . ' An Integrated Reading of 1 Cor 11:17-34." *NTS* 48 (2002): 195–208.

Hendrix, Holland Lee. "Archaeology and Eschatology at Thessalonica." In *The Future of Christianity: Essays in Honor of Helmut Koester*, edited by Birger A. Pearson, 107–18. Minneapolis: Fortress Press, 1991.

Herzog, William R, II. *Parables as Subversive Speech: Jesus as Pedagogue of the Oppressed*. Louisville: Westminster John Knox, 1994.

Hiebert, Theodore. "The Tower of Babel and the Origin of the World's Cultures." *JBL* 126 (2007): 29–58.

Higgins, A. J. B. *The Historicity of the Fourth Gospel*. London: Lutterworth, 1960.

Hippolytus. *Philosophumena*. Translated by Francis Legge. San Diego, CA: Ulan, 2012.

Hofius, Otfried. "The Lord's Supper and the Lord's Supper Tradition: Reflections on 1 Corinthians 11:23b-25." In *One Loaf, One Cup: Ecumenical Studies of 1Cor 11 and Other Eucharistic Texts; The Cambridge Conference on the Eucharist August 1988*, edited by Ben F. Meyer, 75–115. NGS 6. Macon, GA: Mercer University Press, 1993.

———. "Unknown Sayings of Jesus." In *The Gospel and the Gospels*, edited by Peter Stuhlmacher, 336–60. Grand Rapids: Eerdmans, 1991.

Holland, Glenn. "Paul's Use of Irony as a Rhetorical Technique." In *The Rhetorical Analysis of Scripture: Essays from the 1995 London Conference*, edited by Stanley E. Porter and Thomas H. Olbricht, 234–48. JSNTSup 146. London: Sheffield Academic, 1997.

Hollingshead, James. *The Household of Caesar and the Body of Christ: A Political Interpretation of the Letters from Paul*. Lanham, MD: University Press of America, 1998.

Hoppe, Leslie J. *There Shall Be No Poor Among You: Poverty in the Bible*. Nashville: Abingdon, 2004.

Horrell, David G. *The Social Ethos of the Corinthian Correspondence: Interest and Ideology from 1 Corinthians to 1 Clement*. SNTSU. Edinburgh: T & T Clark, 1996.

Horsley, Richard and Patrick Tiller. "Ben Sira and the Sociology of the Second Temple." In *Second Temple Studies III: Studies in Politics, Class, and Material Culture*, edited by Philip R. Davis and John M. Halligan, 74–107. JSOTSup 340. London: Sheffield, 2002.

Huarte, Mercedes. "La Segunda Carta a los Tesalonicenses: El Problema de su Autenticidad: Claves para la Interpretación." *Estudios Eclesiásticos* 75 (2000): 79–100.

Hughes, Anne-Marie. "Marchers Walk Saskatoon's Food Desert." *Prairie Messenger*, Oct. 26 2011.

"Hunger up 21% in Latest Self-Rated SWS Poverty Survey." *Philippine Daily Inquirer*, Sept. 29, 2012. http://newsinfo.inquirer.net/279278/hunger-up-21-in-latest-self-rated-sws-poverty-survey#sthash.Th8ZJtAb.dpuf.

Isasi-Díaz, Ada María. "Communication as Communion: Elements in a Hermeneutic of *lo cotidiano*." In *Engaging the Bible in a Gendered World: An Introduction to Feminist Biblical Interpretation in Honor of Katharine Doob Sakenfeld*, edited by Linda Day and Carolyn Pressler, 27–36. Louisville: Westminster John Knox, 2007.

Jacobs, Jill. *There Shall Be No Needy: Pursuing Social Justice through Jewish Law and Tradition*. Woodstock: Jewish Lights, 2009.

Janowski, B. "JHWH und der Sonnengott: Aspekte der Solarisierung JHWHs in vorexilischer Zeit." In *Pluralismus und Identität*, edited by J. Mehlhausen, 214–41. Gütersloh: Gütersloher, 1995.

Jeremias, Joachim. *The Eucharistic Words of Jesus*. NTL. London: SCM, 1966.

———. *New Testament Theology*. London: SCM, 1984.

———. *The Parables of Jesus*. London: SCM, 1972.

———. *Unbekannte Jesusworte*. Gütersloh: Gerd Mohn, 1963.

Jewett, Robert. *The Thessalonian Correspondence: Pauline Rhetoric and Millenarian Piety*. Philadelphia: Fortress Press, 1986.

John XXIII. *Pacem in Terris* (Peace on Earth). Http://www.vatican.va/holy_father/john_xxiii/encyclicals/documents/hf_j-xxiii_enc_11041963_pacem_en.html.

Judge, E. A. "The Decrees of Caesar at Thessalonica." *Reformed Theological Review* 30 (1971): 2–7.

Junior, Nyasha. "Womanist Biblical Interpretation." In *Engaging the Bible in a Gendered World: An Introduction to Feminist Biblical Interpretation in Honor of Katharine Doob Sakenfeld*, edited by Linda Day and Carolyn Pressler, 37–46. Louisville: Westminster John Knox, 2007.

Justin Martyr. *Dialogue with Trypho.* Translated by Thomas B. Falls. Washington, DC: Catholic University of America Press, 2003.

Kaiser, Walter C., Jr. "Leviticus." *NIB*, 1:1133. Nashville, TN: Abingdon, 1994.

Käsemann, Ernst. "The Pauline Doctrine of the Lord's Supper." In *Essays on New Testament Themes*, translated by W. J. Montague, 108–35. SBT 41. London: SCM, 1964.

Kieweler, Hans-Volker. "Benehmen bei Tisch." In *Der Einzelne und seine Gemeinschaft bei Ben Sira*, edited by R. Egger-Wenzel and I. Krammer, 191–215. BZAW 270. Berlin: Walter de Gruyter, 1998.

Kim, Yung Suk. *Christ's Body in Corinth: The Politics of a Metaphor.* Paul in Critical Contexts. Minneapolis: Fortress Press, 2008.

King, Karen. "Kingdom in the Gospel of Thomas." *Forum, Foundations and Facets* 3 (1987): 48-97.

Klauck, Hans-Josef. *Das Herrenmahl unde hellenistischer Kult: Eine religiongeschichtliche Untersuchung zum ersten Korintherbrief.* NTAbh 15. Münster: Aschendorff, 1982.

Klinghardt, Matthias. *Gemeinschaftsmahl und Mahlgemeinschaft: Soziologie und Liturgie frühchristlicher Mahlfeiern.* Texte und Arbeiten zum neuetestamentlichen Zeitalter 13. Basel: Francke, 1996.

Knight, George A. E. *The New Israel: A Commentary on the Book of Isaiah 55–66.* ITC. Grand Rapids: Eerdmans, 1985.

Koehler, Ludwig, Walter Baumgartner, and Johann Jakob Stamm. *The Hebrew and Aramaic Lexicon of the Old Testament.* Translated by M. E. J. Richardson. 3 vols. Leiden: Brill, 1994.

Kuck, David W. *Judgment and Community Conflict: Paul's Use of Apocalyptic Judgment Language in 1 Corinthians 3:5—4:5.* NovTSup 66. New York: Brill, 1992.

LaCocque, André. "Whatever Happened in the Valley of Shinar? A Response to Theodore Hiebert." *JBL* 128 (2009): 29–41.

Lampe, Peter. "The Corinthian Dinner Party: Exegesis of a Cultural Context." *Affirmation* 4 (1991): 1–15.

———. "The Eucharist: Identifying with Christ on the Cross." *Int* 48 (1994): 36–49.

Lau, W. *Schriftgelehrte Prophetie in Jes 56–66: Eine Untersuchung zu den literarischen Bezügen in den letzten elf Kapiteln des Jesajabuches.* BZAW 225. Berlin: De Gruyter, 1994.

Legaspi, Leanardo Z., et al. "To Live in Memory of Him: One Body, One People—A Pastoral Letter on the Eucharist." Catholic Bishops' Conference of the Philippines, Mar. 21, 1988.

Lenski, Gerhard. *Power and Privilege: A Theory of Social Stratification.* New York: McGraw-Hill, 1966.

Lichtheim, Miriam. *Ancient Egyptian Literature*, vol. 1: *The Old and Middle Kingdoms.* Berkeley: University of California Press, 1973.

Liew, Tat-siong Benny and Gale A. Yee, eds. *The Bible in Asian America.* Semeia 90/91. Atlanta: Society of Biblical Literature, 2002.

Lohfink, Norbert. "Das deuteronomische Gesetz in der Endgestalt: Entwurf einer Gesellschaft ohne marginale Gruppen." *BN* 51 (1990): 25–40.

Longenecker, Bruce W. ed. *Narrative Dynamics in Paul: A Critical Assessment.* Louisville: Westminster John Knox, 2002.

———. *Remember the Poor: Paul, Poverty and the Greco-Roman World.* Grand Rapids: Eerdmans, 2010.

———. "Socio-Economic Profiling of the First Urban Christians." In *After the First Urban Christians: The Social Scientific Study of Pauline Christianity*

Twenty-Five Years Later, edited by Todd D. Still and David G. Horrell, 36–59. New York: T & T Clark, 2009.

Luckenbill, Daniel D. *The Annals of Sennacherib*. Chicago: University of Chicago Press, 1924.

Lundbom, Jack R. *Jeremiah 1–20*. AB 21A. New York: Doubleday, 1999.

Luow, Johannes P. and Eugene A. Nida. *Greek-English Lexicon of the New Testament Based on Semantic Domains*. 2 vols. 2nd ed. New York: United Bible Societies, 1989.

Maclear, J. F., ed. *Church and State in the Modern Age: A Documentary History*. New York: Oxford University Press, 1995.

Malchow, Bruce V. "Social Justice in the Wisdom Literature." *BTB* 12 (1982): 120–24.

Malina, Bruce J. and John J. Pilch. *Social-Science Commentary on the Letters of Paul*. Minneapolis: Fortress Press, 2006.

Malina, Bruce J. and Richard L. Rohrbaugh. *Social Science Commentary on the Synoptic Gospels*. 2nd ed. Minneapolis: Fortress Press, 2003.

Mann, C. S. *Mark: A New Translation and Introduction*. AB 27. Garden City, NY: Doubleday, 1986.

Manus, Chris Ukachukwu. "Luke's Account of Paul in Thessalonica (Acts 17:1-9)." In *The Thessalonian Correspondence*, edited by Ed. Raymond F. Collins, 27–38. Leuven: Leuven University Press, 1990.

Marcus, Joel. *Mark 1–8: A New Translation with Introduction and Commentary*. AB 27. New York: Doubleday, 2000.

Martial. *Epigrams*. Translated by David Roy Shackleton Bailey. LCL. Cambridge, MA: Harvard University Press, 1993.

Martin, Dale P. "The Gospel of Thomas." Video lecture, CosmoLearning, Feb. 4, 2009. http://www.cosmolearning.com/video-lectures/the-gospel-of-thomas-6802/.

Marxsen, Willi. *Der Erste Brief an die Thessalonicher*. Zurich: Theologischer Verlag, 1979.

McConville, J. G. *Deuteronomy*. AOTC 5. Downers Grove, IL: InterVarsity, 2002.

McKenna, Megan. *Not Counting Women and Children: Neglected Stories from the Bible*. Maryknoll, NY: Orbis, 1994.

McRae, Rachel M. "Eating with Honor: The Corinthian Lord's Supper in Light of Voluntary Association Meal Practices." *JBL* 130 (2011): 165–181.

Meeks, Wayne. *The First Urban Christians: The Social World of the Apostle Paul*. New Haven: Yale University Press, 1983.

Meggitt, Justin J. *Paul, Poverty and Survival*. Studies of the New Testament and its World. Edinburgh: T & T Clark, 1998.

Meyer, Marvin W. *Secret Gospels: Essays on Thomas and the Secret Gospel of Mark*. Harrisburg, PA: Trinity Press International, 2003.

———. *The Gospel of Thomas*. New York: HarperCollins, 2009.

Míguez-Bonino, José. "Genesis 11:1–9: A Latin American Perspective." In *Return to Babel: Global Perspectives on the Bible*, edited by Priscilla Pope-Levinson and John R. Levinson, 13–16. Louisville: Westminster John Knox, 1999.

Miller, B. F. "Study of the Theme of 'Kingdom', The Gospel According to Thomas: Logion 18." *NovT* 9 (1967): 52–60.

Miller, Robert J., ed. *The Complete Gospels*. 4th ed. Santa Rosa, CA: Polebridge, 2010.

Mitchell, Margaret M. *Paul and the Rhetoric of Reconciliation: An Exegetical Investigation of the Language and Composition of 1 Corinthians*. HUT 28. Tübingen: Mohr, 1991.

Mitchell, Stephen J. *The Gospel according to Jesus: A New Translation & Guide to His Essential Teachings for Believers & Unbelievers*. New York: Harper Perennial, 1993.

Morrice, William G. *Hidden Sayings of Jesus: Words Attributed to Jesus Outside of the Four Gospels*. London: SPCK, 1997.

Morris, Pam, ed. *The Bakhtin Reader: Selected Writings of Bakhtin, Medvedev, and Voloshinov*. London: Edward Arnold, 1994.

Moule, C. F. D. "The Judgment Theme in the Sacraments." In *The Background of the New Testament in Its Eschatology: In Honor of C. H. Dodd*, edited by W. D. Davies and D. Daube, 464–81. Cambridge, MA: Cambridge University Press, 1956.

Murphy-O'Connor, Jerome. *1 Corinthians*. NTM 10; Dublin: Veritas, 1979.

Myers, Ched. *Binding the Strong Man: A Political Reading of Mark's Story of Jesus*. Maryknoll, NY: Orbis, 1988.

———. *Who Will Roll Away the Stone? Discipleship Queries for First World Christians*. Maryknoll, NY: Orbis, 1994.

Nineham, Dennis E. *St. Mark*. Harmondsworth: Penguin, 1963.

O'Connor, Kathleen M. "Crossing Borders: Biblical Studies in a Trans-Cultural World." In *Teaching the Bible: The Discourse and Politics of Biblical Pedagogy*, edited by Fernando F. Segovia and Mary Ann Tolbert, 322–37. Maryknoll, NY: Orbis, 1998.

———. "The Feminist Movement Meets the Old Testament: One Woman's Perspective." In *Engaging the Bible in a Gendered World: An Introduction to Feminist Biblical Interpretation in Honor of Katharine Doob Sakenfeld*, edited by Linda Day and Carolyn Pressler, 3–24. Louisville: Westminster John Knox, 2007.

———. "Let All the Peoples Praise You: Biblical Studies and a Hermeneutics of Hunger." *CBQ* 72 (2010): 1–14.

Oakes, Peter. "Constructing Poverty Scales for Graeco-Roman Society: A Response to Steven Friesen's 'Poverty in Pauline Studies.'" *JSNT* 26 (2004): 367–71.

Økland, Jorunn. *Women in Their Place: Paul and the Corinthian Discourse of Gender and Sanctuary Space*. JSNTSup 269. New York: T & T Clark, 2004.

Olley, John W. *Righteousness in the Septuagint of Isaiah: A Contextual Study.* Missoula, MT: Scholars, 1979.

Olyan, Saul. "Ben Sira's Relationship to the Priesthood." *HTR* 80 (1987): 261–72.

Osiek, Carolyn and David L. Balch. *Families in the New Testament World: Household and House Churches.* The Family, Religion, and Culture. Louisville: Westminster John Knox, 1997.

Otto, Michel. "οἶκος, οἰκία, ktl." *TWNT* 5:122-161.

Pagels, Elaine. *Beyond Belief: The Secret Gospel of Thomas.* New York: Random House, 2003.

———. *The Gnostic Gospels.* New York: Vintage, 1989.

Pancratius, C. Beentjes. "Recent Publications on the Wisdom of Jesus Ben Sira (Ecclesiasticus)." *Bijdragen: International Journal for Philosophy and Theology* 43 (1982): 191–94.

Patterson, Stephen J. *The Gospel of Thomas and Jesus.* Santa Rosa, CA: Polebridge, 1993.

Patterson, Stephen J., James M. Robinson, and Hans-Gebhard Bethge. *The Fifth Gospel: The Gospel of Thomas Comes of Age*, new ed. . New York: T & T Clark, 2011.

Paul, James A. and Katarina Wahlberg. "A New Era of World Hunger? The Global Food Crisis Analyzed." *Friedrich Ebert Stiftung Briefing Paper* 7. July 2008,

Pervo, Richard I. *Acts: A Commentary.* Hermeneia. Minneapolis: Fortress Press, 2008.

Pesch, Rudolph. *Das Markusevangelium.* Vol 1. HTKNT. Freiburg: Herder, 1976.

Peters, Norbert. *Das Buch Jesus Sirach oder Ecclesiasticus übersetzt und erklärt.* EHAT 25. Münster: Aschendorffsche, 1913.

Petersen, Norman R. *Rediscovering Paul: Philemon and the Sociology of Paul's Narrative World.* Philadelphia: Fortress Press, 1985.

Pilarski, Ahida. *The Textual and Literary Analysis of the References to 'iššâ and nāšîm in the Book of the Prophet Jeremiah*. Ann Arbor: ProQuest, 2008.

Pleins, J. David. *The Social Visions of the Hebrew Bible: A Theological Introduction*. Louisville: Westminster John Knox, 2001.

Pliny the Younger. *Letters and Panegyricus*. Vol.1. Translated by Betty Radice. LCL 55. Cambridge, MA: Harvard University Press, 1969.

Plutarch. *Lives: Pericles and Fabius Maximus. Nicias and Crassus*. Translated by Bernadotte Perrin. LCL. Cambridge, MA: Harvard University Press, 1916.

———. *Moralia*. Translated by Harold North Fowler. LCL. Cambridge, MA: Harvard University Press, 1936.

Pokorný, Petr. *A Commentary on the Gospel of Thomas: From Interpretations to the Interpreted*. Jewish and Christian Texts in Contexts and Related Studies 5. New York: T & T Clark, 2009.

Polan, Gregory. *In the Ways of Justice Toward Salvation: A Rhetorical Analysis of Isaiah 56–59*. New York: Peter Lang, 1986.

Powell, Mark Allan. *What is Narrative Criticism?* GBSNTS. Minneapolis: Fortress Press, 1990.

Premnath, D. M., ed. *Border Crossings: Cross-Cultural Hermeneutics*. Maryknoll, NY: Orbis, 2007.

Priest, J. "A Note on the Messianic Banquet." In *The Messiah: Developments in Earliest Judaism in Christianity*, edited by James H. Charlesworth, 222–38. First Princeton Symposium on Judaism and Christian Origins. Minneapolis: Fortress Press, 1992.

Pritchard, James B. *Ancient Near Eastern Texts Relating to the Old Testament [ANET]*. 3rd ed. with supplement. Princeton: Princeton University Press, 1969.

Pulwarty, Roger, Gary Eilerts, and James Verdin. "Food Security in a Changing Climate." *Solutions: For a Sustainable and Desirable Future* 3, no. 1 (Feb 2012): 31–34.

Quispel, Gilles. "The Gospel of Thomas and the New Testament." *VC* 11 (1957): 189–207.

Rathbone, Mark. "Unity and Scattering: Toward a Holistic Reading of Genesis 11:1-9 in the South African Context." In *Genesis*, edited by Athalya Brenner, Archie Chi-Chung Lee, and Gale A. Yee, 99–106. Texts @ Contexts. Minneapolis: Fortress Press, 2010.

Reiterer, Friedrich V. "The Influence of the Book of Exodus on Ben Sira." In *Intertextual Studies in Ben Sira and Tobit: Essays in Honor of Alexander A. Di Lella, O.F.M.*, edited by Jeremy Corley and Vincent Skemp. CBQMS 38. Washington, DC: Catholic Biblical Association of America, 2005.

Remmert-Fontes, Inge. "Mysticism and Resistance: A Memoir of Dorothee Sölle." http://www.sofn.org.uk/printme/sofia/68soelle.html. Posted September 2004.

Ricœur, Paul. *Figuring the Sacred: Religion, Narrative, and Imagination.* Minneapolis: Fortress Press, 1995.

Ringe, Sharon H. *Jesus, Liberation, and the Biblical Jubilee: Images for Ethics and Christology.* Philadelphia: Fortress Press, 1985.

Rodgers, Daniel T. *The Work Ethic in Industrial America, 1850–1920.* Chicago: University of Chicago Press, 1979.

Roetzel, Calvin J. *Judgment in the Community: A Study of the Relationship between Eschatology and Ecclesiology in Paul.* Leiden: Brill, 1972.

Rofé, Alexander. "The Tenth Commandment in Light of Four Deuteronomic Laws." In *The Ten Commandments in History and Tradition*, edited by Ben-Zion Segal and Gershon Levi. 45-65. Jerusalem: Magnes, 1990.

Ruiz, Jean Pierre. "Abram and Sarai Cross the Border: Reading Genesis 12:10-20 with People on the Move." In *Border Crossings: Cross-Cultural Hermeneutics*, edited by D. M. Premnath, 15–34. Maryknoll, NY: Orbis, 2007.

Russell, Ronald. "The Idle in 2 Thess 3:6–12: An Eschatological or a Social Problem?" *NTS* 34 (1988): 105–19.

Saller, Richard. "Patronage and Friendship in Early Imperial Rome: Drawing the Distinction." In *Patronage in Ancient Society*, edited by Andrew Wallace-Hadrill, 49–62. London: Routledge, 1989.

Sandoval, Timothy J. *The Discourse of Wealth and Poverty in the Book of Proverbs*. Biblical Interpretation Series 77. Leiden: Brill, 2006.

Sarna, Nahum M. *Understanding Genesis*. Heritage of Biblical Israel 1. New York: Jewish Theological Seminary, 1966.

Sauer, Georg. *Jesus Sirach/Ben Sira: Übersetzt und erklärt*. ATD 1. Gottingen: Vandenhoeck & Ruprecht, 2000.

Schneiders, Sandra. *The Revelatory Text: Interpreting the New Testament as Sacred Scripture*. Collegeville: Michael Glazier, 1999.

Schottroff, Luise. *Lydia's Impatient Sisters: A Feminist Social History of Early Christianity*. Louisville: Westminster John Knox, 1995.

Schreiner, Josef. *Sirach 1–24*. NEchtB 38. Würzburg: Echter, 2002.

Schüssler-Fiorenza, Elisabeth. *In Memory of Her: A Feminist Theological Reconstruction of Christian Origins*. New York: Crossroad, 1983.

———. *Sharing Her Word: Feminist Biblical Interpretation in Context*. Boston: Beacon, 1998.

Scott, Bernard Brandon. *Hear Then the Parable: A Commentary on the Parables of Jesus*. Minneapolis: Augsburg Fortress, 1989.

Scott, Christopher A., Robert G. Varady, and Francisco Meza, et al. "Science-Policy Dialogues for Water Security: Addressing Vulnerability and Adaptation to Global Change in the Arid Americas." *Environment: Science and Policy for Sustainable Development* 54, no. 3 (May/June 2012): 30–42.

Scullard, H. H. *From the Gracchi to Nero: A History of Rome 113 BC to AD 68*. London: Methuen, 1982.

Segal, Moses Hirsch. ספר בן-סירא השלם. 4th ed. Jerusalem: Bialik, 1997.

Segovia, Fernando F. *Decolonizing Biblical Studies: A View from the Margins.* Maryknoll, NY: Orbis, 2000.

Segovia, Fernando F. and Mary Ann Tolbert, eds. *Reading from This Place.* 2 vols. Minneapolis: Fortress Press, 1995.

Seitz, Christopher R. "The Book of Isaiah 40–66." *NIB*, 6:498–99. Nashville: Abingdon, 1994.

Shaffer, Harry G. *The Soviet Economy: A Collection of Western and Soviet Views.* 2nd ed. New York: Meredith, 1963, 1969.

Sicre, Jose L. *Con los Pobres de la Tierra: La Justicia Social en los Profetas de Israel.* Madrid: Ediciones Cristiandad, 1984.

Siebert, Charles. "Food Ark." *National Geographic*, July 2011, 108–31.

Skehan, Patrick and Alexander De Lella. *The Wisdom of Ben Sira: A New Translation with Notes, Introduction and Commentary.* AB 39. New York: Doubleday, 1987.

Smith, Dennis E. *From Symposium to Eucharist: The Banquet in the Early Christian World.* Minneapolis: Fortress Press, 2003.

Socias, James. ed. *Daily Roman Missal.* 6th ed. Chicago: Midwest Theological Forum; Schiller Park: World Library Publications, 2004.

Sölle, Dorothee. *The Silent Cry: Mysticism and Resistance.* Translated by Barbara Rumscheidt and Martin Rumscheidt. Minneapolis: Fortress Press, 2001.

Song, Choan-Seng. "Genesis 11:1-9: An Asian Perspective." In *Return to Babel: Global Perspectives on the Bible*, edited by Priscilla Pope-Levinson and John R. Levinson, 27–36. Louisville: Westminster John Knox, 1999.

Spicq, Ceslas. "Les Thessaloniciens 'inquiets' étaient-ils des paresseux?" *Studia Theologica* 10 (1956): 1–13.

Stadelmann, Helge. *Ben Sira als Schriftgelehrter: Eine Untersuchung zum Berufsbild dees vor-makkabäischen Sōfēr unter Berücksichtigung seines Verhältnisses zu Priester-, Propheten-, und Weisheitslehrertum.* WUNT 2/6. Tübingen: Mohr Siebeck, 1980.

Station 20 West Community Enterprise Centre. "Station 20 West: Benefits for All." Http://station20west.org/benefits.html.

Stewart, Jeanette. "Shovels in the Ground at Station 20 West." *Saskatoon Star Phoenix*, July 20, 2011.

———. "Summer Lunch Program Feeds Children in Need." *Saskatoon Star Phoenix*, Aug. 24, 2011.

Still, Todd D. *Conflict at Thessalonica: A Pauline Church and its Neighbours.* JSNTSup 183. Sheffield: Sheffield Academic Press, 1999.

Strong, John T. "Shattering the Image of God: A Response to Theodore Hiebert's Interpretation of the Story of the Tower of Babel." *JBL* 127 (2008): 625–34.

Stuhlmacher, Peter. "Das neutestamentliche Zeugnis vom *Herrenmahl.*" *ZTK* 84 (1987): 1–35.

Stulmann, Louis and Hyun Chul Paul Kim. *You Are My People: An Introduction to Prophetic Literature.* Nashville: Abingdon, 2010.

Sugirtharajah, R. S. *Postcolonial Reconfigurations: An Alternative Way of Reading the Bible and Doing Theology.* St. Louis: Chalice, 2003.

———. *Voices from the Margin: Interpreting the Bible in the Third World.* Maryknoll, NY: Orbis, 1995.

Surburg, Mark P. "The Situation at the Corinthian Lord's Supper in Light of 1 Corinthians 11:21: A Reconsideration." *Concordia Journal* (2006): 17–37.

Synod of Roman Catholics Bishops. "The Word of God in the Life and Mission of the Church." *Instrumentum Laboris.* 12th Ordinary General Assembly. Vatican City, 2008. http://www.vatican.va/roman_curia/synod/documents/rc_synod_doc_20080511_instrlabor-xii-assembly_en.html.

Taussig, Hal. *In the Beginning Was the Meal: Social Experimentation and Early Christianity.* Minneapolis: Fortress Press, 2009.

Theissen, Gerd. *The Social Setting of Pauline Christianity: Essays on Corinth.* Edited and translated by John H. Schütz. Philadelphia: Fortress Press, 1982.

———. "Social Integration and Sacramental Activity: An Analysis of 1 Cor. 11:17–34." In *The Social Setting of Pauline Christianity*, 145–74.

———. "Social Stratification in the Corinthian Community: A Contribution to the Sociology of Early Hellenistic Christianity." In *The Social Setting of Pauline Christianity*, 69–119.

———. "The Strong and the Weak in Corinth: A Sociological Analysis of a Theological Quarrel." In *The Social Setting of Pauline Christianity*, 121–143.

Thiselton, Anthony C. *The First Epistle to the Corinthians: A Commentary on the Greek Text.* NIGTC; Grand Rapids: Eerdmans, 2000.

Thompson, Michael. *Isaiah 40–66.* Peterborough: Epworth, 2001.

Überschaer, Frank. *Weisheit aus der Begegnung: Bildung nach dem Buch Ben Sira.* BZAW 379. Berlin: Walter de Gruyter, 2007.

United States Conference of Catholic Bishops Committee on Divine Worship. *Liturgical Calendar for the Dioceses of the United States of America.* Washington, DC: United States Conference of Catholic Bishops, 2012. http://www.usccb.org/about/divine-worship/liturgical-calendar/.

Uspensky, Boris. *Poetics of Composition: The Structure of the Artistic and Typology of a Compositional Form.* Translated by Valentina Zavarin and Susan Wittig. Berkeley: University of California Press, 1973.

Valantasis, Richard. *The Gospel of Thomas.* New Testament Readings. New York: Routledge, 1997.

Van Wolde, Ellen. *Words Become Worlds: Semitic Studies of Genesis 1–11.* BIS 6. Leiden: Brill, 1994.

Vatican II. *The Pastoral Constitution on the Church in the Modern World, Gaudium et spes.* http://www.vatican.va/archive/hist_councils/

ii_vatican_council/documents/vat-ii_cons_19651207_gaudium-et-spes_en.html

Vattioni, F. "Malachia 3,20 e l'origine della giustizia in Oriente." *RivBib* 6 (1958): 353–60.

Volf, Judith M. Gundry. *Paul and Perseverance: Staying In and Falling Away.* WUNT 2/37. Tübingen: Mohr Siebeck, 1990.

Volz, P. *Jesaja II, Zweite Hälfte: Kapitel 40–66.* Leipzig: Deichert, 1932.

Waltke, Bruce K. and M. O'Connor. *An Introduction to Biblical Hebrew Syntax.* Winona Lake, IN: Eisenbrauns, 1990.

Watts Henderson, Suzanne. "'If Anyone Hungers . . . ' An Integrated Reading of 1 Cor 11:17-34." *NTS* 48 (2002): 195–208.

Weaver, Dorothy Joan. "2 Thessalonians 3:6-15." *Int* 61 (2007): 426–28.

Weber, Max. *The Protestant Ethic and the Spirit of Capitalism.* Translated by Stephen Kalberg. Chicago: Fitzroy Dearborn, 2001.

Weinfeld, Moshe. *Social Justice in Ancient Israel and in the Ancient Near East.* Minneapolis: Fortress Press, 1995.

Williams, Michael Allen. *Rethinking "Gnosticism": An Argument for Dismantling a Dubious Category.* Princeton: Princeton University Press, 2001.

Wilson, J. Kinnier. "Medicine in the Land and Times of the Old Testament." In *Studies in the Period of David and Solomon and Other Essays*, edited by Tomoo Ishida, 339–65. Winona Lake, IN: Eisenbrauns, 1982.

Wimbush, Vincent L. *The Bible and African Americans: A Brief History.* Facets. Minneapolis: Fortress Press, 2003.

Winter, Bruce W. *After Paul Left Corinth: The Influence of Secular Ethics and Change.* Grand Rapids: Eerdmans, 2001.

———. *Seek the Welfare of the City: Christians as Benefactors and Citizens.* Grand Rapids: Eerdmans, 1994.

Wire, Antoinette Clark. *The Corinthian Women Prophets: A Reconstruction through Paul's Rhetoric.* Minneapolis: Fortress Press, 1995.

Witherington, Ben, III. *Conflict and Community in Corinth: A Socio-Rhetorical Commentary on 1 & 2 Corinthians*. Grand Rapids: Eerdmans, 1995.

Wood, Neal. *Cicero's Social and Political Thought*. Berkeley: University of California Press, 1991.

World Bank. "Severe Droughts Drive Food Prices Higher, Threatening the Poor." Press release, Aug. 30, 2012, http://www.worldbank.org/en/news/press-release/2012/08/30/severe-droughts-drive-food-prices-higher-threatening-poor.

Wright, Benjamin G. "'Fear the Lord and Honor the Priest': Ben Sira as Defender of the Jerusalem Priesthood." In *The Book of Ben Sira in Modern Research: Proceedings of the First International Ben Sira Conference 28–31 July 1996, Soesterberg Netherlands*, edited by Pancratius C. Beentjes, 189–222. BZAW 255. Berlin: Walter de Gruyter, 1997.

Wright, David P. "Fast." *HBD*, 306–7. San Francisco: HarperCollins, 1985.

Yadin, Yigael. *Art of Warfare in Biblical Lands in the Light of Archaeological Discovery*. London: Weidenfeld and Nicolson, 1963.

Yamasaki, Gary. "Point of View in a Gospel Story: What Difference Does it Make? Luke 19:1-10 as a Test Case." *JBL* 125 (2006): 89–105.

Yamasaki, Gary. *Perspective Criticism: Point of View and Evaluative Guidance in Biblical Narrative*. Eugene, OR: Cascade, 2012.

———. *Watching Biblical Narrative: Point of View in Biblical Exegesis*. New York: T & T Clark, 2008.

Index of Names

Gregory, Bradley C., 13–14, 89, 210

Gunkel, Hermann, 22

Halmarson, Cynthia, 126
Hays, Richard, 161
Herzog, William, 139
Hiebert, Theodore, 26–27, 30
Higgins, A. J. B., 138, 146
Hollingshead, James, 188
Horrell, David G., 168
Howe, Meagan, vii

Ibita, Marilou S., 14, 159, 211
Irving, David, 126

Jeremias, Joachim, 143
John XXIII, Pope, 85
John Paul II, Pope, 86
José, 152–53

Kaiser, Walter C., 44
Kim, Yung-Suk, 168
King, Karen, 144, 149

LaCocque, André, 27, 33
Latkovich, Sallie J., vii
Lenin, Vladimir, 186
Lenski, Gerhard, 90, 93
Louw, Johannes P., 175
Lundbom, Jack R., 56

Malchow, Bruce J., 101
Malina, Bruce, 129–30
Maloney, Linda, vii, 6, 14, 129, 211

Manzo, J. Laura, 13, 35, 212
Marcus, Joel, 120
McConnell, Ron, 126
McGinn, Sheila E., viii, 1, 14, 185, 212

McKenna, Megan, 122
Miguez-Bonino, José, 31
Myers, Ched, 121, 207–8

Ngan, Lai Ling Elizabeth, 1, 212
Nida, Eugene A., 175

O'Connor, Kathleen, viii, 4–10, 12–13, 17, 68, 111–12, 115, 213

Paul, James A., 59–60
Pazdan, Mary Margaret, 3
Pesch, Rudolph, 119
Petersen, Norman R., 161, 163–64 167

Pilarski, Ahida E. Calderón, 54, 213

Pokorný, Petr, 138, 145–46
Polan, Gregory, 38
Prinz, Julia, 5, 9
Pulwarty, Roger, 62

Index of Biblical and Ancient Literature References

CPSIA information can be obtained
at www.ICGtesting.com
Printed in the USA
FSOW03n0322250815
10227FS